Greening Death

Reclaiming Burial Practices and Restoring Our Tie to the Earth

Suzanne Kelly

ROWMAN & LITTLEFIELD
Lanham • Boulder • New York • London

Published by Rowman & Littlefield
A wholly owned subsidary of The Rowman & Littlefield Publishing Group, Inc.
4501 Forbes Boulevard, Suite 200, Lanham, Maryland 20706
www.rowman.com

Unit A, Whitacre Mews, 26-34 Stannary Street, London SE11 4AB

British Library Cataloguing in Publication Information Available

Library of Congress Cataloging-in-Publication Data Available

978-1-4422-4156-5 (cloth : alk paper)
978-1-4422-4157-2 (ebook)

∞™ The paper used in this publication meets the minimum requirements of
American National Standard for Information Sciences—Permanence of Paper
for Printed Library Materials, ANSI/NISO Z39.48-1992.

Printed in the United States of America

To Joe Kelly

July 15, 1937–February 12, 2000

Contents

Acknowledgments

This book belongs as much to me as it does to the many folks who've worked to build a better movement across the United States and to actively find ways to remake a meaning of human death rooted in the earth.

My absolute gratitude to all those who contributed interviews, information, or other such conversations, including Samuel Bar, Katey Bean, Ed Bixby, Sara Brink, Billy Campbell, Kimberley Campbell, Stephen Christy, Adriana Corral, Amy Cunningham, Robert Fertig, Brian Flowers, Meredith Harber, Ted Hollingsworth, Bob Jenkins, Freddie Johnson, Kate Kalanick, Rabbi Stuart Kelman, Kenneth Kyger, Joellen Lampman, Judith Lorei, Ellen Macdonald, Dyanne Matzkevich, Gordon Maupin, Dr. Bernard McEvoy, Pete McQuillin, Lisa Morahan, Father Charles Morris, Ann-Ellice Parker, Tara Pepperman, Vic Pizzonia, Joel Rabinowitz, John Eric Rolfstad, Andrew Schreiber, Joe Sehee, Kim Sorvig, Katrina Spade, Benjamin Stewart, Rick Touchette, Lee Webster, Liz Woedl, and Mary Woodsen.

I'm most grateful to the Town of Rhinebeck—the cemetery committee and the town board—for a shared belief in the value of natural burial and, also, for a job well done.

Thank you to my team at Rowman & Littlefield, first and foremost my editor Suzanne Staszak-Silva, for believing in my project from the gate, but also Kathryn Knigge, Elaine McGarraugh, and Desiree Reid for readying the book for publication. A special thank you to my friends and their great minds, Jane Caputi, Frances Chelland, Sabra Ciancanelli, and Ellice Litwak, who've listened to me talk about these ideas for too many years and provided me with vital and insightful comments. Also a special thank you to Benjamin Stewart, my new ally in struggle, for offering me fresh perspective in the reading of my chapters.

I'm wholly indebted to those teachers who've gone before, above all Val Plumwood (1939–2008), whose thinking figures prominently in this book, and my mentor Teresa Brennan (1952–2003), friend, colleague, and fellow Australian to Plumwood, who lured me back to graduate school and imparted the ways of daring and drive in pursuing my own work.

Of course, I wouldn't have completed this book without the support of my family with their capacity for love and talent for levity in the face of death. Most especially Mickey Haggerty, whose steady belief in me, as well as the movement, has shored me up for all these years.

Introduction

Waking Up

The process of transformation consists mostly of decay . . .

—Rebecca Solnit

Grief can take hold of us in many ways. It can masquerade as depression or a sense of personal failure. It can bring us closer or farther away from those we love. It can leave us feeling deserted or saved, in service or in need. But where exactly grief will take us is anyone's guess.

When my father died in 2000, I joined the ranks of the bereaved—a clan of straddlers, a liminal sect—awaiting the release of grief's grip and a return to the work of the living. Perhaps it's only when "death's door swings open" and "we can no longer look away"[1] that the lands of life and death can be coinhabited by those who are left behind. With both shores tugging at me in equal measure, whatever energy had given my life full direction seemed to altogether vanish. Grief felt like a kind of nonaction, a recurring derailment. But what I didn't know was that grief had a logic all its own.

While this book is not about grief, or even all that much about me, it was the generous workings of grief that provided the opening through which I came to write what is here. I was thirty, working on my PhD, and preparing for some future life of the mind when my father suffered a massive and fatal heart attack at sixty-two. For some time afterward, I felt wedged between the interests of life and death. But like so many others, the invisible rope tying me to the land of the dead would eventually begin to slacken, just as life's grasp would begin to strengthen. When I finally journeyed back from that liminal place I realized that far from leaving me stranded, grief had actually anchored me back to life with fresh perspective. Indeed, Proust may have been right, that "ideas come to us as the substitutes of griefs, and griefs, at the moment when they change into ideas, lose some power to injure our heart."[2]

Up until then, my scholarly life had been centered on philosophies that tried to make sense of the denigration of matter, of the body in particular, mostly taking form in cultural fantasies of women's bodies and the planet as both playground and dump. Merged with the changing states of my own loss, those same questions began to shift to the dead body—what we think of it, what we do with it, and why. Death would retreat, and my grief, too, would eventually resolve. These questions, however, would remain unshakable by my side, leading me to grapple with the implications of our contemporary death practices at the same time that I become part of a growing movement to change them.

Death was not new to me. I'd grown up with a large cultural mix of Orthodox Greeks and Catholics—Irish, Polish, Italian—and had been attending wakes and funerals since before I could remember. Even in the 1970s, Catholic death practices were fairly uniform, especially in urban places like New York. And because I was not shielded from the corpse, because I was encouraged to see, my gaze had already fallen many times upon that fleshy fact of death. The exact course of my thinking is not so easy to chart now, almost a decade and a half later. But the answers did come, sometimes with great force, clarity, and conviction, and sometimes quietly in shapes and frames that took some sorting out. What I know for sure is that snaking my way down that new trail of questions amounted to a kind of waking up to death.

That waking up to death might come more easily with the fleshy facts available makes sense. Funeral directors will tell you as much—that the point of the wake, or viewing, is to come to terms with the physical loss. Anyone who's ever stood over a casket knows all too well that other reason—the worry that the dead might actually still be alive! I grew up hearing that the word *wake* was an outgrowth of this fear, that our watching was practical, and that we witnessed to ensure that death was in the room. For a time in our history this had its purpose, but medical advances along with the invasive practice of embalming eventually shut out any potential for those mishaps.

Science may have solved the problem of knowing the dead are really dead, yet a good many of us remain observers. *Wake* comes to us from the Indo-European expression meaning "to become alert," and "to watch."[3] When I was a kid, the wake was where the men of the family would circle in on their way back from the corner bar, where the women would keep vigil, and where we children joined together in unrehearsed play. As a witness to the howls of sorrow upon first glimpse of the dead, the intent of the wake was not lost on me. Even then I knew that it had some other purpose. Waking is what the living do.

My father would have the same death rites as his father and his grandfather. Two days of wake followed by a Catholic mass and church burial. Over the course of a week his body would journey that well-trodden path from the funeral home, to the church, and then into the cemetery. We had seen my father off and provided the care to do it. And though, overall, the funeral and familial support helped me say goodbye, I still couldn't get *the body* off my mind.

It's no secret that over the course of the last century the corpse has become increasingly hidden from sight, that the distance between the dead and the living inner circle has grown cavernous. Where funerals once happened in the home, they now occur in a place meant to mirror the home. Funerary viewings are still customary, but their popularity is waning. Nearly 70 percent of Americans die in hospitals, long-term care facilities, or nursing homes.[4] Dead bodies are kept in morgues and transported to funeral homes, and often buried or cremated out of sight of the bereaved. And what funeral directors call "direct cremation," where the body travels en route from the morgue to the crematory, is on the rise.

The more we try to forget, Freud warned, the more it all comes rushing back. Suddenly it seemed the corpse was symbolically everywhere in popular culture. The award-winning HBO series *Six Feet Under* was a hit while crime scene investigations, ghouls, and ghosts haunted television and film. Surely my persistent thoughts couldn't just be a return of the repressed for me, especially since proximity to the corpse was like a right of passage for Catholic families like mine. So why wouldn't the dead just let me be?

Before my father's body was seen through to the end, it would first be embalmed, then placed in a wood and metal casket, and, finally, encased in a reinforced concrete vault that had been inserted in the ground. At the same time that this walled-off city of contaminants prohibited his body immediate access to the elements (and, conversely, the elements access to his body), his body had also become contaminated, poisoned. His body had, in all practical ways, become a problem. It seemed the most sinister of reversals. What kept my mind on *the body* were these facts. What plagued me wasn't simply the lack of cultural proximity to the dead, but, also, the dead body's distance from the whole of nature.

It wouldn't take long to find that what stirred in me was also being felt elsewhere. On the heels of a budding movement in the United Kingdom, the first green, or natural, burial ground in the United States—Ramsey Creek Preserve in Westminster, South Carolina—had opened just two years prior.[5] And because discontent with the status quo is as individually felt as it is shared, the next decade and a half would bring the creation of more green burial grounds throughout the United States, all messaging a rejection of standard funerary forms and a desire to do death differently.

It would be many years after my father's death that I would come to find out that, like me, Ramsey Creek founder Dr. Billy Campbell had his own first inklings of greening up funerary care with the death of his own father back in 1985—although it would take over a decade to cultivate his vision.[6] In those early days I longed for even such small connections. But what I wanted most was to find others who were also *waking up*, and who wished to work together toward the greening of death.

What exactly is this *greening*?

Green burial—also referred to as natural burial—aims to care for the dead with minimal impact to the environment. Where conventional burial typically includes embalming and caskets, often sealed, and manufactured from finished hardwoods and metals and sometimes non-plant-based materials as well as the use of reinforced concrete vaults or liners, whole-body green interment steers clear of all of them. Green burial grounds are on the rise in the United States, hovering somewhere around one hundred at last count.[7] In all of them, rain, wind, and sun are respected in the work of decomposition, as well as the pressure of earth, stone, and roots. Human decay is regarded as good and valuable, as microbes and insects descend to feed on the dead. As food and nourishment for other creatures, the corpse is of consequence to the land and to the species of mammals, birds, amphibians, plants, and insects that inhabit it. In essence, the corpse is of consequence to the planet.

In many ways, green burial is about a return to the past—to the way we buried our dead in the United States over 150 years ago. Simple methods. Dust to dust.

Except that times have changed.

Since Jessica Mitford's best-selling *The American Way of Death* (1963), cremation has been on the rise. The effect of Mitford on cremation rates cannot be understated. Her criticism of the funerary industry hit a chord with Americans—our funerary ways were unnecessarily excessive and expensive, and the funeral industry needed to be reigned in. Over the last forty years, Americans have responded to that sensibility by increasingly making the choice to be cremated. A century and a half ago, that choice didn't even exist. Pyre burning is an ancient tradition, but not one that has been practiced in the United States with any regularity. And the modern crematorium didn't come into being until the turn of the twentieth century, although it would take several decades for it to make any headway. Today, however, nearly half of all deaths in the United States resolve in cremation annually, with some states even higher.[8]

Next to whole-body green interment, cremation is the second most environmentally sound way of disposing of the dead. If it's less than ideal that's mostly because any time something is burned ecological health is at risk.

Still, only about 13 percent of those who choose cremation claim the environment as a reason.[9] All of these years later, Mitford's call to cost and simplicity remain the driving factors. Unfortunately, this call hasn't much helped to curb our unsustainable death ways that pollute, dishonor decay, and sever humans from the earth. In many ways, in not more robustly taking up the charge of our ties to nature, the way cremation has been practiced over the last half a century has left us even more stranded from a meaning of death, and a dead body, that belongs to the planet. In the meantime, conventional death ways have continued in their work of reversals, where flesh, blood, and bone have been turned into contaminants, and pollutants masquerade as protectors.

The greening of death, however, doesn't mean an admonishment of cremation. On the contrary, for cultural, personal, political, and economic reasons, the movement largely regards incineration as a greener option than conventional burial. I say "greener" because cremation does pose some environmental risks. Crematories emit mercury and furans and other by-products of burning while also using a good deal of energy. Still, most green burial grounds do accept interment and/or scattering of cremated remains. The environmental problems of cremation are taken up by green burial advocates (GBAs) by pushing for better crematory filters that would help limit the amount of contaminants transmitted into the air, while also calling for more renewable forms of energy to run them.

The world around us has changed in other ways, too. Environmental destruction has transformed the planet into a very different place than it was when dust to dust was last the norm. Behind us stretches a fifty-year history of environmental activism and, yet, the planet is still on fire. For those of us paying attention, we're desperate for ways to put it out. This is all to say that the movement is interested in not only what goes into our cemeteries, or for that matter what doesn't, but also, how much energy was expended to fulfill an interment? A cremation? Where did the energy come from? What about carbon emissions? Was worker health jeopardized somewhere along the way?

There is also, of course, waste in terms of that other *green*—money. Because the cost of most conventional death care arrangements are wrapped up in expensive caskets and burial vaults that are eschewed in green death care all together, a whole-body green burial should generally cost less. However, depending on geographical location and whether or not the cemetery is using any of the monies for purposes beyond the burial itself, like the restoration of habitat, the price of plots may vary. Which brings me to another movement goal—landscape-level conservation—which fundamentally challenges the standard lawn-park design of cemeteries that requires gridded rows, machine-cut and polished stones, highly manicured turf, and, at least for the larger and more well-funded cemeteries, the use of pesticides.

Of course, the pollution of conventional burial is nothing in comparison to the really big problems facing us, like climate change, water scarcity, and threats to our food system. The green burial movement, however, is doing more than offering more sustainable death care choices that would contribute to a healthier and less wasteful planet. Like me, other folks are waking up to lost ways of knowing death, especially in terms of recovering older practices. Out of this recovery, renewed meanings are emerging—ones that are rekindling our bond with the earth.

And herein lies the greatest potential green burial has to offer—rectifying our severance from the natural world in both symbolic and literal ways. As green-friendly funeral director, Bob Fertig, said to me, "The focus on the environmental aspect [of the green burial movement] is wonderful, but I think what sometimes gets lost in that is the potential for closeness with death and the way that it makes people feel."[10] When GBAs, especially those who deal with grieving families, say that green burial provides great solace to experiences of loss, there's no doubt that such comfort has been born by connection to not only each other, but also to the earth itself.

One of the lessons Green Burial Council (GBC) founder Joe Sehee told me he learned years ago working with Jesuit liberation theologians was that simply knowing something is wrong is often not enough to get people to work against it. "We bring about change," he said, "when we can get behind a vehicle to make things right."[11] He was sure that green burial could be that "vehicle"—a reclaiming of practices that could, once and for all, reform an industry that the American public has never warmed up to.

He hasn't been alone.

Still, the movement's shown to be more slow and steady than soaring. About five years after I set down this path, the shrouded body of Nate Fisher, the prodigal son in *Six Feet Under*, would be lowered into the ground green. A couple of years later Mark Harris's *Grave Matters* (2007) would hit the ground running. I remember thinking *this is it*—a groundswell of support will surely follow. Movements, of course, grow at different paces. For some, there has been a kind of ebb and flow to action where mobilization can run from dynamic to but a whisper. (That's why the metaphor of the wave, for instance, has been used to talk about the women's movement in the United States.) And yet, many of us are still left to wonder why the green burial movement has been more tortoise than hare, and why it still feels as if we're in a slow process of awakening.

Change beckons us as we teeter on the cusp of a mobilized remaking of death care. But plenty of obstacles remain, including a deeply rooted cultural imagining of human life and death that is not a part of nature; an overwhelming distance and denial from end-of-life matters that is only exacerbating death fear and meaninglessness; a powerful death care industry that curbs access to information and a range of death rites while firmly anchoring death care to a market of goods to be purchased; restrictive cemetery rules and state laws; access to land and money; greenwashing (where companies spread false information about what they're selling in order to appear more environmentally minded); structural inequalities that often lead to lack of choices; and an environmental movement that has for too long closed its eyes to human death and decay. Not to mention the encroachment of human doubt that can foil even the most incandescent minded and the most well intentioned of us.

But perhaps, most importantly, what the legacy of movements tells us is that the individual human spirit can see and then soar above the most heinous of realities, but defeating them is a group project. Rooted in this tried-and-true logic of social change, my search for comrades in struggle, all those years ago now, was a matter of practicality. And history. Somewhere along the way I did find like-minded folks, some who had started green burial grounds and were generous enough to share what they'd learned, and others who, like me, wanted to.

In the Women's Studies classroom, I spent years explaining to students how movements take time and that patience is a prerequisite for any kind of lasting reform. I'd tell them that momentum comes from the ground up, from the work of a lot of people doing both big and small things, and not, as we're often told, from the remarkable direction of a few. Indeed, the lack of momentum in the movement is not for lack of leadership. Over the last fifteen years, in places in and beyond Westminster, South Carolina; Newfield, New York; Ferndale, Washington; Gainesville, Florida; Wilmot, Ohio; Goldendale, Washington; and Steelmantown, New Jersey, organizing has been leading the way. In communities large and small, folks have been trying to figure out how to get green burial going.

Bill McKibben has come to call this kind of movement-building "leaderless," not because there are no leaders, but because there are so many. But McKibben also knows, as anyone who has taken part in a grassroots movement also does, that with so many leaders forging the way in their communities, there must be some shared dream. And that dream must be vigilantly guarded, because, without it, any movement is likely to falter.[12] Tensions, frictions, and disagreements certainly run through all movements, and yet the obstacles facing the greening of death will only be overcome through some shared vision, our capacity for organizing, and a belief in our collective power.

Which to my mind means faith in the power of *green* itself.

Green, of course, is now everywhere code for environmental protection, care, and concern. But because greenwashing has in every arena become a problem in a profit-driven market that cares nothing for nature, it's also a word that is now sometimes scorned. Among folks interested in more environmentally friendly death care, much like other environmental issues, some love it while others loathe it. As greenwashing remains a threat, the integrity of the movement is challenged at every step, and the stakes are high.

With burgeoning burial grounds bearing names like Greensprings, Greenhaven, Greenview, Green Hills, and Greenacres, it's clear that the movement has some affinity for green. Still, environmentally friendly death care providers don't all agree on the current usage. Is it green burial or natural burial? For those in the movement who think green is beyond saving, they've settled on the word natural instead.

It's a shame *green* has fallen into such poor favor, as it's a word that's long evoked growth and life. As Jane Caputi has detailed, such symbolic associations extend far back and beyond our own current usage, across world mythologies and traditions that understood that *green* is synonymous with nature.[13] The market did not invent the word, but their appropriation of it should remind us of its power.

After all, the basic building blocks of human life, bacteria, are blue green algae. The color of the fire that died in the eyes of the wolf Aldo Leopold—the so-called father of the environmental movement—was green.[14] We have also seen how the Green Revolution—which sought to feed the world through the spread of monoculture and, more recently, genetically modified seeds—has not only been a catastrophic failure but also a way of assuming the *real* green of the earth for the ends of corporate profits. World-renowned environmental leader Vandana Shiva has argued that efforts to patent strains of rice by corporations like Monsanto are, perhaps, the worst examples of this appropriation.[15] "Green," Shiva says, "has to be reclaimed."[16]

With its rich past of denoting positive environmental action as well as origin, it does seem to be the word that better captures the earthly thrust of the movement. Rather than let the market have it, we ought to do more to own it. But in keeping with the current state of the movement and because there is nothing to object to in the word *natural*, I use the words interchangeably throughout this book.

Two more things about terminology. First, I talk a lot about the human tie, or lack thereof, to "nature." I mean "nature," here, in the way the environmental philosopher Neil Evernden does—as "that great mass of otherness that encloaks the planet,"[17] and not in the way that nature has come to be figured, most especially since the seventeenth century, as an object of our control and manipulation and something that we imagine we are not a part of. Indeed, this entire book is a challenge to that very notion, one I spell out more directly in chapter 1.

Second, I use "conventional burial" here to refer to practices that have taken shape over the last 150 years in the United States—whole-body burial with the use of chemical embalming, sealed hardwood and metal caskets, and reinforced concrete vaults and liners. In my travels, I've heard some GBAs say that what is conventional is really the "old" way, the dust-to-dust methods. But conventional, by definition, means "used and done by most people."[18] And right now, unsustainable death practices are "used and done by most people."

Communities, of course, have their own funerary rituals around the body or lack thereof. Rituals can vary widely, most especially along ethnic, geographical, and religious lines. Ceremonies may be elaborate or simple. Song or prayer or chanting or stories may move mourners along. Contact with the body may be vital or not done at all. Altars may be constructed. Offerings made. But whatever variation may separate cultures and communities from one another is made up for in the uniformity required of the death care industry, an over $15-billion-machine molding American death rites.

As Joe Sehee has said, "Rarely will people go into a restaurant and order something that's not on the menu."[19] If embalming, hardwood and metal caskets, concrete vaults and liners, the modern polluting crematory, and the lawn-park cemetery are "used by most people," that is because those are our available options. And those options have largely cut across lines of race, class, and religious boundaries. Some religions like Judaism and Islam eschew these ways, but even they've been forced to adapt to them sometimes, especially with respect to cemetery vault requirements.

It's these conventions, in their largely universal form, and as they've spread across the states, that the green burial movement looks to redress. How particular communities have, or will, come to challenge these polluting practices is the work of the movement's past, present, and future. For green burial to grow and thrive, it must continue to germinate from the ground up, from the local, bespeaking particular cultural and communal contexts and the rituals that define them.

The power of *green* fires this book in more ways than I can speak it—a book that is as much about moving forward as it is about looking back, as much about laying claim to a new way of caring for the dead as it is about reclaiming one. Reclamation is at the heart of these chapters—recovering not only the word *green* for the future of death but also for practices that were once traditional in the United States that we have now, with vernacular ease, come to call *green*; recouping not only death practices seemingly lost to us but also a meaning of human decay as part of the land that we've been forced to forget; restoring the land not only for the living, as some environmentalists have done in the name of other causes, but also for the rest of nature as well;

retrieving our lost story of connection to the land not only for death practices but also for building a more whole and healthy planetary future.

These chapters are a blend of scholarship and experience and, for clarity of argument, are best read in the order in which they appear. Part I looks at how U.S. funerary practices that turned human decay into a menace took shape within an already existing worldview that had long denied human ties to nature. In admiration, hope, and praise, I call upon feminist environmental thinkers and other such visionaries to help trace the history of ideas behind this severance that has reshaped American funerary practices and turned the dead body into something that doesn't matter to the natural world.

Against a history of severance from nature that has had us running from decay, I turn to look at the shape and future of the green burial movement in the United States whose work, at its best, is struggling to remake a dead body that *does* matter to nature, and lay the groundwork for knowing that we do, indeed, belong to the earth.

In part II, I turn to the green burial movement itself, to those folks who are "waking up" to the problem of our conventional death ways. I look at the some of the meanings both sought and created in the movement, and the recovery of lost knowledge that is getting us to face the fleshy matter of death. I look at how this knowledge is shaping the on-the-ground-work of the movement, especially as it is taking shape in the formation of green burial grounds, and some of the obstacles that are hindering more robust mobilization. In these chapters, I've done my best to bring front and center some of the actors in the movement—those advocates whose work is not only reclaiming lost practices and meanings, but, also, actively tying us to the land.

In the end, I recognize the promise of a shared-earth-based ethic that resituates human decay within nature and that, more broadly, works to resituate humans within the natural world. My conversations with fellow GBAs in many forms—green burial pioneers, cemetery operators and their board members, designers and landscape architects, religious leaders, caregivers of the dead, death educators, municipal governments seeking new ways to green their communities, hopeful grassroots groups, eco certifiers, and land trusts on the cutting edge of thinking of human death in terms of conservation—have been vital to coming to grips with the shape and course of the movement and the challenges that lie ahead. Though I'm but one of many voices in a sea of GBAs, I end the book with one of my own stories; namely, what it took to create a natural burial ground in the small Hudson Valley town I call home, and the promise, as well as the limits, of its potential.

Greening death begins with waking up to *the matter* of death itself. Any widespread transformation in U.S. funerary practices remains incumbent on a change in the living. If there were any question, we only need to look to the movement to find out.

PART I

1

Apart from Nature

"It is more than a little strange," Neil Evernden bemoaned some thirty years ago, "to think of people accepting as normal a view of nature from which they are excluded."[1] But despite pervasive planetary devastation including natural resource depletion; soil, water, and air contamination; species loss; deforestation; ozone reduction; ocean acidification; GMOs; and climate change, that view continues to be deployed in both deliberate and absent-minded ways. As we bear witness to the widespread havoc wrought by some of the worst offenders—hydraulic fracturing, industrial farming, urban sprawl, genetic engineering, mountaintop removal, and fossil fuel reliance—many of us are left scratching our heads in horror. How could such an outlandish, and ultimately destructive, view of nature come to prevail?

Rachel Carson was all too aware of the danger wrought by this *strange* view of nature when she went about exposing the widespread menace that was DDT. "The history of life on earth has been a history of interaction between living things and their surroundings,"[2] she beseeched a skeptical American public to see in her landmark *Silent Spring* (1962). Over the last century, however, humans have gained so much unprecedented power that the fact of this interaction has largely been forgotten. Imagining ourselves outside of nature, our control and mastery has increased to "a disturbing magnitude" as nature is molded to our own needs and whims, ignoring outcomes outside of ourselves, while also forgetting that our actions might come back to harm us.[3]

A little more than a decade before Carson, Aldo Leopold's *A Sand County Almanac* (1949) sketched a similar knowing, with a similar warning. In Leopold's mind, all living things belonged to one community—the land. Unfortunately, "we, in North America," as Thomas Berry has so boldly said, by and large resist living out this knowledge. Instead, we "live in a political world, a nation, a business world, an economic order, a cultural tradition, a Disney dreamland."[4] Power, greed, and self-interest have driven us away from our ability to know the land community, to remember that nature is home to us all. Though we remain grateful for both Leopold and Carson's insights, especially because they gave voice to budding environmental activism in the United States, the mainstream environmental movement has largely failed to observe either of their visions. In fact, since Carson, an environmental politics of protection, economics, and personal choice has only succeeded in positioning the human ever more firmly outside nature's door.[5]

Today, we're in need of ways to expose that *strange* view of nature for what it is, while also finding ways to reposition ourselves in relationship to the more-than-human[6] in the name of a healthier earth. Leopold's cure was cultivating a concept of the land community we could live by. Only "when we see land as a community to which we belong," he said, "may [we] begin to use it with love and respect."[7] Leopold was deliberate in fashioning his concept in terms of ethics, because "all ethics," he said, "rest upon a single premise; that the individual is a member of a community of interdependent parts."[8] By replacing separation with relationship, humans are turned "from conqueror of the land-community to plain member and citizen of it."[9]

With humans no longer in a position to wield power indiscriminately against a homogenized and detached nature, everything is apt to change. It's a guiding logic that still remains our best hope for halting the unsustainable path we've been traveling down for too long. Which is to say that leading with a concept of the human that is part of nature remains as much a priority as ever.

In taking up that charge, it's time we took human death along for the ride. As the environmental feminist philosopher Val Plumwood declared some three decades ago, a "major philosophical challenge" to perceiving humans as part of nature "is to reconceive and interpret both death and the significance of human life in ways which are both life—and nature—affirming and death accepting."[10] And so, if it's within our current *strange* view of nature that the footings of our most pressing environmental concerns can be found, it's also within this view that we can find the foundations of our alienating, polluting, and unsustainable funerary practices.

Over the course of writing this book, I asked many fellow green burial advocates (GBAs) what they thought the message of the green burial movement was all about. Answers overlapped and varied. GBAs talked about better choices in death care, cost savings, matters of sustainability, land conservation, giving something back to the earth, comfort, remembrance, community building, and family involvement. Freddie Johnson, executive director and one of the founders of Prairie Creek Conservation Cemetery, spoke about some of these messages too, but said that if he could "sum it up in just one way it would be about a return to rationality."[11] Of all the responses I received to this question, in all the ways I came to ask it, Johnson's cut to the problem of our conventional death practices like no other. And that's because if what's rational is what's reasonable, adhering to these practices does defy rationality—at least in an everyday sense of the word.

This "return to rationality" can be heard in the voices of those who upon hearing about green burial for the first time were nothing short of invigorated by the idea. Like Marge Thomas of Wooster, Ohio, who was so "struck with the 'rightness' of " it that she ran out and bought a burial plot.[12] Or that of working cemeterian Brian Flowers who was all but floored by the possibility of offering green burial where he worked, not because it seemed so novel, but, rather, because it was so in keeping with what he'd felt to be right all along. "That's always what I've said I wanted," Flowers recalled, "but I didn't think was possible. Or legal." That "it just makes good sense," as Kimberley Campbell put it as she extoled the pioneering green burial work of her husband, Billy Campbell, and the reasons why they came to build the first green burial ground in the United States—that it has a certain undeniable logic to it—is unquestionably one of the reasons GBAs are growing in number and more and more green burial grounds are establishing roots across the nation.[13] Former executive director of Foxfield Preserve Cemetery, Gordon Maupin, couldn't agree more, saying people are choosing Foxfield precisely because "the modern burial thing just [doesn't] make sense to them."[14]

Still, there's something else to this story of "a return to rationality"—something less on the surface and substantively more paradoxical that might cause us to wonder whether rationality is what we really want to return to after all. Because even though our everyday use of the word may be synonymous with an innate logic that allows the "rightness" of green burial to become clear, rationality's history in the centuries since the Enlightenment has ironically tied it to a cultural perspective that has not been particularly kind to nature.

In fact, rationality, as it has been organized and applied over the last few centuries in the West, has been understood to be the very quality of the human mind that sets us off from nature. As such, the rational, human mind is positioned in an oppositional and superior position to nature, creating a hierarchy—human above and nature below. It's a dualism that's long operated in favor of the human world, though, as it turns out, such favor has befitted and benefitted some humans more than others.[15]

For a long time, rationality was consigned to white men in particular, as well as all those qualities associated with them—including culture, selfhood, subjectivity, spirit, agency, and, of course, power. Early European feminists such as Mary Wollstonecraft fought back against the likes of Jean-Jacques Rousseau for not believing in women's intellectual capabilities, in the promise of women to develop the faculties of mind so favored by eighteenth-century European culture.[16] Her struggle may seem part of a past we can barely touch now, lodged in the social milieu and dictates of a culture that no longer bear out real meanings for us. And yet, those attitudes still have a place in our sexual politics today where the prizing of mental aptitude stands in contrast to the disdain and disrespect for the chaos of the flesh.

Women's bodies are still more revered than their minds, their emotions still play as fodder for political commentary, and their biological processes—childbirth, menstruation, and menopause—are still unruly things to be controlled and overcome. The effects of this kind of rationality not only continue to play out on the bodies of women, but also on all those bodies stigmatized as lower, other, deviant—bodies marked by racial, ethnic, class, gender, sexual, and age differences, by nation of origin and ability status, as well as all those qualities labeled feminine both in us and all around us—the emotions, the passions, disease, chaos, and, of course, death. This is all to say that by virtue of the way certain bodies are stigmatized by the culture, some of us are still considered to be closer to a mindless nature that always seems to be falling short.

Regardless of which bodies, beings or attributes have been relegated to the realm of nature, nature has been defined as all that is primitive, chaotic, wild, and fecund—as those Edenic spaces openly available to human whim and consumption. Outside civilized, rational culture but also below it, nature has been engendered for human pleasure—as scene and atmosphere. Val Plumwood describes the human/nature dualism responsible for rationality's banishment from nature as one rooted in a master/slave dynamic so a part of Western thought that it appears to us as essential and "natural."[17] But this dualism is not, in fact, original to the world.

Although we have the Enlightenment to blame for its current form, its roots can be traced as far back as ancient Greece and early Christianity, eventually coming to take on a life of its own with the rise of the Scientific Revolution and, later, the development of capitalism. While some feminists point to Plato as the source of this dualism (Plumwood is one of them), his ideas haven't been the worst of it. Even so, Christianity has done its part too; namely, in setting the world of spirit apart from matter. Though matter would not fare well throughout the centuries, there was still a bit of hope for nature. Christian thinking made some room for a nature that mattered and of which humans were a part. We can see this in biblical passages that recognize the necessity in returning humans to the earth in death and even in some practices like the early modern cult of relics that so embraced the sacredness and power of the body.[18]

But whatever dissent there might have been, whatever hope was there for nature, was all but eradicated by the seventeenth century, ushered in with the ideas of Francis Bacon (1561–1626) and Rene Descartes (1596–1650), who both infamously downplayed matter in favor of a mind that could live without it. If any truth was to be gleaned from nature, it was only in "learning to overcome it."[19] Yes, by the time Francis Bacon called for a future "race of heroes and supermen who would dominate both nature and society," and Descartes declared, *cogito ergo sum*, promising a future where we would become "masters and possessors of nature," the dualism had already made some inroads.[20] But the Scientific Revolution would shift human perception away from thinking of nature as nurturing, providing, and whole and into a machine with disparate parts—objects that should and could be managed and profited from.[21] In the end, this symbol of nature as machine—empty of mind or reason—but also agency and spirit too, would initiate a modern sensibility that, unable to cope with the disorderliness of nature, ultimately sought ways to overcome it.[22]

Conceptualized in this way, nature was turned into something we could merely experience, use, maintain, or regulate. Not something we were a part of. Not something we were in relationship with. Void of the possibility of connection, we would come to interact with nature as an "It" to be known, in theologian Martin Buber's terms, and not a "Thou" with which we could build a living bond. Buber believed the central way we forged meaningful lives was through our relationships. But what meaning is to be found in a nature that has no capacity for it?[23]

Of course, viewing nature as beyond or beneath us not only renders any potential relationship with "It" impossible, but, in a more general way, also renders the full context of our living invisible to us.[24] Indeed, as David Abram reminds us "we are only human in contact, in conviviality, with what is not human."[25] But the human/nature split keeps our ability to know as much out of reach. As our perception of nature continues to be determined by a logic of disconnection—the *strange* view of nature Evernden lamented—ecological devastation goes on leaving us to wonder, how? Just how does such an abstract and fleeting concept come to bear down on nature—to do such damage?

Plumwood describes five key features that enable the human/nature dualism to do its work. I explain them here for two reasons. First, they provide insight into the power of ideas to shape how we see and know the world. Second, I'll refer back to them later, most especially throughout chapter 3, when I illustrate how they've come to shape our death practices over the past 150 years.

1. *Backgrounding*—or denying the importance of nature for the human world's survival. In denying dependency, the human world is figured as not only self-invented but also generative, repudiating the very source of goodwill and energy that has allowed it to survive.
2. *Radical exclusion*—or hyperseparation of nature from the human world, named "culture." Maintaining strict lines between humans and nature is required so that the human world of culture and reason maintain their sense of distinctiveness, a distinctiveness or difference built on separateness that guarantees that humans are not only not part of nature but also that, conversely, reason is securely excluded from the realm of nature.
3. *Incorporation*—or a relational definition of nature, in which nature is defined in terms of what it is not—the world of human culture.
4. *Instrumentalism*—or perceiving nature as only a means to an end of human culture and never as an end or good in itself.
5. *Homogenization*—where all of nature is seen as one thing, denied of any complexity.[26]

The greatest to the smallest environmental threats can all be directed back to the deployment of these features that, when applied, work to keep nature subdued and confined to the parameters of human will and making. From fracking to SUVs on the road, from fossil fuel consumption to food waste in landfills, nature is, to one degree or another, *backgrounded, radically excluded, incorporated, instrumentalized*, and *homogenized* by human culture.

So herein lies the problematic foundation to our prevailing *strange* view of nature. How do we undo these features? Where do we even begin?

Confronting rationality is a start.

Everywhere we turn today we hear that the environment is *the* crisis of our time. But some twenty years ago Plumwood insisted that the real crisis facing us is not one of ecology, but one of reason,[27] and that any path we take to heal this broken earth must include an interrogation of our prevailing construction of rationality—that form of reason the dominant culture continues to desperately cling to. Our perceptions of what's *really rational*—of what reason is and where reason resides—calls for radical renewal. By reimbuing nature with its own sense of intelligence—all those things that our current form of rationality has stripped from it—we can begin the long road back to care and respect for the earth.

If I'm partial to the ideas of Plumwood, here and elsewhere,[28] it's mainly because her work stands apart from other environmental thinkers, as well as activists, who have largely ignored the fact of human death for environmental concerns. It's also because Plumwood comes from a feminist theoretical tradition that brings all of the problems of multiple oppressions to bear on the exploitation of nature. One of the lasting criticisms of the environmental conservation movement has been the absence of the consideration of bodies and lands occupied by those most affected by environmental pollution—namely, women, the poor, and people of color. The environmental justice movement has worked to redress these omissions, but, on the level of ideas, these intersections remain vitally important for us to take up. They're also essential, as I will discuss in chapter 7, for building the robust green burial movement many us dream is possible.

Though Plumwood didn't exactly take on the problem of our conventional death ways in *Feminism and the Mastery of Nature* (1993) or *Environmental Culture* (2002), she did make the argument that any hope for a future ecological identity hinges on our capacity to fully accept death as a part of life.[29] Some years after the publication of those two books, Plumwood began writing more along these lines, questioning whether polluting and unsustainable cemetery traditions could change and arguing that a path to a renewed perspective is to be found in repositioning humans within the food chain.[30] Had Plumwood lived longer (she died in 2008), her work might have expanded to include the kind of consideration I put forth in chapter 3, especially as it might have been related to her Australian homeland. In that chapter, I suggest that it's no coincidence that the death practices beginning to take root 150 years ago in the United States would reflect the hardening of the dualism and the qualities of *backgrounding, radical exclusion, incorporation, homogenization,* and *instrumentalism* that have been with us for so long. And furthermore, that these qualities would find a home in American death practices and, just like other aspects of nature, begin to enact control over the dead body.

But there is an upside to all this. Because if there were ever a set of practices that challenged our prevailing strange view of nature and gave credence to the philosophy Plumwood calls for, it would be those offered through green burial. The pollution of our current mainstream ways of death care may not be the dire matters of hydraulic fracturing, climate change, species loss, or environment injustice, but they're still part of a grander picture, a piece of which gives life to the logic of dualism, that enables that *strange* story of separateness to go on and to perpetuate the other terrible damage many of us spend our lives trying to curb and clean up.

If green burial practices "just make sense" to people, it's because they fundamentally affirm reason in nature. In that way, Freddie Johnson was right. Green burial is a return to rationality. Not the damaging kind we've lived with for too long, but the kind that equates with the good sense of nature. In breaking down the walls between humans and nature, it's also a rationality that enables us to see that, living or dead, we do, indeed, belong to the earth. After all, the *eco* in *ecology* comes from the Ancient Greek *okîos*, which means "home." What could make us more aware of this home than unobstructed, sans pollution, returning to it when we die?

Of course, understanding all of this is one thing, but coming out from under such a damaging form of rationality is another. The twentieth-century philosopher Herbert Marcuse understood as much, cautioning us against this form of reason that finds a way to seep into every crevice of our lives. As we become more constrained by what it requires of us, the more "unimaginable" it can be to trust that we can actually break free of it.[31] And so, the task before us is great.

But not impossible.

Leopold said, we need "a mode of guidance,"[32] an ethic, that will lead us to live in communion with the earth. *A thing is right when it tends to preserve the integrity, stability, and beauty of the biotic community. It is wrong when it tends otherwise.*[33] Living humans, as well as the human dead, are part of that biotic community. And the green burial movement is helping us to remember. In guiding the living to do right by the dead—to do what just makes sense— an earth-based ethic of human death resituates rationality back inside the ring of nature while renewing human interconnection with the earth.

2

Dead Bodies That Matter

Not long after my own awakening, I was confounded by a whole host of news stories in which the dead had been violated in some way. While none of them touched on greener death ways or challenged conventional death care in any substantive way, I somehow knew that grappling with them was important for this overall project of greening death. And so I wander here a bit in order to do some of that sorting, so as to be absolutely clear what I mean when I say green burial does right by the dead.

DOES THE DEAD BODY MATTER?

Perhaps the most bewildering of these stories was the breaking news of the Georgia crematory operator who failed to incinerate hundreds of bodies left to his care, a discovery made quite accidently by a propane deliveryman making a last-minute pit stop in the woods surrounding the facility. There he glimpsed a gruesome scene that even the Appalachian forest couldn't contain—the scattered remains of the human dead.

Though the worker reported what he'd seen to his boss, who then called the local sheriff's office, it would be two years before the EPA and the FBI would fully uncover the crimes, and the crematory operator, Ray Brent Marsh, would be arrested and charged. A total of 334 corpses would be recovered from the Tri-State Crematory—some in caskets, others still wearing hospital gowns—all in varying stages of decay. The recovery would test the limits of forensic science, as some of the bodies were there for as long as five years, making identification difficult. Not all the bodies were found strewn in and among the wilds of nature, however. Many were stacked in a nearby garage.

One lay inside an unused hearse, and another partially inside the crematory's oven chamber.[1]

Not long after that, several stories of the thriving black market in body parts were big news in the Northeast,[2] most notably with the arrest of former New Jersey dental surgeon turned mastermind ghoul, Michael Mastromarino. Hatching a plan for the procurement, dismemberment, and sale of human tissue, skin, nails, and bones to the tune of millions, Mastromarino pulled together the supply of funeral homes with the demand of the medical industry, one acquiring the dead and doing the dirty work of butchering and the other paying for it.

To make matters worse, many of the bodies were diseased—some with cancer and AIDS—the effects of which continue to play out among donees today. Mastromarino unsuspectingly preyed on the poor, sourcing most of his cadavers via the direct cremation crowd in low-income communities, but the story splashed the headlines in 2006 because one of the bodies that fell under his knife was a celebrity—*Masterpiece Theatre*'s Alastair Cooke. His daughter, a Vermont minister who arranged for the cremation, said that while her father might have appreciated the "Dickensian" quality of what became of his skin and bones, he also had a deep aversion to dissection.[3] Mastromarino paid for his crimes. He, along with a former nurse who ran the "cutting crew" and three New Jersey funeral directors, were all arrested, tried, and convicted.[4] And in an ironic turn of events, Mastromarino developed metastatic liver cancer in prison, a fast-acting malignancy that quickly spread to his bones and killed him.[5]

In more recent years, I've followed the criminal investigations emerging from a number of cemeteries throughout the United States, including three owned by Service Corporation International (SCI), the largest conglomerate provider of funeral services in North America. In those three high-profile cases, SCI was accused of overselling plots, digging up gravesites, and removing remains to make room for new burials, all done without the knowledge or consent of the families involved.[6]

Though the sensational aspects of these stories make them newsworthy in a culture that feeds off human indiscretion, they also tug hard at us because we understand that the dead are somehow due our respect. Sent into a tailspin of worry over what exactly we mean when we say the corpse matters to us, such events can leave us feeling morally stranded as we search in vain for answers as to how they could happen at all.

Greed, power, and corruption may clear up some of the motives at the SCI cemeteries as well as the ghoulish crimes of Mastromarino and his co-conspirators, but because Marsh had nothing to gain from not cremating the bodies left to his care, the reasons for his behavior remain less clear. Many of the families of the dead long to hear Marsh explain his actions, because in the decade or more that has passed, and with little time left on his prison sentence, he has yet to offer one. With the likelihood of never knowing why, we're left living in the aftermath of violations that can't be undone, where, very often, the only source of justice is to be found in the courts.

In legal terms, all of these events involved a failure to fulfill fiduciary responsibilities and provide services for which they were paid. In some cases, not only were the dead not granted the disposition they were promised while they were alive, but families, duped into believing their loved ones were interred for eternity, were conned by the very folks expected to adhere to an idea of the dead that actually matters. Though our laws provide some indication that such violations against the dead are wrong, what causes us to cry out against them is not mere negligence and harm, but a breach of inviolable trust—that silent contract of care that the living expect from others who take on the responsibility of tending to the dead.

All these years after the grisly discovery at the Tri-State Crematory, public sentiment remains raw.[7] And that's because Marsh's crimes weren't just deceitful and fraudulent. Yes, he failed in what he had been assigned to do, lied to the families about promising to incinerate their loved ones, and perpetuated those lies by handing back boxes of cement powder in place of human ashes. But Marsh broke more than just the law. He shattered what caregivers of the dead regard as a sacred charge assigned to them on behalf of the bereaved. "The bodies of the newly dead are not debris, nor remnant, nor are they entirely icon or essence," funeral director Thomas Lynch reminds us, "it is wise to treat such new things tenderly, carefully, with honor."[8]

Disbelief, disgust, and indignity are likely to move in us when they're treated otherwise, whether we're directly affected or not. Whatever any of us may believe about what happens after death, about the existence of souls, and the worth of departed spirits, such deeds defy some essential logic of reverence, something most of us struggle to get our heads around. Indeed, lack of regard for the corpse betrays more than our sense of right and wrong, more than just our trust. It cuts to an ineffable wisdom Lynch implores us to never forget—that like a newborn baby, the dead are worthy of our care. If Tri-State and the other stories push us to question whether the dead body matters at all, it's only because in the deepest, most whole parts of ourselves, we know that it somehow does.

Perhaps we've not lost hold of what Durkheim proclaimed to be true, that "the dead man is a sacred being"[9]—sacred, not because the dead are tied to religion, but because the corpse is part of the extraordinary and beyond-the-social aspects of human life that we can never know for sure, and not a member of those ordinary and commonplace things that we can know for certain—the profane.[10] If we treat the corpse well it's because it evokes in us

feelings of apprehension and dread, feelings that surface from its mysterious-
ness.[11] In other words, not being certain of what the dead are prompts us to
do right by them.

After all, every culture has rites for the dead[12] with proper disposition an
expectation that can be traced back to the earliest of civilizations.[13] Though
in ancient Greece the soul may have reigned over the body, the lack of proper
burial was still imagined as an affront to human dignity.[14] Antigone, who
took great personal risk by defying her uncle and out of love and respect for
her dead brother buried him on her own, continues to be read as a reminder
that even in the worst of circumstances—like facing the death of someone
whose life may have been lived with a propensity for cruelty or evil—there's
always value in putting the dead to rest. President Barack Obama sent this
message—sans love—in 2011 when he insisted that the treatment of Osama
bin Laden's corpse be in keeping with Muslim tradition, and ultimately "respectful of the body."[15]

But expressions of respect are complicated, because what looks like reverence in one culture can be read as defilement in another. Ideas of corpse
violation can even vary within the same culture, a fluctuation in meaning and
practice that is often politically motivated. For example, although we may
detest what happened at the SCI cemeteries, Native American burial grounds
have long been sites of condoned mass disruption, a practice that persists
today by way of state- and corporate-sponsored real estate development.[16]
In 2011, activists were arrested protesting a state construction Kaua'i park
project to build a septic leach field that continued to move forward despite
evidence of native burial. In response to the desecration, one of the protest-
ers, James Alalem, remarked, "What are we, the toilet? Our sacred sites are
toilets."[17] So violated are the living native people of Hawaii by the dislocation
of their ancestral dead that a rethinking of the sacred tradition of whole-body
earth burial in favor of safeguards against future violation is afoot, as some
say that many native Hawaiians are now considering cremation in order to
avoid desecration.[18] Though the 1990 Native American Graves Protection and
Repatriation Act requires that cultural items, including human remains, be
returned to native people, burial grounds continue to be disturbed today. Unlike the crimes of SCI, however, this disturbance is more often than not sanc-
tioned at the federal and state levels, leaving no real recourse for the living.

Another most recent example of how power and politics shape the treatment
of the dead includes the story of Michael Brown, an eighteen-year-old black
man who was shot and killed by a white police officer in Ferguson, Missouri, in
August 2014. For four, some say as long as five, hours, Brown's bloody body
lay in the street in the "unrelenting summer heat," and, for a long portion of
that time, undraped and available for public consumption. The spectacle of his

violated body was reminiscent of a history of lynchings—when not so long ago black men were murdered without recourse in the light of day, and their bodies were left to be openly gazed upon to remind southern blacks of the threat of white power. Many say that the public disrespect of Brown's body was one of the contributing factors that led up to the ensuing riots.[19]

What's considered gravesite desecration endures as a thorny question in other places too, like in forensic investigations following wartime atrocities. Whether it's the murdered daughters of the Madres de Plaza de Mayo, the massacred of Jedwabne, Poland, or the slain civilians and soldiers in former Yugoslavia, or the Congo, tensions have surfaced between religious leaders and the human rights workers sent in to find evidence to be used against those standing trial for war crimes.[20] Not unlike the native Hawaiian reaction to the digging up of ancestral burial grounds, there are many global cases in which religious leaders have spoken out against disturbing the dead, claiming the work of forensics teams as a form of desecration itself. This in spite of the fact that the dead had already been violated in innumerable ways, most often through mass grave burial, and that the charge of the war tribunals was to seek justice for the horrors done to those bodies. But some religious communities and their leaders have not always been convinced that humanitarian work contributes to a dead body that matters. Instructions to humanitarian aids in a 2003 Red Cross report in the former Yugoslavia included a directive to "respect the remains; they are part of the deceased person and as such are in *some way* sacred."[21] As the religious leaders themselves may have wondered, in what *way*, exactly, might that be?

In the United States, examples of shifting and conflicting ideas of defilement shaped by increasingly powerful institutional forces include two practices now widely accepted, embalming and dissection. Prior to the Civil War, embalming was perceived as an unwarranted and unthinkable practice, in much the same way it's still regarded by Muslims and Jews today throughout the United States and other parts of the world. What would become the widespread use of embalming was also politically fueled, as chemical companies that manufactured embalming fluid hired teachers to spread their science to others. Eventually, some chemical companies set up mortuary schools, training new undertakers in the novel and highly praised practice of preserving the dead.[22]

Similarly, whether it's for determining cause of death, organ donation, or gross anatomy labs, dissection in the form of autopsy is routine today. And yet up until the early nineteenth century cutting into the dead was considered a mark of disrespect for the person performing the task and "a fate worse than death" for the corpse subjected to it.[23] That the first bodies made available for dissection were those of criminals—namely, the dead sourced from workhouses of the poor—was not a mere matter of convenience. Anatomists were able to do their cutting precisely because, in Durkheim's terms, they were no longer thought to be in the realm of the sacred. Their social status had already recast them into the everyday, the knowable, the profane, making them fair game for science's pursuit of knowledge.[24]

By the 1940s, all of this had changed—the dead would no longer need to be removed from the realm of the sacred in order for medicine to raise its scalpel. Within one hundred year's time, dissection would be transformed into a kind of benevolence, a form of "public goodwill toward medical progress and toward fellow citizens."[25] This stark shift in attitude didn't go unnoticed by medical schools responsible for it as they recognized that in order to get students to do "the willful mutilation of the body of another human being,"[26] they would need to be trained in the suppression of their own physical and emotional responses. While the dead would be remade into a locus worthy of scientific inquiry, the dissector would also undergo transformation; they would need to think differently in order to do differently. They would need to find a way to detach.[27] This change in attitude, and practice, would amount to a radical departure in terms of what would count as violation.

Even before the rise of anatomists, though, there were exceptions to the rule that all dissection was, in fact, an act of defilement. The most notable of these was the early modern Christian cult of relics, where bodies of mostly holy people were boiled, buried, and disemboweled and then placed on display in places of worship throughout Europe.[28] Fast forward to today. We might be okay with dissection, but the public display of human remains? Seems rather inconceivable. Except that in some cases, it's not.

I couldn't help but think of Jeremy Bentham—the British moral philosopher whose mummified corpse and skeleton have been on view at the University College London since 1850—when I went to see Gunther Von Hagens's controversial *Body Worlds 2.*[29] Before his installation of permanently preserved human corpses went on tour, von Hagen was perhaps best known for performing the first public dissection in 170 years in an East End London gallery.[30] Much like that public evisceration, but through a process called *plastination, Body Worlds 2* and his initial *Body Worlds* invite the public in to see with their own eyes, to "discover the mysteries under [our] own skin."[31] Though *I* experienced *Body Worlds* as a violation of the dead, the veneer of science seemed to overwhelmingly trump any widespread outrage. On a global scale, it has been wildly popular, with the only real objection that some of the cadavers might have been illicitly procured from a Chinese prison.[32]

And so, what counts as care for the dead is a knotty thicket, made all the more so by the range of values given to bodies—alive and dead—mainly because even the dead are not exempt from the enduring politics of race, class, and sex. Not to mention science and religion. And though the dead may be sacred, though desecration remains a problem for us, what's actually violating toward the dead is culturally specific, sometimes even personal, and readily open to change. But despite the bearing context has on what counts as reverence or defilement, what seems fairly certain is that how the dead are treated still very much matters to us.

If stories of violation aren't enough to remind us that the dead body matters, we can always count on the doubters among us to help us remember. Cultural historian Thomas Laqueur traces the skepticism of the dead body's worth back to the Greek philosopher Diogenes the Cynic, who called for his own dead body to be thrown over the city wall to the dogs.[33] Diogenes might have scorned the acts of Antigone and the whole of ancient Greece, but he might still share something in common with at least some Americans today who believe there's nothing much about the corpse to fuss about. As one client told it to his elder law attorney in response to his preferred funeral plans, "just put me out with the trash."[34] Perhaps because it's the living who will eventually act on behalf of the dead; to think about the value of one's own corpse can be a different project than thinking about the value of another's.

Whatever the reason, these doubters stand in contrast to what Laqueur suggests is some original wisdom that marks human beings' "step away from nature" into culture. Because the dead were once alive and rooted in culture, because they still have ties to the living, and because they act as the living's touchstones for history, they are, he says, "more than just matter."[35] And yet, being "*more* than *just* matter" brings us right back to that troublesome human/nature dualism—that *strange* view of nature that sets humans apart and above it. If we take Laqueur at what he says, then our doing right by the dead hasn't been the result of their flesh, blood, and bone. Rather, it's only because the corpse rests within the meanings of culture that we are apt to care about it at all.

And herein lies the problem.

DOES THE DEAD BODY MATTER TO NATURE?

The well-dressed and adorned body in the fancy casket may have been all satire to Jessica Mitford, who poked fun at the practice of putting lipstick on a corpse in *The American Way of Death*.[36] But those practices were—and still are—expressions of respect and care for the dead, just as the less ostentatious and more affordable practice of direct cremation and dispersal of ashes are, too.

And yet, as we've been "doing right" by the dead through these conventional forms of care, in both tending to them and still believing they are in need of our concern, we've all the while been unable to see how the dead body is *matter* too, one that has value all its own, and one that matters not only to us but also to the whole of nature. And this is regardless of whether conventional whole-body burial or cremation is practiced. As I'll discuss in the next chapter, though cremation has had less of an impact on the environment than conventional burial, the rising tide away from conventional burial to cremation has not yet done much to bring us back to a dead body that matters much to nature at all.

Thwarting the trajectory of the dead at every turn, U.S. conventional death care has denied the very sense in dead matter, its very flow—its essential direction. Rendered mindless nature, the corpse is treated much like other parts of the natural world that are also imagined to have no necessary design of their own. Through the perfunctory use of embalming, sealed hardwood and metal caskets, concrete vaults, meticulously manicured lawn-park cemeteries, and, even to some degree, incineration, death care in the United States has been all about ignoring the very logic inherent to the process of decay, making it seem as if it has no place, or value, in the natural world. It's in these most basic ways that conventional death care has not been doing right by the dead.

Whatever is at play in the dead body's matter—transformation, return, the flow of life, decomposition, rot, or, most simply, decay—it's a kind of sense we've long lost sight of, but one we can get a glimpse of by looking at the truth of ecology. Dead bodies—as *matter*—matter in a similar way that, for instance, food waste matters. Like any organic substance, dead bodies will rot and return to the elements.

Environmental conditions will determine the how and when, but unless a body is frozen, preserved, incinerated, or annihilated through some newly developed disposal process like alkaline hydrolysis, promession, or the Energetically Autonomous Tactical Robot (EATR),[37] a corpse will break down, nourish the land, and contribute to the flourishing of other life. Drawing from the knowledge of her Pueblo ancestors, Leslie Marmon Silko explains it this way: "You see," she says, "that after a thing is dead, it dries up. It might take weeks or years, but eventually if you touch the thing, it crumbles under your fingers. It goes back to dust. Nothing is wasted. What domestic animals or wild scavengers can't eat will be fed to the plants. The plants feed on the dust of these few remains."[38] It's a truth we've long been at odds with.

A central roadblock to embracing it, Plumwood said not long before her own death, is that human beings are figured as the exception to the rule of predation. "Dominant concepts of human identity," she says, "position humans outside and above the food chain, not as part of the feast in a chain of reciprocity. Animals can be our food, but we can never be their food."[39] It wasn't until Plumwood was thigh high in the grip of a crocodile's mouth that she was seized by this bare bones knowing. There, she "glimpsed a shockingly indifferent world in which [she] had no more significance than any other edible being."[40]

A tale as chilling as it is rare, modern culture has done its best to do away with the predator/prey relationship of humans and more-than-humans. Apart from extreme reality television that reminds us otherwise, the uncommon bear, shark, cougar, or crocodile attack—of human demise and devouring—is practically faraway fiction. Most of us will live lives free of predators looking for their next meal. Whatever sense of our own "foodiness" such experiences may have once lent to us has been lost to us in life, as well as in death. But alive or dead, humans are food, too.

Within seconds of death, fleshflies and blowflies are drawn to human matter through a "universal death scent." Scientists who study bacterial decay, taphonomists, have tracked this process, especially in the open woods where the insects are more readily summoned.[41] The color green may be symbolic of money and greed, nature and growth, but it's also long signified decay. So it comes as no surprise that the hub of the corpse—the abdomen—greens up once putrefaction has set in.[42] This is just one of the five stages of decomposition, as the body moves from internal to external breakdown, bacterial consumption and gases that melt away flesh, to flesh that becomes mold, to dried-out flesh that, at last, disappears. Former surgeon Richard Selzer describes it as "a feast" where "a rich table has been set." Where "guests have already arrived, numberless bacteria that had, in life, dwelt in saprophytic harmony with their host . . . now . . . press against the membrane barriers, break through the new softness, sweep across plains of tissue, devouring, belching gas."[43]

Decomposition, however, is an inexact process. Dinner *will* be served, but it could be fast food or fine dining. An array of determinants can speed up, halt, or delay it, like temperature, humidity, soil type, burial depth, cause of death, and even what the dead had for breakfast. What, if anything, the body was encased in and whether or not the body was embalmed are, of course, factors, too.

Today, the work of taphonomists can be found at some five "body farms" throughout the United States—open-air anthropological research facilities where decomposing corpses are objects of scientific study.[44] Science's goals are meant to be objective, and the body farms' aims are no different—to get to the detailed facts of human rot under different conditions. Justice is another. Driven by forensics, these body farm scientists study human decay in order to help prosecutors win cases.[45] Important work, but that still largely continues to dodge the problem of our burial practices for the environment.

Taphonomy comes to us from the Greek words for *burial* and *law*. Taphonomists, then, essentially study the law of burial. And the law of burial is decay. But for too long now we've been breaking that law through the standard American funeral that has inhibited and temporarily arrested decay—that has, in essence, created a kind of prohibition against decay itself. While scientists have convincingly shown that soils exposed to the repeated burial of cadaveric material create hospitable environments for more decomposition, not unlike a compost pile, further gravesoil ecology could certainly help in better understanding the health and integrity of the land to which the dead are rendered.[46] It could also help to highlight this injustice—that over the last 150 years American death care has come to position human death outside the cycles of nature, crafting a false story in which the "decay of the body is of no significance."[47]

Conventional practices have not exactly stopped decay in its tracks. Embalming fluid will dissipate, and nonbiodegradable enclosures will, in time, bend to the forces of nature. But preserved, encased, and sealed, the corpse's breakdown will look very different had none of these practices been used. When a corpse is hostage to an environment void of oxygen it will likely produce a host of properties that, under oxygenated conditions, would have been transformed and released as carbon dioxide or water. Within such an anaerobic environment, however, things such as "lactic acid, butyric acid and acetic acid as well as butyl alcohol, ethyl alcohol, acetone methane, hydrogen, hydrogen sulfide, . . . and cadavarine . . . a toxic compound" are likely to find their way into the soil.[48]

The cost of these practices is even greater than the sum of these compounds. Through the erection of barriers between the corpse and the rest of the living world, decomposition is not only preempted and altered, but nature is profoundly polluted—corpse and all. The offenders—embalming, hardwood, sealed and metal caskets, and concrete vaults—all have their own histories, their own reasons of how they came into perfunctory use. What each use shares in common, as I will spell out in the next chapter, is that none of them could have come to flourish and to remake a dead body that does not matter to nature without a radical shift in how we think about human decay.

Undoubtedly, the newly dead are as mysterious to us as few things have ever been. That same awe, the last time I checked, did not include our own excrement (unless maybe you're a toddler!). Science has changed some of that. And yet myth, superstition, and religion still surround the dead body. As much as we might like to think otherwise, we're still largely beholden to the spell of the liminal corpse.[49]

Of course, human decay stands apart from other dirty, but tolerable, parts of living. And good and practical reasons exist for why humans wouldn't want to live in the midst of putrefying flesh. Smell is one of them. But unless a corpse is harboring certain kinds of pathogens—like Ebola, Creutzfeldt-Jakob disease, cholera, or haemorrhagic fevers—proximity to human decay won't cause the living irreparable harm.[50] That's true whether the corpse is at home, in a morgue or mortuary, or even in the ground.

Granted, dead bodies have always been regarded as horrific and worrisome, and fear and dread of the dead drench cultures in ways few things do.[51] It's a shared dread—this corpus of ensuing rot—that comes from the need to draw lines between the pure and the polluted, the dirty and the clean.[52] Building on Durkheim's ideas of the sacred and the profane, Mary Douglas's important anthropological work, *Purity and Danger* (1966), urged us to see that there's no such thing as absolute dirt. We do a bit of organizing as a culture to make clear which things are clean and which things are not, an organizing that is meant to bring order and unity to the living world. It should come as no surprise that the corpse most often comes to fall on the dirty side of things, and that it's expected to be dealt with so that cleanliness and stability can return. Cultures respond with rituals that offer to purify the living's space of those fleshy facts so that all may endure. And as we've seen, it's expected to be done with toleration and care.

But if drawing lines between the pure and the polluted, the living and the dead, is what cultures have in common, what's not culturally shared is *how* the *pollution* of the corpse comes to *do* its polluting. The corpse may always be regarded as *dirt*—so to speak—but the manner in which it's imagined to be a threat is time and space specific.

One hundred and fifty years ago colonial practices may have also rendered the corpse a pollutant, but disposing of the dead through proper ritual was more a symbolic gesture meant to ensure well-being on both sides of the life/death divide. But as I'll detail in the next chapter, by the 1830s human decay began to be regarded as especially perilous to the living.[53] This deep unease lodged itself in actual disintegration, in the fear that human death could physically contaminate, harm, and possibly even destroy living bodies. By the turn of the twentieth century, scientists would show this to be a false fear rooted in misinformation, bad science, and superstition. But most folks would not come to know it. Instead, the spell of this phony panic would linger, fueling toxic and unsustainable practices for decades to come, and with poor outcomes for the environment. Reimagined as an actual, bodily danger, funerary practices developed to inhibit its wrath. The living would need to safeguard. Boundaries would be built. But these fortresses of protection would have dire outcomes. Any notion of a dead body that belonged to some kind of planetary order, that was part of our ecological vision, that mattered to nature—*as matter*—was on its way out.

The danger of this pollution saturates our culture in ever increasing ways that extend beyond what is actually taking place in our death practices. The embodied dead flood plotlines of television and film—zombies carry assault rifles; vampires rage against the living for rights, access, and recognition; and medical cadavers stump the initiated with illness and accident that mere mortals seem incapable of solving.[54] Animated or not, the dead are disgusting invaders, powerful foes, cunning and creepy lovers, and sites of scientific intrigue and discovery. The dead appear as threats for us to deal with. And yet, we can't seem to get enough of them.

Perhaps that's because watching helps us to deal, at least on a symbolic level, with all those matters of life that frighten us most. The feminist film theorist Barbara Creed suggests as much, arguing that the reason why images of femininity often take shape as frightening forms in horror films—castrating female monsters, preternatural adolescent girls, bloodthirsty vamps—is because we loathe, run from, and then seek to control all that is *the monstrous-feminine* in real life.[55] Of course, the corpse already shares something in common with the abject living bodies of women and other feminized people.

In U.S. culture, live bodies are regularly made "other," and marginalized by way of sex and gender, not to mention race, ethnicity, class, nation, and ability status. The bodies of women, queer and transgender people, people of color, the poor, and people with disabilities are both feared and ostracized through state-sponsored programs, social norms, and everyday practices. The abject can take many forms depending upon the culture it inhabits, functioning to oppress and harm others, to maintain the status quo, and to regard certain bodies with suspicion. In this way, the oppressed share a curious commonality with the corpse. Julia Kristeva evokes as much in her influential *The Powers of Horror* (1981)—a work Creed actively draws upon in order to make her case—claiming the corpse as one abject form universal to all human experience. Confronting a corpse, as she famously says, "I am at the border of my condition as a living being, my body extricates itself, as being alive, from that border. I am forced to recognize my own mortality, yet unable to do so at the same time, thus, I must repel it, reject it, abject it."[56]

Distance has done its part, too, in making the pollution of the corpse even more terrifying. There has been a deepening divide between the dead and the living over the last 150 years that makes the living's meeting up with the dead not only frightening but also rather novel. In watching, we're not only encountering a danger, but also, it would seem, a stranger. In psychoanalytic terms repression is at play, as what has been buried climbs its way back to the surface. What this means is that coming face to face with the dead in popular culture culminates in a confrontation of the return of the repressed in the form of death itself—an encounter that gives us the opportunity to ritually redraw the lines of life and death. When the dead do reemerge, however, how do we receive them? This seems an important question, because these representations, while potentially full of connection and revaluing of the dead and their attendant decay, also run the risk of making death both scarier and more sinister, so hostile and troubling that we may do nothing more than push it back down.

The good news is that our feelings about human decay are not fixed and forever. They're flexible and change in contexts and over time and, so, we can remain hopeful that our feelings can be swayed once again. Though popular culture may be a double-edged reminder, it does have the potential to help us along the way. But we'll need to do more. I say *we*, because in spite of our differences—e.g. ethnic, gender, racial, religious, sexual—despite the cult of individualism that fills the veins of American life, our funeral practices are oddly ubiquitous and shared. We are, en masse, a culture terrified of human rot. And we've done our best to shun it.

As green burial offers back to us a relationship with nature that's long overdue, it demands a rethinking of human decay. For too long now attention to decay—to "human foodiness" as Plumwood calls it—has been considered "tasteless," vulgar, wrong.[57] And it's hard to discuss. It's time we brought those putrid facts out into the light of day. This doesn't mean that we look to create practices that leave us living with rotting corpses. But it does mean seeing to our physical place in the food chain and rethinking our relationship to the earth in our living as well as our dying. It means respecting the intelligence within nature so we can find our way back to union with the earth.

Recognition of our "human foodiness," however, should not be mistaken for simple function or utility. This isn't about falling into what philosopher Neil Evernden identifies as a "modern environmental trap" of justifying the parts of nature that are "good for something."[58] This isn't about reducing the value of the corpse to an instrumental scientific valuation—like soil health, for instance. Though that value may be tied to some functional good that human decomposition has to land, it still skirts the deeper question of the dead body's force, flow, power—of its intrinsic worth within the order of things.

The resistance to its worth—the taboo against decay itself—runs deep. *Decay* comes to us from the Latin "to fall," to descend. In a culture that imagines human identity apart from nature, where body is below and mind is above, to go down is a frightening and forbidden trajectory. And what of *decomposition*, which literally means to separate into parts, to lose wholeness? Our nonearthly identity could never comply with such possible disintegration, as it defies a sense of distinct and contained individuality we imagine makes us fully human. *Rot*, of course, also means decay. But it also means *nonsense*. It's adjective relative, *rotten*, which means something has already decayed or has degenerated beyond what's good for human consumption, also denotes something that's "bad" or "morally corrupt." With such negative connotations in our everyday language, it's no wonder we have such an aversion to what the corpse is meant to do. But what the corpse does is neither bad nor corrupt. It has a worth beyond its use for the living, and it's anything but nonsense. Indeed, the corpse has a sense all its own.

Dead bodies may be mysterious to us; they may be part of us, and, for these reasons, may still very much matter to us. But by cutting reason off from matter and the worth of matter off from our meanings of death, we've also been cut off from being able to see that the dead body matters for other reasons too—for the ecologies to which the dead are rendered as well as to the living's sense of their enduring ties to nature. To fully know this wrongdoing, we'll need to track the great wave of ideas and attitudes that came to shift our death practices into ones that, by turning decay into a menace to be managed, have not been respecting the very matter of death.

3

Wrath of the Corpse

There was a time before all this. A time before human decay was robbed of its own sense and purpose—before the perfect storm of practices wiped away a dead body that mattered to nature. Indigenous peoples of North America rendered their dead in earth-friendly ways and within a cosmology that figured humans as part of the larger whole of the natural world.[1] When colonizers first settled onto the land, they, too, buried their dead with simple, natural methods—an unfinished wooden box, a hand-dug hole, a mound of soil. Bodies were prepared for burial mostly by the women of the family, wrapped in the care and strength of their community, and later interred in the family plot or local church graveyard.

This was before the dawn of communal cemeteries, before the word *cemetery* was even used. This was before industrialization and manufacturing, before plastics and polymers and lab-born bound chemicals. Before concrete, steel, and chrome. It goes without saying that not having these things made it possible not to use them. That when they became real and available we did tells us something about the fragility of our thinking in the face of new forces. Even though we once buried our dead green, without yet having the words to say it, human separation from nature was already making inroads into budding American culture, already shaping a view of nature that could turn the dead body, and ultimately our meanings of death, sharply away from the earth.

Like rain and wind bend the land, we're shaped by ideas old and new. On the crag of a changing culture, very old ideas were not very far away. Greek and Judeo-Christian divisions of reason and passion, body and soul provided potential for the damaging practices we would come to call our own. Urban expansion and a budding funeral industry, bent on controlling the reigns of one of our most intimate and meaningful rites of passage, favorably responded to the nascent ideas of the Scientific Revolution that were rapidly turning matter into a problem to be managed.

Death rituals have always varied in the United States, especially with respect to race, ethnicity, class, nation of origin, and religion.[2] And yet, we have only two methods of disposition to call upon in the United States—interment and incineration. And even that distinction's debatable, as the bone that's left from burning must be placed *somewhere*. Most dead will be embalmed. Most will go into the ground inside reinforced caskets and concrete vaults. The others will be cremated.[3] Apart from one location in Colorado that offers a limited number of open-air whole-body incinerations every year, cremation in the United States is practiced by way of crematorium, a high-temperature combustion machine that reduces the dead to bone fragments.

In the American narrative, the philosophies underlying these practices are depicted as wholly unlike each other, as different as the bedrock of Democrats and Republicans. And in many ways they are. But with a closer look we can see that much like politics they do, in fact, share some common ground. Over the last 150 years, burial and cremation—to a greater and lesser degree—have both been shaped in response to the problem of decay. And both of them, in their attempt to manage that problem—to thwart the direction and flow of human death—have clandestinely operated as the real wreakers of havoc, contaminating the dead and the ecosystems of disposition as well as our relationship to nature.

One of the central motivators of my research, as well as my green burial advocacy, has been to grapple with how it is that we ended up where we are. And time and again, what I've come up against is this basic truth—that if our apartness from nature was building strength by the eighteenth century, it soon enough began to show in our death practices. Waking up to an earth-based ethic of human death will mean traveling the long path back to locate some fissure, some moment when human decay first began its creep away from the natural world. Retelling the history of this creep through our funerary practices exposes the routine propensity to feed the human/nature split—to fuel the qualities that arm our separation from nature, the very ones Plumwood warned about—*backgrounding, radical exclusion, incorporation, homogenization*, and *instrumentalism*—attributes, that when deployed, bear down on nature and cause destruction.

It's time we retraced our steps.

Everywhere, it seems, *the* defining shift in our death rites is to be found in the post–Civil War era, when bodies first began to be embalmed and, later, when embalmers tried to professionalize their service in order to sell it.[4] Embalming did have a profound influence on the way we eventually came to care for the dead, but it didn't single-handedly create distance between the dead body and nature, or all on its own transform the way we came to think about human decay. There were other factors, too, some that came before, like sanitation reforms that forced burial outside the town and city walls and away from matters of everyday life. And some that came after, like revived purification arguments that hoped to sell cremation.

GRAVEYARDS, RURAL CEMETERIES, AND LAWN-PARK CEMETERIES

And so, this story begins before the war, around the turn of the nineteenth century when, on the heels of sanitation reforms taking place in Great Britain and France, the United States began their own war on filth. Expanding urban growth and increased immigration collided with new findings in medicine and science that warned of a grubby world that could cause the living irreparable harm. The key offenders were tied to the workings of the human body—what was ingested, excreted, and what ailed us. Health reforms tore through cities, creating new municipal systems—water, sewer, and garbage—as well as hospitals and sanitariums equipped to both efficiently and effectively deal with the specter of disease. Amid a century filled with the human rights struggles of slavery and suffrage was also the battle for cleanliness—a kind of mission to find a way to live without the ominous problem of dirt.[5]

It's no surprise that sanitary reformers would eventually set their sights on that other bit of flesh—the corpse. When medical reports first began to question the polluting factor of the dead, they focused on the spread of diseases, like yellow fever, measles, and cholera, which swiftly moved through urban settings and began to fill graveyards to capacity. Fearful of more of the same in the days or years to come, broken and grieving families were left desperate for answers, while city officials began to think about health in public terms.[6]

Unfortunately, these epidemics were mostly misunderstood at the time. Before we knew that disease was caused by microorganisms too small to see with the human eye, scientists and medical professionals held to the idea of "miasmas"—that foul-smelling odors could travel through the air and cause people to get sick. Even die. "We need nothing but noses to know there is something rotten in the street," the *New York Daily Times* reported in 1852.[7] If the stench of things—garbage, human waste, rotting corpses—could be eradicated, the theory went, the living might fare okay. And so elimination of the problem became the essential remedy for sanitary dilemmas. Quarantine became a popular solution for the sick, deportment for the suspect. Because immigrants were often scapegoated for the influx of disease, sanitary science became as much about the demonizing of certain bodies marked by nation of origin, race, class, and creed as it did about the scourge of the human body more generally.[8]

Up until the 1830s—in cities throughout the twenty-four states—most dead bodies were interred in the churchyard. Outside of cities, the dead were buried in church graveyards, too, or sometimes also in family plots. These burial grounds, especially those inside larger cities, came to be so poorly managed, and burial space so overcrowded, that remains were often dug up to make room for fresh bodies. Boston's population, for example, tripled in forty years, so that by 1830 there was little room left to bury anew. And though living with the odor of human decay had been a fact of life in early America, as it also had come to be throughout much of Europe, burial grounds increasingly came to be seen as not only public nuisances, but also physical threats. In the streets and in the air, panic over reputed "miasmatic vapors" transformed into a full-fledged public health issue.[9] The dead would need to be dealt with.

Fear of the corpse's rot soon enough made relocation of the dead seem the only logical solution. Cities and small towns everywhere began to pass legislation banning human burial within their borders. In some places, bodies were also disinterred, and if families were well-heeled enough to pay for it, they were individually reinterred somewhere else. In places like New York City, resistance to such practices coupled with protests from churches that wanted to keep the dead in their midst kept the conversation about the infectious qualities of the human dead going for decades until a final decision was made to "exile" them.[10] New York finally banned burial within the city limits in 1823, with many other cities and towns eventually following suit.

By the late 1800s the public would come to know that it was germs, and not stink, that was the real source of infection. The miasma model gave way to a theory of germs, and discussions about public health devolved into personal problems of hygiene. And yet, attitudes toward human decay only worsened. Like immigration reforms (1882 and 1891) that focused on ridding the nation of the bodies of the sick, the dark, the poor, the criminal, and the insane, health reformers focused on "cleansing the nation of the dead."[11] In other cases, remains were moved, en masse, to communal, and often unmarked, gravesites. The terror of the dead was only exacerbated by the death of "undesirables." Those who in life were imagined to pose a threat to community stability were still considered a threat in death, relegated to their separate burial grounds otherwise known as "potter's fields," or, later, sections within new cemetery spaces that were set aside from the more "respectable members of the urban community"[12]—upper-class white folks.

As the United States began to grow and define its boundaries and character, to lay claim to an identity all its own, the dead were also going through their own redefinition. The liminal status of the corpse—its in-betweenness—had long marked it as a kind of social pollution the living had to "put in its place."[13] But the danger the corpse now posed to the living was so severe—so literal— the dead would need to be *radically excluded* in order to be "put to rest."

As this *radical exclusion* happened everywhere, the impact on death practices was sweeping. In my hometown of Rhinebeck, New York, for instance, a burial ban within the village limits was fully passed in 1858.[14] Cemetery plots in some of the churchyards were disinterred and then reinterred in the new "rural" cemetery that was slowly, but surely, forming on the outskirts of town. It's unclear whether the overcrowding was real or simply fueled by spreading sanitary anxiety. But what we do know is the population of Rhinebeck in 1850 was 2,816,[15] a far cry from that of New York with a population nearing eight hundred thousand.[16]

With the urgent need to reform our burial practices, the rural cemeteries that would come to replace the festering mess of the churchyard would be guided by new ideas. Horticultural and landscape design anchored their development, with the first of them, Mount Auburn in Boston, established in 1831. Others just as grand soon followed, like Laurel Hill in Philadelphia; Mount Hope in Rochester, New York; Green-Wood in Brooklyn; and Spring Grove in Cincinnati. Until about 1865, the style flourished in these majestic examples, as well as in more modest ones that took form all over the nation.

Love of "god, nature and the dead"[17] may have collectively grounded their design, but nature was always, by far, front and center. However abhorrent decay might be, reformers recognized the need to do right by the dead by burying them with an expedience that could only be tempered by the peaceful setting of the countryside.[18] Moreover, by resituating human burial away from religious moorings and squarely within the heart of nature, the Rural Cemetery Movement succeeded in doing something else—building common nonsectarian burial institutions. Abandoning the name *graveyard*, which summoned images of waste and disease, for the less menacing word *cemetery*, the Greek for "sleeping chamber," people from disparate backgrounds responded to the call to spend time in these newly designed garden spaces.[19]

But while returning to nature was a vanguard idea of the Rural Cemetery Movement, it's sometimes easy to forget that the movement's genesis was inspired by separation. Exiled from where humans did the regular work of living, being in the midst of the dead would now mean venturing out to visit them. So, too, for the rest of nature. Rendered somewhere "out there," nature was not to be found in the homes or in the streets, in the backyards or in the churchyards of village and urban life. In many ways, the Rural Cemetery Movement wasn't so different from other sanitary measures happening at the same time, particularly the creation of asylums—those bucolic oases sequestered away from the reasonable human world.[20] And so, although nature may have been celebrated and the dead's place within it certain, *radical exclusion* of the dead was, in effect, turning the living into tourists of both.

This radical exclusion combined with a still prevailing fear of decomposing flesh would come to trump the Rural Cemetery Movement's call back to the land and ultimately preempt its longevity. That the movement had such a short go of it is, perhaps, more a testament to the strength of the new status of decay as a physical threat—the one that drove the dead out into the countryside to begin with—than a failure to sell the concept of common burial in the garden. If the strength of the concept withered in the face of an exiled contaminated corpse and an increasingly mechanized culture that only amplified distancing in other parts of our lives, it's because under the gaze of science the corpse never really stood a chance.[21]

By the late 1800s cemeteries across the United States would begin to become both more "standardized and mechanized,"[22] paving the way for a more functional cemetery look—the lawn-park and later, the memorial park cemetery. As time went on, these new cemeteries would appear more like the emerging organized suburban landscapes that were cropping up around the United States and less like the romantic English gardens that inspired them. Rural cemeteries may have been more park than these new lawn-parks could ever be, but the lawn-park would find a way to co-opt the language of the green commons to its own ends.[23] Upending terrain marked by serpentine paths of dappled shade, increased tree cover, blooming shrubs, teeming ponds, and a range of birds and other creatures that navigated their shifting borders, the emerging lawn-parks were built as "proof . . . against the powerful forces of nature constantly at work."[24] Cemetery superintendents were known to compete with each other by manipulating "the natural in nature," so that the lawn-park became not only less and less about actual nature but also less and less about the living's place within it. Though the living would still visit the dead, folks were no longer urged to spend time in the "park," creating ever more distance between humans and nature. And, ultimately, between the living and the dead.

Not only were the dead *radically excluded* from the living but, also, *instrumentalized*, reduced to a means to an end—an end that was all about the order of cemetery standardization and maintenance.[25] With their focus on both—the gridded rows, the manicured lawns—any bond the Rural Cemetery Movement hoped to forge between the corpse and nature was increasingly under siege. Indeed, the war on decay was anything but over.

EMBALMING

If there was any doubt that it was, the Civil War came as a forceful reminder that the problem of decay still very much remained a problem of the day. In fact, the dreadfulness of decay only fueled the Union cause. While abolishing slavery was part of the political arguments driving the North, Union narratives that foretold the terror of corruption wrought on the battlefield were often steeped in racist rhetoric. A war correspondent reporting on one particular battle described the dead—all white—as "so black" that they "all looked like negroes, as they lay in piles where they had fallen, one upon another . . . [filling] the bystanders with a sense of horror."[26] Symbolically tying the bodies of African Americans, living or dead, to visual cues of rot only further substantiated the growing view that decay was something to be feared.

As soldiers died on the battlefield far and away in the South, the Union army had to figure out the most thoughtful and efficient ways of caring for them. War dead would either need to be buried where they expired, or somehow—some way—shipped back home. But transport was costly and slow, and, depending upon the time of year, very hot. New preservation techniques, as medical professionals trained in arterial embalming presented them, promised to outwit time, space, and environmental conditions. They promised to do just what needed to be done—forestall the inevitability of decomposition. Newly trained civilian medical professionals were called into action, and over four years' time, as many as forty thousand bodies were embalmed.[27] For those families who wanted it, and who could also afford it, bodies were shipped back home for burial.[28] Responding to the illogic of war, and in spite of the long-held prohibition against it, embalming was taken up as a temporary solution to rampant rot.[29]

But embalming would not be left on the battlefield. When Abraham Lincoln died, his body was "hollowed" out, crafted into a shell, pumped with preservation fluids, and paraded around a country of mourners for all to see.[30] Until the Civil War, embalming had been considered a violation of the dead, but by the time the war broke out and cast upon the land thousands of fallen soldiers sanitary arguments were well underway. No doubt the prevailing fear of filth made it easy for a nation, so in pain and so in need of "overcoming the violence enacted on it," to look upon the preserved body of Lincoln with respect and hope.[31] Because, in a sense, Lincoln's embalmed corpse was also about overcoming. Overcoming not just the carnage of war, and the hate and injustice that had cruelly parted a nation, but of nature, too.

Which is just how funeral directors—who eventually needed to be licensed in the new practice—began to push embalming onto a growing urban public already schooled in the problem of decay. By 1920 funeral directors set their sites on honing their techniques on the body, directing their aspirations in one direction: to make the dead body, in one funeral director's words, "look to me as natural as though they were alive." The rationale was the "memory picture," that only an embalmed body—funeral directors argued—could offer the living. In trying to convince the public that embalming could conquer "the horrors of the grave," funeral directors made specious claims about the potential of the new science, saying, for instance, that if bodies were dug up they would look as fresh as when the living got their last look.[32] But the promise of preservation was ultimately built on a lie, because no amount of embalming fluid can keep a body in that faux fresh state forever. After awhile, even Abraham Lincoln's body showed signs of decay that no amount of chemicals could fix.[33] Indeed, embalmers understood the limits of preservation—knew there was no overcoming the flow and direction of nature. And yet, it would be many decades before the public would really come to believe it.

Jessica Mitford was the first to publicly blow the whistle on this lie. Her interview with California pathologist Dr. Jesse Carr sounded an alarm in the early 1960s when it exposed how "(a)n exhumed embalmed body is a repugnant, moldy, foul-looking object."[34] Despite this disclosure, and the ensuing public awareness born from Mitford's best-selling *The American Way of Death*, preservation remains one of the driving forces behind the mainstream practice of embalming. But it's not the only one, and it's not the only reason why it came to sell in the first place. Indeed, questions of sanitation were still very much in the air when embalmers first came onto the scene with their arsenic-based embalming fluid, patented in 1856.[35]

Centering on issues of disease and the use of embalming fluid as a hygienic precaution, embalmers' sanitary arguments were more than familiar.[36] With a helping hand from the funeral industry, fears around sanitation augmented the social belief that embalming was a necessary health measure—the corpse would be cleansed of its own filth in order to produce a less dangerous one to the public. Medical professionals, urban planners, and funerary personnel accepted this promise of disinfection, and eventually, too, so did the public, opening the way to rituals in which newly relegated caretakers would eradicate the dirt of the dead.[37]

Which brings us to another lie promulgated by the funeral industry—that embalming is a sanitary practice. Not only is there nothing much about the corpse that needs disinfecting, but even if it did, embalming chemicals don't act as cleansers. Dead bodies, like live bodies, can carry pathogens, but most of them die with the body. Ebola and Creutzfeld-Jacobs disease may send up red flags, but whatever danger may lurk poses more of a threat to those who handle the dead than to air, soil, and water.[38] But even if such pathogens pose a threat, they won't be remedied through embalming.[39] In fact, as the Centers for Disease Control (CDC) suggests, embalming could actually exacerbate the spread of some infectious diseases, particularly Ebola.[40]

The social belief that the dead body is an actual pollutant—one that can bring real harm to the living—lingers. Until the 1980s, the World Health Organization (WHO) operated on just that idea, saying that in the aftermath of natural disasters, large numbers of dead could actually cause such harm.

Over the past thirty-five years, however, WHO has been working to dispel that myth, and to reeducate the public, The media, unsurprisingly, has not done much to support WHO's endeavor.[41] And neither has the funeral industry. In spite of evidence that's exonerated the corpse of its perilous status, the practice of preservation masked as sanitation has become widespread and, for some reason, imagined to be necessary. The effect of this sanitation lie runs deep, as the dead body is *backgrounded*, denied its own direction and flow—it's own intrinsic value and purpose.

To deal with the fictitious wrath of the corpse, caregivers of the dead would now need to be skilled, to possess a certain kind of "scientific acumen," to ensure the social good.[42] Not only did states begin to pass legislation that required as much,[43] but some chemical companies, who desperately wanted to sell their products, set up schools to train teachers in the new science of death care. Aided by new publications that glorified embalming's many attributes—disinfection, preservation, as well as the guarantee that being buried alive would no longer be a problem—company teachers traveled the United States proselytizing their good word.[44] The National Funeral Directors Association (NFDA) emerged at this time, too (1882), a trade organization that, among other things, promoted the wonders of embalming while wishing the work of the embalmer, in all his scientific prowess, be granted a kind of professional status.[45] That status never fully materialized in the United States. But the embalmer as funeral director/funeral director as embalmer did. Launched by the promise of sanitary science and the will of commerce, these new caretakers of the dead would, with authority, grab the reigns of our death rites.

Tasking caretakers of the dead to deal with the fake wrath of decay marked a sharp departure from how the dead had been cared for both before and after colonizers first ascended the banks of North America. Preparation of the body was not set apart, but tightly interwoven into the tapestry of early American communities.[46] Because death most often took place in the home, those duties were long confined to domestic life, although sometimes an outsider, such as a midwife came in to do the work. Still, it was more often family, mostly women, who washed, clothed, and prepared the body for burial. In many ways, death care was merely an extension of other home-based work, including childbirth, child rearing, and caring for the sick. But the science of embalming would come to change all that. As death labor moved away from the domestic realm, men's care of the dead would become formalized, while women's would become discredited and forgotten.[47]

A shift in who cared for the dead, and how, would not be the only outcome of the new practice of preservation. Because embalming would eventually require the removal of the body from the home, domestic space, as quasi-public grieving space, would eventually become a thing of the past. Combined with new crowded urban settings, a growing loss of community wrought by immigration, and an increase in wealth among those upwardly mobile folks for whom paying for death care suddenly didn't seem so strange, more and more distance would be created between the dead and the bereaved.[48]

Though it was upper-class white communities that would first begin to pay for this care—hiring newly trained professional men who were also white—it wouldn't take long for those services to spread into communities of color. When they did, however, white undertakers were often known to neglect and disrespect the bereaved. Combined with a history of violence at the hands of whites, especially among African Americans, professionals would begin to emerge from within their own ranks. African Americans, in particular, saw not only opportunity within the emerging funerary trade but also a moral obligation to their neighbors, kin, and friends to care for their own dead. But it would be slow going. In 1900 less than 1 percent of the undertakers in Manhattan, for instance, were "colored."[49] And retribution from white undertakers who sought to corner the market was not uncommon, making death care choices, especially for those in ethnic immigrant neighborhoods, narrow and unsafe.[50] The eventual licensing required for funeral care lodged a wedge between communities and their dead, one that would only come to be undone through struggle. Fighting to become a legitimate caretaker of the dead would also mean taking on the new practice of the trade. And take it on they did.

In the end, regardless of race and class contexts, the same fears around sanitation that drove the dead away from the living also catapulted the widespread practice of embalming. Together, they began to radically redraw the lines of dirty and clean, remaking the decay of the dead body into an actual physical pollutant. At a time when other institutions, such as schools, hospitals, and prisons,[51] had become increasingly successful at disciplining the bodies of the living, the funeral industry, medicine, and science were finding their own ways to discipline the matter of death—a disciplining that would have repercussions for the human as well as the more-than-human.

And that's due to the simple fact that the embalming process relies on chemicals. Until the early 1900s, arsenic was the key ingredient, a mineral whose meaning comes from the Greek words for "masculine" and "potent." And arsenic has staying power. Although arsenic would later be named a human health hazard and eventually banned, remnants of the chemical have been known to show up in "groundwater 'downstream' of [many] late-19th century cemeteries."[52] Arsenic in embalming fluid may be a thing of the past, but embalming fluid still relies on chemicals. Today the key ingredient is a form of formaldehyde, along with "42 other federally regulated" substances.[53] In its vaporous state, formaldehyde is a known carcinogen, and so proper precautions must be taken when handling the fluid. Which is to say that worker health is always at risk.[54]

But what's perhaps most alarming about the way embalming has developed over the last 150 years is that by dosing the dead body with toxic chemicals the dead have become poisoned, In its quest to eradicate filth and safeguard the living, the use of embalming has effectively succeeded in turning the dead into something dangerous, a real pollutant. An astounding reversal.

Despite this contamination, formaldehyde *is* biodegradable, meaning that through contact with sunlight, heat, oxygen, and the presence of bacteria it will eventually break down into smaller molecules. Few studies have been done to learn under what conditions formaldehyde is most apt to break down, or what threat formaldehyde and other toxic chemicals in embalming fluid precisely pose to soil, water, and air. But whether the environmental risk is severe or mild, with 4.3 million gallons of embalming fluid used each year by the funeral industry[55] it still amounts to a considerable slowing down of bacterial decay.

And that's because decomposition of an embalmed body takes quite a different course than one that is not embalmed, with the larger muscles affected first, like the legs. Studies also show that flies and beetles, which are by necessity drawn to dead bodies, are not attracted to those chemicals, staying away until much of the fluid has dissipated.[56] Ocean life is also repelled by the smell of embalming chemicals, and so an embalmed body buried at sea will take longer to decompose.[57] Again, what these studies show is the deep ramification of the perfunctory use of embalming—more and more, and yet, more *backgrounding* of decay.

CASKETS, VAULTS, AND LINERS

If burial now happened in a sphere of nature outside of the realm of the living in a place that symbolically eschewed the disorderliness of corruptibility (the lawn-park), at the very least the dead were returned to nature through actual burial. But coupled with embalming, the dead body's distance from nature would only be further hastened by the use of sealed hardwood and metal caskets, and vaults and grave liners.

Until the nineteenth century, bodies were largely buried in simple wooden boxes made by family members or furniture makers. Some of these furniture makers morphed into informal undertakers who, because they made and sold coffins, were in a fitting position to be paid for other services like transporting the body and, later on, preparing it for burial. As funeral directors organized and turned death care into a business of services, manufacturing companies saw an opportunity to make and market death commodities to those who now sold them. One of the first casualties of this commodification was the coffin. Crafted to contour to the human shape, the coffin elicited the gloomy rank of the graveyard.[58] This in contrast to the casket—with its rectangular design and sophisticated style—that functioned to shift attention away from the "dangerous" qualities of the corpse.[59]

One of the early casket companies, Stein Manufacturing Company, also published a funeral trade journal—a professional rag—that targeted industry movers.[60] Like the chemical companies selling embalming fluid, Stein set out to convince funeral directors that their caskets could also produce a good-looking corpse. And so, not only were caskets turned into the opulent containers Jessica Mitford would later deplore, but the design of the caskets would be such that the living were now promised that the dead would be protected for an eternity. With grave robbing a real fear during this time, many early casket makers secured their new burying boxes with locks and elaborate lids. But by the late 1880s, companies began to secure their caskets for other reasons—worry that the surrounding environment might infect the corpse. Casket makers began offering "air-sealed metallic caskets" that were not only "air-tight" but also "water, vermin and germ-proof."[61]

The legacy of caskets as preservation endures today, still sold to the bereaved with the promise of shielding the body from the elements that surround it. The world's largest casket company, Batesville Casket Company, markets both hardwood and metal caskets with gaskets and sealers that promise invincibility to soil, air, and water—to protect the flesh. Yet another fib crafted by the funeral industry. Like embalming, no container is able to "preserve the body in a life-like condition forever."[62] Not only will any casket, metal or otherwise, eventually bend to the forces of nature, but as Mitford exposed long ago now, confining decaying matter to an airless space only speeds up putrefaction.[63] The body will produce gases, and with no place to go, containers will leak or possibly even burst.[64] Companies such as Kryprotek and Ensure-A-Seal know this, of course, as they manufacture protective coverings for caskets that are inserted into mausoleums.[65]

Nearly all caskets that go into the ground are first placed within another container of some kind—the burial vault or grave liner. Unless we've been in the market for one, it's likely most of us have never seen a vault. And that's primarily because when mourners arrive at the cemetery for burial the vault has already been installed in the ground. With the faux grassy drape cloaking the surrounding dirt and the casket hovering over the hole, the vault is all but invisible to those in attendance. And distracted by the weighty matters of the funeral itself, few probably notice the vault cover lying on the ground nearby.

Though almost always used, there's no law that requires a vault for burial. And yet, most cemeteries insist upon it—a rule born from the maintenance needs and methods of the lawn-park style. Because caskets will eventually settle and leave an impression that makes lawn mowing tough to navigate, vaults have become a routine part of the burial process. Makeshift vaults and grave liners were, like metal caskets with their locks and sealed lids, initially used to hinder grave robbers and also to prevent sinkholes,[66] but they eventually found widespread purpose in the even lawnlike atmosphere that came to be one of the defining features of the lawn-park.[67] And that purpose, born out of an attempt to counter subsidence, has succeeded in *instrumentalizing* the corpse—turning it into a means to an orderly end for the cemetery. Vault use is also a way of *homogenizing* the dead, of rendering the dead uniformly the same—neatly spaced within "incorruptible" boxes—and not uniquely positioned to succumb to the contours of the land.

This *instrumentalism* and *homogenization* has even interfered with the rites of Jews who hold tight to religious law that calls for earth burial. The first Jewish green burial ground in the United States, Fernwood in Mill Valley, California, opened in 2010. Qualifying any Jewish burial as "green" may seem unnecessary. And yet many Jewish cemeteries have been requiring concrete vaults for decades, either with holes pierced through the bottom or with the bottom removed. Muslims, too, have struggled to maintain their dust to dust rites, in some places forced to adhere to cemetery rules that require a vault or liner.[68]

That dust to dust burial is not a root value of the vault requirement should come as no surprise, as cemetery vault manufacturers are all about dismissing the dead's tie to nature. Like sealed coffins, vaults are sold with a promise of protecting the dead body from its own decomposition back into the earth. "Grave contents will not be compromised by insects, water, or other natural elements," Wilbert, the oldest vault company in the United States, boasts. Because there is "nothing to prevent groundwater from entering the box and damaging the contents inside," many families, according to Wilbert, find comfort in knowing their loved ones are protected.[69] But it's a reckless sort of protection, as even the most reinforced of vaults will eventually, like the casket, give way to the forces of nature. Moreover, by *radically excluding* the corpse from contact with the elements—in trying to protect decay from its own direction—the very matter of death is *backgrounded* once more.

To make matters worse, these practices have made dumping grounds of our cemeteries. Each year twenty million board feet of hardwood and sixty four thousand tons of steel are buried.[70] In one cemetery study, geologists demonstrated elevated concentrated levels of "iron, lead, copper, zinc and cobalt"—all metals, the first four of which "are commonly used in casket construction"[71]—in the silt loam. And because most vaults, like the ones Wilbert sells, are made from reinforced concrete, there's also impact for the more-than-human. The Green Burial Council estimates that the funeral industry buries over 1.6 million tons of reinforced concrete each year. But reinforced concrete is not the only by-product of this dumping. Vaults can also be made of copper, plastic, and asphalt—a semisolid form of petroleum.[72] When it comes right down to it, burial vaults not only catalyze some of the worst attributes of the human/nature dualism, but of all the conventional funerary practices, the common use of vaults persists as a top environmental offender.

CREMATION

Mostly because ideas spread like wildfire—one spark and the whole forest is down—cremation in the United States was not spared the effects of sanitation arguments. Since 1876 when the first so-called modern cremation was performed in the small town of Washington, Pennsylvania,[73] cremation reformers have used a range of arguments to sell the practice. The earliest of these—like other methods of disposition throughout the nineteenth century— were driven by the promise of purification. Indeed, reasons for cremation rested in the same thinking of the day—that interment jeopardized the health of the living as germs from decaying bodies infected water supplies and seeped into the air.[74] Unlike cemetery reformers who were a bit derailed by the new emerging theory of germs, cremationists deliberately preyed on these images for their pitch, conjuring the festering germiness of moldering flesh in the ground that might stick around "for years."[75] Burning would purify what could never be made clean by burial.

Early cremationists liked to draw inspiration from Greece, Rome, and India, to say they were reviving an "ancient rite."[76] But their new way of burning also eschewed the embodied experience of bearing witness to the pyre and the smell of burning flesh that came with it. Throwing over open-air burning for the oven chamber, cremation in the United States would, instead, be sterile and mechanized. Unlike ancient pyres in which the temperature of the fire was not hot enough to fully vaporize the body, the new burning machines would reduce matter to "purified" crushable bone the living could actually touch. This new form of cremation could do something entirely new—annihilate the problem of decay and erase any trace of pollution, thus making the initial goal of the crematory to control the contaminant through its unmaking—by *backgrounding* and *radically excluding* it from its maker.

In ancient traditions, as it continues to be practiced in many parts of India today, burning was the soul's vehicle out of this world, and the living were expected to bear witness to that transformation. But in this new American cremation story, the direction of the dead, or what's good for the dead, is not part of cremation's goals. Rather, the dead are fully *instrumentalized*, as the ends of cremation becomes all about securing an orderly culture that imagines it cannot maintain its purity without total obliteration.

But unlike lawn-parks, embalming, and the caskets and vaults that would come into being through the quick success of sanitation arguments, cremation was much slower in capturing the American imagination. The central reason had to do with religious questions—largely Christian. To what degree did the dead body matter after death? Before 1920, most Americans thought the practice too extreme. Sanitation might have been a good enough reason to accept the technology of embalming and to create new spaces for the dead and the dead alone, but it wasn't good enough to overcome the fears associated with burning it—corporeal destruction at the cost of the human soul.[77] As practices blossomed to respond to the new status of decay as contaminant, cremationists still failed to convince a worried public—who were now running from the dead—that burning the body was the answer.

Though cremation didn't sell in the way that reformers had initially hoped, it also didn't retreat. In fact, by the turn of the twentieth century more cremations were performed in the United States than any other Western nation.[78] As religious moorings began to loosen and with sanitation concerns still very much present, the utilitarian arguments of cremationists were just enough to keep it within the public consciousness.[79] Growing quite gradually through the better half of the twentieth century, cremation lay in wait for the moment when it could finally find its wings.

Just years before the cremation numbers would begin to rise, Jessica Mitford would set the funeral world ablaze in her own way by deploying a critique of the standard American funeral as an expensive and vulgar charade. As folks had been yearning for less costly and simpler ways of dealing with death, the public responded with vigor. The *American Way of Death* (1963) would open the floodgates to a new venue of disposition—the crematorium. In order to avoid the trappings of costly caskets, and funerals, too, cremation began to gain steam due to simple economics.[80] Although cost would drive the practice, it would be simplicity that would, in the end, give it the strength to endure. In that post-Mitford end-of-life logic, if conventional burial was extravagant then cremation was prudent. And so, the public face of cremation would begin to change. But like many things American, the turn toward cremation would be more a matter of style than substance.[81]

If Mitford's success was won on style, it was perhaps her style of writing more than anything else that fueled the use of crematories and the building of new ones across the nation. Cynicism and not sincerity, simmering anger and not solicitude, is what would finally rally Americans to the new practice of burning. "Gradually, almost imperceptibly over the years," Mitford disapprovingly cajoled "the funeral men have constructed their own grotesque cloud-cuckoo-land where the trappings of Gracious Living are transformed, as in a nightmare, into the trappings of Gracious Dying."[82] Echoing Diogenes as well as more modern-day satirists such as Ambrose Bierce, who had just decades earlier called embalming a way "to cheat vegetation by locking up the gases upon which it feeds," and "(t)he modern metallic burial casket . . . a step in the same direction," for "many a dead man who ought now to be ornamenting his neighbor's lawn as a tree, or enriching his table as a bunch of radishes. . . ,"[83] Mitford sought to undo the "professionalism" of funerary practices through disclosure and ridicule. But unlike Bierce who, though also irreverent, saw the thwarting of decay in emerging funerary practices as a problem, Mitford was content to focus only on the charade the industry had made of death and how much lighter our pocketbooks were for it.

Indeed, there's much to be cynical about, and cynicism can sometimes be useful as a way of coping with suffering in a time of deep uncertainty. But cynicism also often bears the mark of apathy—of not really taking on the problems of the world while only criticizing them from a distance and fundamentally changing nothing. That's why irreverence and cynicism eventually falter as a method of resistance, because resistance needs a mode of caring to carry it. While Mitford's tongue-in-cheek analysis inspired the development of memorial societies all over the United States and, likewise, individual people to see themselves as funeral consumers with more power than they once thought, the cheeky tone of *The American Way of Death* did little to help us re-mean our death practices in any significant way. Unhappy and critical with the state of funerary practices, we have for too long opted for meaninglessness in place of transforming meaning. If mockery has its limits, it seems we have at last run up against them. Mitford's thinking, her style, and the style of resistance we've adopted in her wake have taken us as far as we can go.

With all of its focus on style and the consumer's right to choose their own panache, there's been little effort to pull cremation out of the market and into a narrative of nature of which humans are a part. By the time Mitford came along, many Americans, especially those who saw themselves as outside the mainstream or part of the counterculture, had had enough of the over-the-top rituals of American death.[84] All around the country, the bereaved began to lay claim to their consumer voice as blossoming memorial societies anchored their new attitude. In fact, "the style of simplicity" that cremation offered might never have been fully known without the collective organizing of funeral consumer advocates. But as simplicity became the new art of death care, questions of the environment casually fell into the background. Failing to attach itself to an environmental voice in which constructive changes in the form of policies, as well as practices, might take place, the language of simplicity as a style of death that we could each now choose for ourselves proved to be no force to address our destructive death practices, or to provide an earthly meaning of death we could feel good about.

Still, it's not as though no voice has ever been heard on the ecological problems of standard American death rites (prior to the green burial movement, that is). The budding environmental movement of the 1970s lent a hand to what many cremation advocates had been arguing since the late 1900s—that the land was no place for the corpse. But before 1970 that argument had all but failed to convince the American public that burning the corpse was the solution to the environmental problem of human death. When the numbers began to shift upward—in 1970 from a creeping 4.6 percent to a leaping 40 percent by 2010[85]—it seemed that a strong environmental voice was afoot. But the truth is that cremation's popularity has had less to do with the environment than with opting for something other than the meaningless and costly death rites wrought by the industry.

Of course, environmental health concerns have played some role in driving up cremation rates. Unease over the overconsumption of land through human burial as well as knowledge of the poisons that are part of the typical American funeral have been reason enough for many to choose cremation.[86] And in fact, cremation uses far fewer resources than conventional burial and, in that way, presents as a more ecologically sound option. Indeed, up until quite recently, cremation was praised as the only valid ecological answer to conventional death care's despoiling of the earth.

Some may say it makes little difference what reasons lie behind cremation's increased popularity. If cremation *is* the environmental solution, then the more folks choose it, the less damage done to the earth. But in the last decade questions have surfaced regarding just how environmentally sound cremation really is. Energy consumption is one consideration. Pollution another.

Incinerating just one body is estimated to be the equivalent of driving six hundred miles.[87] Through the burning of any number of contaminants that eventually make their way into the atmosphere—embalming fluid, mercury from dental fillings, surgical devices, radioactive isotopes, prostheses, metal plates, screws and sutures, and silicone from breast implants—cremation poses notable risks to the environment.[88] Crematories release a range of by-products via fossil fuel combustion, including dioxins, hydrochloric acid, hydrofluoric acid, sulfur dioxide, carbon dioxide, nitrogen oxides, carbon monoxide, particulate matter, mercury, hydrogen fluoride, hydrogen chloride, and other heavy metals.[89]

Older crematories with a lack of filters that could prevent some of these pollutants going airborne are the worst offenders, but no crematory is free from polluting effects.[90] Increased environmental awareness has shifted city planning in places throughout California, such as Livermore, San Rafael, and San Leandro, where cremations run as high as environmental consciousness.[91] Some effects of these emissions could be curtailed with stricter regulatory controls and crematorium filters, as has been done in parts of Europe.[92] With the national average inching its way toward 50 percent, and in some states, such as Washington, nearly 80 percent,[93] the polluting effects of cremation are no longer marginal.

Some of these effects were brought to light in the most abhorrent way back in 2000 with the discovery of over three hundred bodies strewn through the woods at the Tri-State Crematory. Though the crematory operator, Ray Brent Marsh, eventually pleaded guilty to the crimes, publicly apologized, and then firmly stood behind the Fifth Amendment without offering an explanation, Marsh's lawyers did proffer their own—mercury toxicity.[94] Elemental mercury from amalgam dental fillings is a common by-product of crematory emissions. In Minnesota, it's estimated that as much as 3 percent of the state's airborne mercury comes from crematoriums.[95] In places where thorough studies have been done to demonstrate the relationship between dangerous levels of mercury pollution and high rates of cremation, regulatory practices have come to include amalgam extraction prior to incineration. Such is the case, for instance, in Scotland.[96] Even though legislation has been proposed in several places in the United States, no such requirement yet exists.[97]

This is despite universal agreement that elemental mercury can wreak systematic havoc on the body when breathed as a vapor. If that happens, a host of poor health outcomes are possible, including "tremors, emotional changes, insomnia, weakness, muscle atrophy, twitching, headaches, disturbances in sensations, changes in nerve responses, and performance deficits on tests of cognitive function."[98] And death. But Marsh didn't draw the mercury into his lungs the way someone might if they smashed open an old-fashioned thermometer and the silver liquid suddenly became airborne. He inhaled it as a by-product of burning, and, on U.S. turf, the capacity for elemental mercury to do damage to the human body through the alchemy of fire remains contested.

While investigators found that the crematory was in poor shape, albeit functional, that lax state regulations and lack of emissions controls contributed to unhealthy working conditions, and that, additionally, Marsh's own father, Tommy Ray Marsh, was forced to retire from the Tri-State Crematory in 1996 due to health problems that many say were due to "classic mercury poisoning," the mercury toxicity story was never put forward as a defense. All these years later, families and the public at large are still looking for answers.

Mercury eventually dissipates from the body, often making tests inconclusive. As Marsh has never given a reason for his crimes, we'll probably never know for certain whether the alleged poisoning played a role in his violation of the dead. Still, the possibility remains unsettling. If it was mercury, and not malice, that turned Marsh into what his lawyers called "a modern-day mad-hatter,"[99] then environmental pollution played a role in that desecration, to the shame brought upon that small northwestern Appalachian community, and to the suffering experienced by the families involved.[100]

To many environmentally minded, it may come as a shock that cremation has not turned out to be the best and only answer to our damaging death practices. Exacerbated by a cultural silence around the environmental toll of human death, our blind faith has endured and, until rather recently, kept us from looking to other solutions. This is mostly because the environmental arguments for cremation, as weak as they were by the 1970s, focused on land scarcity and the idea made plain in the slogan "Save the Land for the Living."[101] Certainly, conventional burial uses land in ways that make even the most lighted-hearted environmentalist cringe. But rhetoric over land loss did nothing to create a culture of belonging to it. That language has just been another vehicle for distance and denial from death where the more-than-human continues to find belonging to the elements but where the human's best gift to the environment is only to be found in transcendence from it.

Of course, burning the corpse is not inherently land distancing or nature denying. Ashes to ashes or dust to dust, the body is broken down either way and returned to the play of earth, air, fire, and water. Whether incinerated remains are buried in the ground or given to the wind, the cremated corpse doesn't actually transcend nature. The rhetoric of land loss, as it has been raised to buttress the good choice of cremation, has offered the corpse up as a kind of token of environmental goodwill, a sacrifice made on behalf of human polluters. But it's a tired story that has only aided *radical exclusion*—transcendence, disconnection, and disaffection. It's only made us more convinced that the best we can do for nature is stay away.

Sanitizing decay through lawn-parks, embalming, sealed hardwood and metal caskets, and reinforced concrete vaults and liners, and, ultimately, through the crematory may have been a way of protecting the living—first through a lack of knowledge, later through lying, and later still through laziness. What all of that has ultimately amounted to is a way of distancing the dead body from its own decomposition and eradicating the ecological value of its reintegration into the cycles of nature. In sum, the drive to separate the dead body from its own decay—to *background* its purpose, to somehow get us to think that decay is not necessary for life to thrive and to *radically exclude* it through methods of distance and separation—not only from humans but from the rest of nature too—to *homogenize* it through uniformity and mechanization, and to *instrumentalize* it through treating it as a means to an end of human desires, has created a prohibition on returning the dead body to the elements.

This prohibition is, for the most part, not based in the legal system, as there are no state laws that require embalming, sealed hardwood, or metal caskets, or outer burial containers.[102] However, now perfunctory, these practices have grounded human death in a hyperdistance, producing a dead body that simply no longer belongs to the more-than-human world. Whatever meanings we have held on to during this shift—religious, personal, communal or otherwise—come to be overshadowed by the grip of these practices in which the dead body simply no longer matters to nature.

There's one more attribute of the human/nature dualism that I've yet to touch on—*incorporation*. *Incorporation* is a kind of relational definition whereby nature is only ever defined in terms of what it is not, the human world of culture. If human culture is orderly and reasonable, then nature—decay—is void of both. In a worldview that perpetuates such *incorporation* the idea that a green burial ground could, through the respect of decay, express its own order and direction would be impossible, as the very concept of what the corpse *is* can only be understood in terms of what it *isn't*. All of these practices as they've grown over the last 150 years contribute to *incorporation*, to a defining of the corpse only in terms of a culture that has had the power to name it.

GBAs are, one step at a time, challenging these damaging attributes, reminding us that decay does have a reason all its own. Letting decay have its place, to be and do its own thing, would not only halt such damage but also open another window to a rekindling of a bond that has for too long been broken. Bit by bit, that bond is regenerating around the nation as GBAs recover forgotten knowledge, and forge renewed meanings that tie us back to the earth.

PART II

4

Reclaiming Knowledge

"**M**y first burial included my very first a cappella performance," recalls Jodie Buller, cemetery manager at White Eagle Memorial Preserve Cemetery. "The family wanted a bagpiper but I couldn't find one so I learned how to sing 'Danny Boy.'" A thick layer of hoar frost covered the unpaved and hilly road leading down to the canyon gravesite, leaving the impression there had been a snowstorm the night before. Had there been, arrangements would have been made with a nearby funeral home to keep the body on ice until things cleared up. "Though we've never had to do that," Buller told me. In the end, the frosty February roads were passable, and the burial went on as planned.

The widower drove his wife's body out to White Eagle in his Subaru. Bags of dry ice under her shrouded frame, they moved her to a ranch pickup and made their way as far as the road could take them. Family and friends then followed alongside the person-drawn cart that carried her body the rest of the way. At the graveside, Buller sang, the family read, and someone played a song on their iPhone. Her body was lowered inside the hand-dug grave, and pine needles and woodchips were spread out on top. "It makes for a lighter and fluffier first layer," Buller said. "And it also helps with the composting." Shovel by shovelful, the family filled in the hole.

"You'd never done a burial before," I said to Buller. "How'd you know what to do? Or are you just fearless by nature?" I wondered, half-joking.

Buller laughed. "Well," she said, "curiosity is the antidote to fear. That's something my father always told me. Something I've never forgotten."[1]

THE NEED TO KNOW

If the dead body has had us running the other way, some deeper desire to know is getting us to stop and turn around. We may call on courage to confront what frightens us most, to quell uncertainty, and to summon strength, but curiosity catalyzes in us what can't be mustered by will alone. At the heart of the green burial movement lies a stirring—it seems our lust for lost knowledge is bringing on a reckoning with decay.

Indeed, "people are hungry to know," as New Hampshire–based home funeral guide and fellow green burial advocate (GBA), Lee Webster, attests, some of them even ravenous.[2] Mary Woodsen has experienced this hunger firsthand, learning about green burial in 2000, collaborating with others to form Greensprings Natural Cemetery Preserve in Newfield, New York, in 2006, and, since then, finding ways to feed that hunger by speaking about the promise of green burial whenever she can.[3] Woodsen and Webster are just two of a growing number of GBAs around the nation who advocate for the cause through education, wherever folks are likely to gather—community centers, churches, schools, hospitals, libraries, and town halls (and conferences and not-for-profits, too).

Freddie Johnson was originally inspired to develop a green burial ground in his area because of a talk he attended about the little-known practice. Since then, he has developed his own presentation and returns that gift to others throughout his region.[4] While green burial founders and operators often bring their experience to bear, funeral directors sometimes do too, like Amy Cunningham, who gives regularly scheduled talks at the Park Slope Food Coop in Brooklyn, New York.[5] Although most of these lectures are happening at the grassroots community level (indeed, I offer the same in my community), some GBAs, like Green Burial Council founder Joe Sehee, also share what they know with folks within the industry and across greater distances. Armed with what the twentieth-century philosopher Michel Foucault called *subjugated knowledges*—or ways of knowing that are discredited and forced to go underground to survive—GBAs place the power and possibility of reclaimed knowledge in the hands of the people.[6] As Joe Sehee has said, "I've talked to a couple thousand consumers over the last four years and I know what's driving them . . . it makes people's eyes sparkle."[7]

Other social movements verify this truth. Over forty years ago, women's health advocates took to the streets with their diagrams and speculums, with the hope of giving back to women the knowledge of their own bodies that a misogynistic medicine had all but stripped them of.[8] It wasn't only a matter of birth and reproduction, but sex too—women fearlessly securing the rights to their own desire free of shame. Current agricultural and locavore movements are fueled by a similar inquisitiveness—wanting to know the where, how, and what of their food, as well as by whom its been cultivated and cared for. GBAs are doing the same for our death rites. Giving talks about the history of U.S. funerary practices, what exactly green burial entails, where one can get it, and how to go about planning for it, GBAs are not only laying the ground for reclaiming a dead body that matters to nature but also giving back forgotten ways of dealing with death.

Of course, consciousness raising and education have been key drivers of other social movements, like the second wave of feminism. And we can see just as much happening with green burial, strengthened only by ever-expanding DIY (do-it-yourself) death care efforts. Back in 2000, my initial search for allies in struggle led me to Jerrigrace Lyons who, at that time, was one of the only so-called death midwives in the nation. In 2002, I was so eager to know just about *anything* related to alternative death care I flew out to Portland, Oregon, for the Association for Death Education and Counseling Conference with one of my main goals being to meet her. I did eventually find her, purchased her booklet of home- and family-directed funerals, and read it over and over again on my flight back East.[9]

Since then, home funeral guides, like-minded funeral celebrants and funeral directors, and other death educators have been growing exponentially, evidenced in the 2010 creation of the National Home Funeral Alliance (NHFA), a 501c3 that advocates for families' rights to care for their own dead by supporting and educating folks on how to do it.[10] Home funeral advocates are an organic fit for the green burial movement, and many of them, like NHFA president Lee Webster, are committed to both with equal energy. "Both are trying to reform the funeral industry," Webster told me. Right now, "many of us may not have the knowledge," she said, "but it's there, and people are *waking up*."[11]

In the shadow of a history of mortuary school training that has not included care of the body without the use of embalming, some funeral directors are also waking up to what green burial has to offer, thinking about how their services might be adapted to provide greener care to families. When Brooklyn-based funeral director Amy Cunningham was a student at the American Academy McAllister Institute of Funeral Service in 2010, there was no training on how to care for the dead "naturally." Since then, and in spite of increased awareness around green care, the training has changed unremarkably. Cunningham told me that at McAllister they're now offering a unit on green burial, but merely as an "oh by the way your customers might mention this."[12]

New Jersey funeral director Bob Fertig had been in the funeral business for over a decade when he first heard about green burial from his wife, Denise. He initially dismissed the idea. but, eventually, he found himself researching the possibilities. His first green burial was transformative. "The whole formality was taken out of the process," he said. "We pulled out a large map of the burial ground to look for plot locations [it was Steelmantown Cemetery in southern New Jersey]. We ended up sitting on the floor together," sorting through possibilities. By then, Fertig was no longer merely intrigued. He felt called to provide green burial to families who wanted it. But that experience changed him on a more personal level, too. He knew, without question, that green burial was what he wanted for himself.[13]

Moves to unearth such knowledge are often indicators of shifting frameworks, omens of things to come. Such was the case when, on the heels of the women's health movement of the 1960s and 1970s, many women began to rescue birthing practices from the clutch of medicine. The resurgence of midwives at this time was not just about restoring old methods, but about laying claim to certain wisdoms that were demonized and forced to the margins— ways of knowing that had retreated, but not disappeared for good.[14]

Inevitably, knowledge that is too primary or elemental will find a way to be recognized. Just look at some of the recurring stories in popular culture that over and again give us a glimpse of the matter of human death and its attendant decay struggling for acknowledgment. Zombies—the embodiment of rot gone viral—are an especially prevalent brute-force reminder that all our efforts to distance and eradicate the flesh cannot outdo the forces of nature.[15] Because they come in the form of stories, popular culture is a most palatable form of communicating these terrors. But whatever role popular culture may play in the recooperation of knowledges that underlie our death fears, what's most clear about the green burial movement, and perhaps movements more generally, is that the desire to know eventually becomes stronger than the fear that's been keeping us in the dark.

Today, this curiosity can be found in other places beyond the recovery of family-directed funerals and the reclamation of greener disposition. Over the last forty years, hospice has made inroads in demystifying end-of-life matters— at least for those within its immediate reach—and in urging us to see death as a necessary part of life. Ellen Goodman's The Conversation Project echoes some of this philosophy, with its focus on the value in getting us to think about advanced directives (end-of-life legal documents) and finding ways to talk to those we love about "the last taboo."[16]

Death practices in the United States may fundamentally know no bounds in terms of race, class, and sex, but conversations focused on changing business as usual can look different depending upon the community that's having them. For example, San Francisco Bay area death educator and counselor Ann-Ellice Parker spends a lot of time working to empower families in end-of-life discussions in her African American community—especially about advanced care planning—although she offers home funeral guide services too, and provides information about greener death care. But despite Parker's optimism about the potential of these conversations, she told me she's not feeling much of an impact. "I wish I could say that these things were making a qualitative difference in the people who are coming to me for my services," Parker said with a bit of laugh, "but I don't find that it is—yet."[17]

While it's true that green burial is still marginal in most communities, even the most cursory look at the movement—the pioneers and growing advocates, the grassroots folks, and players from within the industry—reveals a lack of ethnic and class diversity. Much of this may be a matter of history.

As I mentioned in the last chapter, death care has not been exempt from the marks of disenfranchisement and discrimination. Many so-called skilled trades excluded nonwhites, as well as all women, and the funeral trade was no exception. For instance, before the 1930s, Chinese Americans were barred from becoming funeral directors, leaving their experiences of death, as well as their death customs, in the hands of white actors.[18] Fraught with power, these relationships reflected larger systems of inequality taking shape across the nation. Not surprisingly, taking back the right to care for their own dead became essential for communities of color.

Discrimination extended into places of burial, too. Slaves and, later, many poor African Americans were buried in potter's fields, which were sometimes separate or situated on the periphery of existing cemeteries.[19] Unmarked and unmemorialized, many of these sites, as well as their histories, are still being uncovered today. Burial segregation, however, continued long after the perfunctory use of potter's fields. Until 1968 it was legal for cemeteries to refuse to bury bodies on the basis of race.[20] Though the United States Supreme Court would eventually rule against segregation in death, local laws and ordinances were often slow to get on board.[21] And though the laws may now say otherwise, self-segregation is an ongoing reality in both funeral homes and cemeteries.[22] This has been largely true for African American communities, but segregation has also been a reality for other communities as well, Native Americans in particular.[23]

As these divisions gave way to African American funerary traditions, they, "for better or worse, [kept] African American folk customs alive."[24] While the black church has played a pivotal role in fortifying these traditions and in solidifying community identity,[25] the death care industry has played a central role in these rituals, too. For Ann-Ellice Parker, this represents the so-called worse aspect of the equation for her community, as these customs have largely embraced the waste, excess, and expense of the American way of death. And yet, holding strong to these traditions in spite of their polluting ways has been central to speaking out against the injustice wrought against African American bodies, against the idea that African American lives don't matter.

Of course, moving away from polluting practices does not mean that other rituals, ones that celebrate the value of the body for instance, must change in any substantive way. Funerals can still be highly, and specifically, ritualized. Or not. Even though we've all been forced to embrace these polluting and earth-distancing practices in one way, or another, waking up to them doesn't have to amount to an admonishment of our cultures, our customs or our contexts.

GBA, Adriana Corral, seems sure of this. Working as a licensed funeral director, funeral celebrant and home funeral guide, in and around Miami, Florida, has fed a calling to tend to the bereaved. And yet, the pull of her Mexican American community in El Paso, Texas, is only increasing with time. Corral plans to one day return to Texas for good, and bring greener death care with her. "I need to go back to my roots," she told me, "to bring green services back to the many generations of families that still live there." As she does now in Miami, she plans to do workshops and online consulting to educate and inform. And though she says that funerals are still quite conventional in her hometown, she's hopeful for a good response.[26]

Still, questions remain: How are communities of color, in particular, and other disenfranchised groups not now well represented in movement building making sense of green burial in terms of their own histories? And in what ways will multiple cultural and community perspectives come to shape the movement as grassroots work continues to grow?

Such context and histories can help us to better understand some of the resistance to change, but there's another more shared reason why change might be slow to happen. Talking about these matters doesn't necessarily equate to doing things differently. A good example is the more recent development of Death Café, where people gather "to eat cake, drink tea, and discuss death" with the goal of raising awareness about death in a more general way.[27] Death Café encourages folks to get more up close and personal with death, to address what the organizers in my region call "the elephant in the room."[28] But unlike hospice that is clearly challenging a health care system committed to immortality at all costs, some say that Death Café's sharpened focus on personal sharing often ignores looking at the institutions that have alienated us from death in the first place. Lee Webster is one of them. Webster has a long history as a hospice volunteer and sees some differences between what Death Café is doing and what home funeral and green burial advocacy is all about. "Death Café helps people process their fears and feelings around death by talking" about them, Webster said to me. "We're really coming from quite another place. What we're talking about is action."[29]

She means action leveraged at the level of institutional and structural change. This tension reminds me of the many classroom discussions I had teaching women's studies for over a decade—trying to get students to grasp what we mean when we say "the personal is political"—that what happens in our personal lives is very often a reflection of larger societal forces. In order for our personal lives to feel and look different, the larger culture needs to change too.

No doubt transformation of personal consciousness is key to changing business as usual, but not simply because our sense of self is made better for it. Conversations like the ones fostered through Death Café are beneficial in that they get us to think about what we want and what's important to us. But in the end, what's our knowledge good for? If we don't buck the system—alter who's controlling the flow of knowledge and the implementation of those wisdoms in terms of our available funerary options and our ability to access them—then whatever's important to us may ultimately have little reflection in the world around us.

KNOWLEDGE LOST AND FOUND

The green burial movement's recovery of dust to dust knowledge might feel phony in light of Muslim and Jewish traditions that have never abandoned this sensibility. Muslim law, *shariah*, requires the use of a shroud for burial.[30] And Jewish law, *halachah*, maintains that the dead must be buried in the earth.[31] Genesis provides the evidence for this directive—"the Lord God formed man of dust from the ground" and "from dust you are and to dust you will return."[32] But modern cemeteries (as I talked about in chapter 3) have often impeded these Jewish as well as Muslim death rites, forcing the use of inverted or three-sided concrete vaults and a manipulation of the meanings of earth burial.

In response to this manipulation, the "first green Jewish cemetery," Gan Yarok (which is Yiddish for "green garden"), opened in 2010. Located in the San Francisco Bay area, this "green garden" developed through the collaborative cross-denominational efforts of several Bay Area congregations and Fernwood Cemetery, which provides the land for the now consecrated ground. One of the organizing members, Rabbi Stuart Kelman, told me that in Israel "they use concrete for everything" and that the head of one of the burial societies in Jerusalem actually said "that concrete is 'green' since the ingredients it is made from comes from the earth."[33] But the Gan Yarok Burial Association believes otherwise. Concrete vaults or liners or monuments are not allowed.[34] Another Jewish green burial ground, Prairie Green at the Greenwood Cemetery in Milwaukee, Wisconsin, opened in 2014. Unlike Gan Yarok, however, Prairie Green is unaffiliated with any synagogue or burial society.[35]

"Dust to dust" teachings aren't exactly foreign to Christians either. Jesus, after all, was buried in a shroud, and Christian liturgy supports the dead returning to the earth. "By the sweat of your brow you will eat your food until you return to the ground," Genesis 19 famously reads, "since from it you were taken; for dust you are and to dust you will return." These teachings, however, have been ever sidelined in actual practice. But whatever the reason for leaving the promise of dust to dust at the church door, countering these practices has become imperative to at least some ecotheologians. Benjamin Stewart urges Christians to heed the Orthodox liturgical words of humans' tie to the earth—"Open wide, O earth" to "receive this body, O earth, as it is your own"—ties that have been severed over the past century or so and that, at least in Stewart's assessment, the green burial movement is "recovering— largely ahead of ecclesial renewal movements."[36] In trying to identify teachings that support overcoming the cultural obstacles that have led to the literal walling off of the body from the earth, theologians like Stewart are finding support for green burial within their own traditions.

To these ends, there's been at least some on-the-ground movement among eco-minded Christian pastors and parishioners. For example, in 2012 Most Holy Redeemer Cemetery in Niskayuna, New York, opened a green burial section, Kateri Meadow Natural Burial Preserve (KMNP), because several members of the church were asking for it.[37] Rick Touchette, executive director of Albany Diocesan Cemeteries, told me that they wanted to offer a dust-to-dust option to Catholics and their families "that was in keeping with the order of Christian funerals." While situated inside Most Holy Redeemer Cemetery, KMNP is a stand-alone section abutting the 140-acre Lisha Kill Natural Area held by The Nature Conservancy. Lisha Kill boasts several miles of walking trails set within a rare example of an old-growth forest, especially for such a developed area. The diocese also worked with the Vermont Wildflower Farm to come up with the right mix of perennial seed for KMNP, and salvaged vintage cobblestones from another cemetery they manage in nearby Troy to be repurposed as markers. KMNP is proving popular; over 10 percent of the available plots have already been sold.[38]

Michigan-based priest Father Charles Morris was also moved to create a green burial ground in 2009 when he was pastor of St. Elizabeth's Church and administrator of Mount Carmel Cemetery in Wyandotte. He'd long been involved in the environmental movement, most notably around issues of renewable and sustainable energy, "and so it made sense," he told me, "that the cemetery would follow with this kind of statement." They carved out about a quarter acre from the twelve-plus-acre cemetery for green burial. "About 225 graves," he said.

To date, there are three green burial grounds in Michigan and, interestingly, two of them are Catholic. The other, The Preserve at All Saints, is located in Waterford. Catholic green burial grounds have emerged in other states, too. Of the nearly one hundred green burial grounds that now exist in the United States, about 15 percent of them are religious affiliated. About two-thirds of those are Catholic. Father Charles Morris didn't seem surprised by this. "Because the Catholic tradition is very sacramental and highly ritualized, there's a sympatico maybe more so than other Christian traditions."

Even though Father Charles's environmental activism was integral to the development of Mount Carmel, the thought of green burial actually surfaced when he was a child growing up in Xenia, Ohio. Something struck him in those days, playing in the farm fields just beyond his yard and witnessing the regular cycles of birth and death on the land. And so, although curiosity may be largely firing this "dust to dust" recovery, not all GBAs have been or will be initially propelled by some deep desire to know. Some may be prompted into thinking about death ways in renewed green terms through some sort of experience that gets them to see the world in a different way.[39]

This certainly seems to have been the case for Billy Campbell, who in 1985 was "inspired" by the death of his father to consider a more "wild setting" for burial.[40] And this was certainly true for me who, through my contact with the body and my subsequent grief was swept up in the lost knowledge of the corpse's tie to the earth. Why do some immediate experiences speak to us so powerfully—wash over us with a force that wipes away what we once knew to be true?

David Abram points to the power of our contact with the more-than-human—being enveloped in the "spell of the sensuous," breathing world—that, if we're paying attention, can drive knowledge to the surface.[41] Thoreau went to the woods with the hope of deepening what he already knew, but such knowings aren't so easily willed—that kind of inner revolution is rarely so strategic.[42] Val Plumwood's story of surviving a crocodile attack while paddling her canoe through Australia's Kakadu National Park provides a good example. Plumwood, who'd spent her life advocating for the planet and thinking about the human's place within it, would alight upon something fresh in the aftermath of that life changing event—understanding her place in the food chain, seeing herself as prey.[43]

Much has been made of Aldo Leopold's ecological conversion, if only because he named it and set out to get others to understand what he experienced. And yet all of these years later we still have much to learn from his transformation, as well as his message. After he killed the old wolf and "watch[ed] the fierce green fire dying in her eyes, there was," he said, "something new to him in those eyes—something known only to her and the mountain."[44] What Leopold saw may ultimately be beyond words, but what he most clearly walked away knowing was that the wolf's life mattered.

Seeing might come because we're inquisitive, and the knowledge is there, just waiting to be grasped. With less acute force and, perhaps, more slowly, our interest might lead us to the toll of funerary pollution, and the history of practices that has forged its way. But it might also come from an encounter with death itself—as it did for me—and the contradiction between the worldview I so believe in and the practices that support the dominant *strange* one that's driving our environmental woes. It might come by attending a funeral, caring for the dead, writing a sympathy card, digging a grave, or bearing witness to a passing. It might come through an encounter with the opulent green washing over this planet in all its beauty—birdsong along the shore, mist over an ochre meadow, sunrise, sunset, the rippling brook and the windshook rain—or in all its pain—oil spills, GMOs, ozone depletion, toxic smog, poisoned streams, and acidified ponds. As GBAs will attest, waking up can come in many ways, but however it does, whenever it comes, it carries with it a renewed kind of logic, the kind "that just makes sense."

It's time to "throw off the illusions of the past,"[45] as Plumwood urged, to write a different story of death that returns humans back inside the circle of green. GBAs are taking us there. One by one, in both small and large communities, they're helping us, as Thomas Berry said about our ties to nature more generally, "recover our vision."[46] At the very least, this recovery is necessary to keep this knowledge above water.

How we keep it there remains to be seen. If the strategy is simply to get folks to buy greener death care, that knowledge, as I'll say more about in chapter 7, is likely to falter. The potential of such an earth-based ethic of human death won't be found in its capacity to offer environmentally sustainable end-of-life options. Its greatest promise lies in stimulating a change in the way people see themselves in terms of being a part of, and not apart from, nature.

Over the last fifteen years I've grappled with the *strange* worldview that has had us running from the dead in the best ways I know how—in the written word, the work of my community, the garden that needs tending, the classroom, the farm field, the wisdoms in deep slumber, long walks, and waking dreams—in all the facets of life that have allowed the world to rush through me with questions. And answers. With all the lessons learned from all of the teachers before me, what surfaces time and again is that something must change in us to begin to defy a separation that has become so normalized.

"It's something I never imagined myself doing in a million years," Brian Flowers has said about how he came to be involved in the movement. Having heard about green burial in passing, he started "waking up in the middle of the night thinking about the possibilities." Eventually he realized he "had to do something."[47] Likewise, Freddie Johnson ventured with others to develop Prairie Creek Conservation Cemetery after he heard about the burgeoning practice. "It's just something I had to do," he told me.[48] Mary Woodsen's story bespeaks a similar transformation. Developing Greensprings Natural Cemetery Preserve was a life turn she couldn't have anticipated. Indeed, "I spent several long decades being terrified of death," she's said to me on more than one occasion.[49]

The desire to start a green burial ground, care for the dead in greener ways, set standards for greener death care, engage the earthbound liturgy of one's faith in death rites, spur on other land-use folks into thinking about disposition, or speak and write about the cause harken both a practical response to an unsustainable situation and a deeper sense of calling. However that change comes, GBAs' resurrection of forgotten ways of knowing are preparing the ground for people to have their own greener experiences of death, ones that value the sense in decay and acknowledge our connection to the earth.

5

Renewing Meaning

Decay may be rattling our imaginations, prompting GBAs to recover lost ways of knowing and to return a sense of reason to the fleshy matter of death. But this rattling, recovery, and return is anchored to yet another force for change, something that home funeral guide Lee Webster has sensed from the many kitchen tables she sat at over the years talking to folks about end-of-life matters. If people are beginning to wake up, it's only because of a deeper yearning—a hunger "for more meaningful death practices."[1]

Right after my father died, I remember wrestling with the desire to defy the conventional wake and burial and opt for something else. I'd long been fed up with what felt like imposed funerary practices that left me feeling confused and alone. Some of my dissatisfaction was environmental, but less concrete feelings of disconnection plagued me, too. Even the funeral home seemed foreign and wrong. Some of my feelings had to do with swallowing the Mitford consumer critique that had produced in me a suspicion of anything having to do with those who cared for the dead. But even with Mitford and all of that questioning, no good alternative surfaced. Not one that seemed to make more sense.

Burning didn't pose an ethical or spiritual problem for me, but the crematorium left me cold. Where would my father's body actually *go*? And *who* would be there to witness it? As far as burial was concerned, the cemetery would not allow it without a vault. And without embalming, the funeral home would unlikely provide an open casket funeral, something my mother very much wanted. And without the body, what would the funeral *be*, exactly? And without the funeral, where would *we* go, with all our tears and sadness, without the support of family and friends in a time when we needed it most?

Many fellow GBAs have shared with me similar feelings about the lack of embraceable alternatives. Freddie Johnson once planned to be cremated, but only because "dust to dust" wasn't an option where he lived.[2] What green burial is doing for people like Johnson is "offering them something they actually want," as Jodie Buller so plainly said to me, "and not just something they can live with."[3]

In the digital age, this quest for meaning is paradoxically palpable with online memorials sometimes more crowded than funerals. And for a long time now, the funeral industry has said folks are finding meaning through new rituals of personalization and services geared toward the individual.[4] But the truth is that much of that individualization is actually created *by* the industry and its markets, like extreme embalming—where bodies are superpreserved and then posed with props—and other business ventures that commodify death, such as cremated remains transformed into jewels, stuffed into shotgun shells, or tattooed into the skin of the grieving.[5]

The desecularization of death practices has only exacerbated this approach, leaving people unmoored from communal understandings of end-of-life matters. Organized religion and spiritual traditions still provide meanings for those tied to them, but secular American culture is increasingly absent a place to root some shared sense and/or value around the dead. Freedom to and from religion grounds our nation and the cultures built up within it leaving us all freer, but without a collective place to anchor a sense of death we've been able to live with. Today, whatever meaning is to be found is mostly left to individuals to sort out on their own.

It's no wonder we're looking for meaning.

After all, humans are meaning-making beings. Suspended in what the anthropologist Clifford Geertz called "webs of significance," we're in an ongoing process of deciphering those meanings, and then finding ways to express them so that they become real to us. And that's because the abstract idea and the expression work in tandem, reinforcing each other, becoming what Geertz described as "fused" together—inseparable.[6] And so, if we don't find ways of expressing the thought that is the meaning, then meaning itself will find a way to elude us altogether.

Of course, that's the key reason rituals matter in the first place. Rituals aren't simply show and fancy, display and theater. Rituals fortify who we are, what we believe, and how we are to live. They essentially weave the substance of our living. And so, if we take on death ways of separation, of environmental pollution, of extravagance or style, those will be our meanings of death. And if we eschew them all together, think them too primitive, too flimsy, too silly to bother with or care about, we're left with no meanings at all. Over the last 150 years our meanings of death have been on such a collision course. Aided by the rise of a funeral industry that has had a stronghold on final disposition and decay, but, also, a growing Mitfordesque logic that has ignored a quest for meaning apart from what's good for our wallets and our sense of style, what has become of what we think of death is just what Plumwood said it is—"a nothing, a void, a terrifying and sinister terminus, whose only meaning is that there is no meaning."[7]

Forged from both the curious and the converted, and a quest for meanings that "just make sense," greener death ways are growing rituals that are restoring a human bond with the rest of the living world. They're also reminding us of our common ground—the whole of nature itself. GBAs aren't exactly the creators of these rituals, but more like the preparers of sites of meaning for renewed ones to take place—ones that encourage respect for decay and for the human's place within the environment.

LANGUAGE

Perhaps the most glaring site of meaning making is the language used to talk about green burial. GBAs may say the dead are recycling themselves, replenishing the planet, returning or giving themselves back to the earth. Numerous news stories and promotional materials echo this reclamation. Jay Castaño plans to be buried in the Congressional Cemetery in Washington, D.C., as it now allows interment without embalming fluid, hardwood or metal caskets, or burial vaults. "I want to be part of a tree, be part of a flower—go back to being part of the earth,"[8] Castaño told the *Washington Post*. Touted by some GBAs as "the ultimate recycling project,"[9] the powers of regeneration are summoned. "We enjoy the outdoors," says Foxfield Preserve plot owner Roberta Angerman. "We like our fruit trees and our vegetable garden. We have a compost heap. In light of this it makes sense for us to let our bodies return to the soil naturally."[10] It's that cycle that Aldo Leopold most famously captured in his round river concept, that biotic stream, that current, that loops back around from whence it came. "A rock decays," Leopold says, "and forms soil. In the soil grows an oak, which bears an acorn, which feeds a squirrel, which feeds an Indian, who ultimately lays him down to his last sleep in the great tomb of man—to grow another oak."[11]

Whatever we want to call this cycle, GBAs make plain the essential role of the corpse within it. Like so much of living nature that has given itself over and again to us, very often against its will, the language of green burial says we have something to offer in return. Ramsey Creek plot owner Babs McDonald typifies this view when she says, "We've got to give back to the earth. It supports and provides for us . . . and our bodies provide nourishment."[12] And

Cynthia Beal, owner of The Natural Burial Company,[13] an online source for ecoburial containers, reverberates these sentiments, saying that "we spend our entire lives eating and building our bodies. It's the ultimate insult to not give anything back."[14]

If it's insulting—and it is—that's because reciprocity is a vital part of gift giving, something the French social scientist Marcel Mauss (1872–1950) suggested nearly a century ago. We've just somehow forgotten. Anthropologists Douglas Davies and Hannah Rumble, who have been charting the flow of green burial practices in the United Kingdom—otherwise known as woodland burials—say that "the appeal of gift giving" is a key motivator for those who choose the practice, one only heightened by the marketing of burial grounds looking for plot sales.[15] Though the idea of gift giving may mean different things to different people (like charity or love or honor), there is "at the very least," Davies and Rumble say, "some symbolic reciprocal gesture" at play in the practice. But as Mauss also saw it, reciprocity only really matters because that's how mutual relationships are built. As Davies and Rumble suggest, the earth gives and we summarily create and fortify connection by giving back to it through the gift of our own bodies.[16]

Our obligation to "give back" is core to an ecological ethic or to recovering ways of "feeding the green," as Jane Caputi phrases it,[17] rather than continuing on our path of taking, using, discarding, of consciously or unconsciously trying to kill it. The language GBAs use to talk about green burial bespeak this acknowledgement, while fueling a kind of resistance, both real and symbolic, to the *strange* worldview Neil Evernden bemoans. In the United Kingdom, Davies and Rumble describe folks choosing green burial as a mere "gesture of what life should be about, rather than what it already is."[18] But such symbolic gestures, when forged through practice and ritual, have great potential as they can rewrite new meanings of our place in the order of things.[19]

And that alone seems good enough reason to welcome them in.

Luckily, green burial practices offer up other sites of meaning making that render such gestures possible—including the journey to the grave, the body, the open grave, the burial mound, and, of course, the land itself. Graves will be dug by hand or by backhoe and filled in with or without the help of family and friends. Some folks may get there by foot, others by car or even by horse. Bodies, locations, and lands will differ and burial sites, cemeteries, and the paths we take to them will as well. Some bodies will go into the ground whole while others will return as ashes—scattered, buried, or somewhere in between. Some land will be arid and others humid, balmy, and soaked with rain. Some will be wide open, others dense with snags and invasive ground cover. Soils may be loamy in one place and clay and boulder in another; some will be depleted while others will be rich and diverse. But despite these variations, greener death ways are, in sum, coming to define the burgeoning practice through these sites of meaning while reclaiming our sensible relationship with the more-than-human world.

JOURNEY TO THE GRAVE

The hand-drawn cart was already adorned with Joe Pye weed and wild daisies when I arrived for the burial at Steelmantown Cemetery, a natural burial ground cradled in the Pine Barrens of New Jersey's southern tip. No roads take you into the cemetery, not even into the diminutive old section with its graves dating back to the 1700s. Instead, mourners park their cars and gather along the wooded perimeter, waiting just outside the cemetery gates to hear what's next.

Nine states in the United States impede DIY funerals, requiring families to obtain the services of a licensed funeral director. New Jersey is one of them. Not only does the state require a funeral director's signature on the death certificate but also their presence at the final disposition of the body.[20] The family had hired Bob Fertig, a green burial–friendly funeral director from outside the Philadelphia area. Fertig parked his minivan, checked in with the family and Ed Bixby, owner and operator of Steelmantown, and then commenced the procession to the grave. Ed and Bob lifted the body from the vehicle and, along with a couple of family members, carried and slid it onto the cart—a repurposed prewar vegetable wagon that never creaked when it was empty.

At some green burial grounds, mourners can easily drive up to the grave and make their way out to the site in the same manner they would at a conventional lawn cemetery, but at many others, like Steelmantown, gravesites can't be reached by cars, and so the procession must travel on foot or on wheels that are no wider than the paths that lead them there. I followed behind the forty-person procession, sticking with the three gravediggers Ed had called to assist him that day. Along with Ed and Bob, family members pushed the cart along the narrow, mossy path, wheelbarrow style, until it narrowed even more and the roots and curves of it prevented the cart from moving at all. They lifted the body from the cart and led the group along the sun-dappled trail—the cart creaking, the trees singing, and the sweet, acrid smell of autumn closing in.

We arrived at the prepared grave together, the hole having been hand dug that morning. Bookending the left and right of the grave were wide hemlock boards that made for a sturdy platform. The family rested their loved one over the hole, the edges of the boards keeping it afloat.

Before the rise of the lawn-park and a funeral industry that seized hold of our dead, families, friends, and religious groups accompanied the body of their loved ones to the final place of rest. But in conventional burial, communities rarely journey to the grave any longer. The dead are most often already there when we make our way to the cemetery. What meanings might be rescued through reclaiming this journey?

Strength in community certainly seems to be one of them. Transporting the body to "the place of disposition shows that this act involves the labor of many hands,"theologian Thomas Long reminds us.[21] And, indeed, green burial ground owners and operators report a high level of family involvement that challenges the *radical exclusion* of the dead from the inner living circle so common in conventional burial practices.[22] Such involvement is what's rallying at least some GBAs to the cause. "Our main purpose here is for the families," Ed Bixby said to me about operating Steelmantown, to facilitate their role as "participants and not spectators" of death. "That's the true meaning of it for me."[23] At White Eagle, Jodie Buller has witnessed as much, most surprisingly with children. She told me that "not having yet been impacted by the taboos around death, it's amazing to see the way kids respond." One of her line-item budgets for the coming year is to buy kid shovels. "Breaking down that barrier between participant and observer, that's something we're able to offer."[24]

Lee Webster confessed something similar, that while the environmental components of green burial are crucial, it's been its potential for community building that's tugged at her most.[25] In fact, her greatest green "aha" moment came when she attended a lecture by GBA Cynthia Beal, who talked about local artists making shrouds, building pine caskets—creating not an economy of goods around greener death ways but, rather, an economy of care. "How do we tend to the living," Webster said to me, "how do we create connection to each other?"[26] New Jersey funeral director Bob Fertig, who has done quite a few burials at Steelmantown, agrees. He has witnessed firsthand how "getting up close to the experience can bring people together."[27]

Recovering the act of the journey provides the living with at least one other important potential meaning, one that won't be found if we're only thinking in terms of where the journey might be headed. Benjamin Stewart suggests that it's, perhaps, the passage itself—the actual *transit*—that matters most. For what is transit if not transitory?[28] What are journeys if not fleeting moments on the way to some place, some thing? Okay, so we've all heard it before, "it's not about the destination, but the journey," a saying that's meant to remind us that all we really have is the present moment. A cliché to be sure, but one supported by the easily forgotten and stark truth of our temporariness. Recapturing the journey to the grave is a kind of rejoinder to the modern quest for immortality, an act of facing the facts—that we, too, are finite.

THE BODY

The presence of the body in whole-body green interment also has the potential to deepen meanings around our finitude. Funeral directors have long held that there's great value in having the dead present prior to final disposition. Much of this value has centered on the "memory picture" born from the "viewing," which is meant to aid the living in coming to terms with a particular death as well as with the naked truth of immortality more generally.[29] Of course, the Mitford critique said otherwise, that the viewing was just another funeral industry invention deployed to sell stuff to a vulnerable public and that, in the end, the viewing succeeds in doing just the opposite of this said intention, as the embalmed body only further buries our temporality.[30] Green burial, however, inserts an interesting wedge in this impasse.

Before Bob Fertig opened the doors to the minivan, he told the crowd of mourners what they would expect to see. The deceased's body was wrapped in a shroud, he explained—a large piece of cloth—and because of that it may look different from anything they'd seen at a funeral before. "You'll see the outline of———'s body, his shoulders, his head." Fertig said. "His feet." His body was wrapped in a white shroud, partially cloaked in burlap and adorned with the same wildflowers that graced the cart. As I far as I could tell no one looked away.

In the previous chapter, I mentioned how before the casket came into being, the coffin was the burial container of choice. The new "casket" makers rode the emerging wave of death care, mindful to distance themselves from the doom and gloom elicited in the body-contoured shape of the coffin and favoring a rectangular-shaped casket that could, in essence, be holding any kind of valuable good. Except it's not just any kind of valuable. It's a dead body—a fact the new casket design succeeded in downplaying. Today, many of the biodegradable burial containers on the market may continue to mirror this rectangular design—whether it's wicker, soft wood, or cardboard.[31] But other ecoburial container makers (like Ecopod,[32] that is manufactured in the United Kingdom and made from paper) are coming onboard, defying this distance by bringing the shape of the body back into view. In foregrounding the body and its dissolution, these containers eschew the *backgrounding* and *radical exclusion* of the conventional casket and the accompanying vault.

Moreover, according to the green burial ground owners and operators I've spoken with, shrouds are also a popular choice. Although it remains to be seen what type of burial container will come to prevail in the movement, and whether such meanings of bodily finitude will triumph along with it, the green burial movement seems to be attracting the shroud crowd—the most body conscious of burial containers.

In a story told to me by Brian Flowers, burial coordinator for The Meadow Natural Burial Ground at Moles Greenacres Memorial Park, such meanings of bodily finitude are unambiguous. Flowers first shared this story when we met in 2011, walking through the Galisteo Basin in Santa Fe, New Mexico, on land that was purportedly slated to become a green burial ground at some point in the near future (although to date that has never happened).[33] Some years later I called him to hear it again.[34]

Not long after The Meadow first opened, Flowers facilitated the burial of a man who died as the result of a violent crime three days short of his nineteenth birthday. In planning for the burial, the father of the young man requested something wholly unconventional, even by green burial standards—to view the face of his son all the way to the grave. "His grief process involved maintaining visual contact for as long as possible," Flowers said. But for all kinds of reasons; namely, that the journey to the grave would take place while the cemetery was open to visitors and might cause discomfort to those not involved with the burial, The Meadow could not accommodate his request. They could, however, meet him halfway. The young man was to be buried in a wooden box designed by his father. The box lid was removed and fashioned "as a prop system," Flowers explained, "that lifted his son up in the casket . . . so you could see him in profile."

The Meadow uses a hand-drawn caisson for funeral processions, similar to Steelmantown's cart in function, and during the procession the dead young man's body and face were covered with a pall. Although his father was unable to gaze at his son's face for the entire journey, the pall was removed at the graveside, at which time the funeral continued as planned. The lid, however, was never resecured to the top of the box. As Flowers explained it to me, "There was no way to close it because the lid was fastened underneath the young man," something the grieving father had intended by design. To soften the blow of dirt to the uncloaked and uncovered body, Flowers lay down about two feet of biomass. "It made for a much more graceful experience," he said. On a bitter January day, after music and prayers had ended, and in the midst of about four hundred people, the dead young man's father filled the hole back in by himself.[35]

No doubt this story is one of a kind, and not all green burials will be carried out with a shroud like the one I witnessed at Steelmantown. Still, what these stories of the body offer up is the suggestion of renewed meaning making around death that has as much to do with our ties to nature as it does with that unique knowledge of being human—that although we may do our best to deny it, all of our bodies will someday return to dust. With the body no longer *radically excluded*, green burial and the rituals born from them offer new ground for the fortification of this knowing, for the making of this meaning.

THE OPEN GRAVE

In both of those burials—at Steelmantown and The Meadow—the funeral ended in the same way. The body was lowered into the grave and the dirt shoveled back in, though in the former case the family and staff did this shoveling, and, in the latter, one member of the family did it alone. Because family involvement is both encouraged and often eagerly desired by family members, the closing of the green burial grave and the laying back in of the dirt often happens at the hands of the bereaved inner circle. This is in contrast to most conventional burials (sans traditional Jewish and Muslim ones) where the closing of the grave happens with the use of a backhoe by a skilled gravedigger. But while family involvement is encouraged in green burial grave closings, for practical and safety reasons most green burial grounds do not allow families to open graves. And yet, whether the grave is opened or closed by family members, the open green grave still bears out potential meaning for the living.

Not long after full-time physician and green burial pioneer Billy Campbell first established Ramsey Creek Preserve in 1998, he began digging each and every grave by hand, by himself. "My first attempt created a hole eight feet long, four and half feet wide and six feet deep," Campbell told me. "I was so proud of it." But that satisfaction quickly wore off as he realized that a larger hole only meant more work to fill it back in. Today, the graves at Ramsey Creek are only three-and-a-half to four feet deep and the length and width just enough to fit a coffin. "We basically have a template that folds up," Campbell explained. Having participated in digging nearly one hundred graves, creating the guide gave Campbell and his wife Kimberly the push they needed to hire a part-time digger, though Campbell admitted he still starts most of the gravesites himself. Indeed, he says, "there's just something meditative about digging a grave."

The practice of hand digging at Ramsey Creek began for practical reasons. "When we first started we were using a mini backhoe," Campbell said. Even though it was a small piece of equipment, Ramsey Creek had to rent it, which made for an added expense. But for Campbell, that wasn't the worst of it. One of the areas where many of the burials take place is mostly "heavy clay with a sandy crust," making it "very fragile," he explained. In fact, a burial from when they first opened in which a minibackhoe was used is still "not back to where it should be," Campbell lamented. If there were downsides to the backhoe, Campbell soon realized there were upsides to hand digging. Not only was it gentler on the land, it was also a lot easier to fill in. "When you use a backhoe the soil comes out in big chunks," he explained. And because families often participate in filling the grave back in, those chunks need to be broken up in order to be shovel ready.

Campbell's attention to the biological health of the gravesites has only deepened over the years, and not only with respect to whole-body burial. Ramsey Creek, like many other green burial grounds, also offers burial of cremated remains, although Campbell says they're trying to get away from doing cremation inurnments and "move toward a more modified scatter burial of ashes." Cremated remains are mostly made up of salts that, in a concentrated form, are fairly hostile to plant life. Right now Ramsey Creek doesn't do a lot of real scattering because, he says, "you end up with white stuff all over the plants" and if there's a drought, or the burial ground happens to be situated in an arid climate, "well," Campbell says, those ashes aren't "going anywhere for a long time." His plan for scatter burial is to "take about half a square meter and dig the ashes in about that amount of ground," he explained. That way there's a lower impact to any one area of soil.[36]

Interestingly, thirty-five-year funeral service veteran Bob Jenkins and his wife, Annette, have recently developed a product for market that addresses the hostile quality of cremated remains. It's called Let Your Love Grow. Bob told me that some plants are able to tolerate more salt than others. For those that can't, they react in a similar way the human body does, "swelling, organ failure and possibly death." Their product claims to lower this risk by diluting the sodium and "allowing the good agricultural nutrients found in the bone to become plant life." "In simple terms," Jenkins told me, "Let Your Love Grow jumpstarts a Mother Nature that the cremation process stopped."[37] In both of these examples, cremation is not only "greened-up" but also deliberately tied back to the earth, something green burial grounds are now having a hand in.

With respect to whole-body green burial, Billy Campbell has developed a method for disassembling the layers of earth and for reassembling them in a way that, in his words, "accelerates restoration." "First we roll up the forest floor strips, then take off the top soil and put it in a separate place, and then the subsoil—the red clay and rocks—that goes in a different pile, and then, of course, they all go back in that order."[38] But before that reassembly can happen, the body must first be placed inside.

Many natural burial grounds like White Eagle in South Central Washington, Duck Run in Virginia, and The Meadow at Greenacres in Western Washington place what they call biomass—sticks, twigs, boughs, or other remnant organic matter from the surrounding area—inside the grave. Duck Run's Kenneth Kyger and Ed Bixby at Steelmantown both use cedar boughs. Kyger explained to me that they help create a certain amount of airflow below ground so the aerobic decomposition that functions to turn something once living into food for other living things can happen as fast as possible.[39]

They started using biomass at The Meadow for two reasons, Brian Flowers said: to soften the blow of the dirt to the body—especially if it's shrouded—

and to "inoculate the grave environment with microbes, oxygen and moisture to expedite decomposition."[40] Unlike the confined space of the vault and sealed casket that creates conditions for putrefaction to quickly set in, the nesting quality of the twigs creates a prime environment for organic break-down. Sticks from the forest floor are placed inside the graves at Ramsey Creek not to "add nutrients," Campbell insists (indeed, the dead body has enough of its own), but to "make the nutrients from the body come back into the living layer easier."[41] Maintaining and restoring the vegetative structure of the gravesite has become as much a part of the green burial imperative for Campbell as using human burial as a land conservation tool (of which I'll say more in the next chapter).

His emphasis on the flow of nutrients in and through the soil—on restoration, rather than depletion—remarkably echoes alternative approaches to agriculture that are part of a rising tide of public conversation and practice today. The problems of pesticide use and fossil fuel reliance in industrial agriculture are well known. The problem of monoculture—of planting a single crop in the same place over consecutive years—has slowly made its way into this public conversation. Though thinkers like Wes Jackson and Vandana Shiva have condemned monoculture for decades, the stronghold of global agribusiness continues to thwart efforts to increase biodiversity that would restore nutrients to what we grow and, ultimately, to what we eat. Michael Pollan's popular and wide-reaching work has emphasized how "monocultures in the field lead to monocultures in the diet."[42] But what's underneath all that is what Jackson's been pointing to all along—that the planting of monocultures has led to massive soil erosion around the world and the closing of what he calls "a long line of ecosystems stretching back thirty million years."[43] Jackson is from Kansas, a geographical vantage point that has enabled him to see the firsthand destruction of those ecosystems—the obliteration of the Midwestern prairie—the actual roots of which were cut through and destroyed for modern farming and the outcome of which has been overwhelming soil and fertility loss.

That we could do this to the soil without remorse and without expecting repercussions has a lot to do with our ideas about soil in the first place. Soil is considered both earth and excrement, land and refuse. Green thumbs may chide the uninitiated with the difference, but soil has long been synonymous with dirt in the English vernacular. With soil's dual meaning, it should come as no surprise that, in our *strange* view of nature, dirt is deemed disgusting, not decent, obscene, not acceptable. In fact, the word *obscene* comes from the Latin root that means "dirt."[44] As that which is part of nature, dirt is something we are expected to overcome—disregard at best—not honor or value. Just think about the idiom "to hit pay dirt." In order for dirt to have value at all it must be modified by the "green" of the market.

The green burial grave isn't just about reclaiming decay, but of dirt more generally—of imbuing value into the soil that we have for too long maligned. Current moves toward organic farming, backyard composting, and no-till gardening bespeak this truth, too. Green burial is yet another set of practices that enable the value of dirt to shine. When the mourners arrive at the gravesite of a green burial, the dirt has not been temporarily hauled off to some far corner of the cemetery or cloaked with some faux grassy drape. There's no vault to impede the view of dirt, its attributes, its hues and contours, even its smells. The mound of dirt is openly waiting nearby.

In the case of Ramsey Creek there's a system to filling, to the mounding, to the closing of the grave. Others have their systems too, like Steelmantown that separates the subsoil from the topsoil and also replaces any plants that may have been dislocated during digging. At other green burial grounds, especially where machines do the digging, there's no such system in place. But, even then, the dirt is not *backgrounded*, it's value and purpose are not denied. The dirt front and center.

THE BURIAL MOUND

Some green burial grounds may treat the filled-in green grave in the same way they do conventional graves by following the burial with grass seeding of the bare ground and the laying of a granite, machined-cut, and polished slab. Most green graves, however, are not tended in this way. Markers are minimal at best, often flush with the ground (although not always) and made from local natural stone or sometimes wood. Usually, green graves are mounded and left to regrow on their own. Subsidence is heeded—the body decomposes, the grave settles. The soil is allowed to restore, or with the help of stewards, like Billy and Kimberley Campbell, aided along in its restoration. Sometimes the graves will need to be remounded, though the green burial groundskeepers I've spoken with say that has never been necessary.[45]

As there tends to be more family involvement, the filling in of the grave is often done with the help of family and friends. Flowers said that in his experience that's also what typically happens at The Meadow. He told me that immediate family will step up initially, and then eventually someone will tap them on the shoulder and take their place. The filling in will continue like that until some, or all, of the grave is made whole. "It's communal and it's pretty intuitive," he explained. Gordon Maupin, former executive director of Foxfield Preserve Natural Cemetery, has been critical of the resistance to this communal ritual. "People in the cemetery business say, no, you never want to let that happen. Someone could get hurt."[46] But at Foxfield, as is done at many other green burial grounds, this option is frequently offered mostly because people ask for it. The green burial I attended at Steelmantown went this way, although the family left before it was fully completed and the caretakers and I finished mounding the soil and laying back the topsoil and, finally, any plants that had been removed.

Maupin describes his first grave closing: "People just lined up like they would at a Jewish funeral and everyone took a turn putting a spadeful of soil into the grave. It became a labor, but there were so many people helping that they barely broke a sweat. They closed the grave and mounded the soil up." One of the more surprising aspects of these grave-closing experiences for Maupin has been the sheer number of people who've walked up to him afterward to shake his hand in gratitude. "That's the reaction we get," he said.[47] "People actually thank us." Flowers told me the same. After the grieving father of the nineteen year old boy completed the mound, the other mourners "forming a circle around him and bearing witness" to his labor, he walked up to Flowers and said, "I know this is going to sound really strange, but thank you. This was a pleasure."[48]

On a more practical level, green burial ground stewards and/or operators will tell you that the same amount of soil they took out of the ground goes right back in. And that's whether it's a pine box, cardboard box, or shroud burial, or whether there was a little or a lot of biomass sprinkled into the hole. The mounding of the grave is not necessarily about anticipating subsidence, but about restoring the location and origin of the dirt. The return of the dirt to that space leaves—even when there is a system like Campbell's—an elevated spot, a mound that is as long and wide as the hole that was dug. And unlike conventional burial plots, it is one that is unique to the burial and not *homogenized* via casket and vault methods that get in the way of the mound settling at its own pace with its own shape. Moreover, green gravesites are not imagined as a means to an orderly end for the burial ground, not *instrumentalized.* At Greensprings Natural Cemetery Preserve, mounds are often decorated with perennials and annuals approved for planting in the meadow, although natural grave markers are permitted and many have both.[49] At Steelmantown, no plantings are allowed in the forest, but natural grave markers are often used, though they differ by size, shape, and stone type.[50] But all around these mounds the forest and meadow go on as before, growing upward in spring and dying off come fall.

When I first began thinking about green burial and turned to look at Val Plumwood's work on our separation from nature to guide me, Plumwood was alive and well and in the throes of completing *Environmental Culture: The Ecological Crisis of Reason* (2002). Nearly a decade later, Plumwood would die quite suddenly from natural causes, and her friends would rally to defy Australian law in order to bury her "green" on the land she called home. Interestingly, her work had taken a turn in those very recent years before her death toward envisioning more sustainable cemeteries in her homeland, critiquing the symbolism embedded in "the concrete slab" of the modern cemetery. "This use of stone to affirm transcendence of life," Plumwood railed, "forgets that we are bodies, plain members of the ecological order, and that our life is a gift from an embodied community of prior others we must nurture."[51] For her friends, green burial was the *only* way to honor her life. After she'd been lowered into the ground and the hole filled in, one of the attendees described the end result of "the large completed mound" as a lozenge of earth covered in bright garden flowers"—flowers that had come from Val's garden.[52]

No matter what's permitted or actually done, the mound is a necessary outcome of green burial. It's also the last and final reminder of the purpose and promise of dirt. This ritual space is especially evident at places like White Eagle and Greensprings, where mounds are sometimes kept as ovals or circles or defined with stones or sticks, where the mound itself is the memorial. Of course, most green burial grounds allow for some kind of marker—often stone. And some, like Foxfield, also allow for trees.

Whether one's navigating the vegetation, rocks, and roots of Steelmantown or the open meadows at Greensprings, these changing burial sites impart more than the knowing that the dead are buried in the woods. Decay is happening. And it's essential. Along with the other signs of death and rebirth in those vibrant and, sometimes, diverse ecosystems, humans are undergoing the same process. For those not in attendance at a green burial or for those who might pass by later—as I've done at so many green burial grounds in recent years—the mound tells the story of this process, and of our shared and fated place within it.

In challenging our *strange* worldview, green graves are slowly, but surely, restoring that place. At last, decay is not *incorporated*, not defined only in terms of what it *isn't*, but, rather, its order and direction and own sense defines it for what it *is*. Sparked by our desire to know as well as our need for meaning, these sites of green burial provide common ground for death rituals that heed the green, ones that return some sense to dissolution and to the fecundity of dirt. By turning away from the *radical exclusion, backgrounding, homogenization, instrumentalism*, and *incorporation* of conventional burial, green burial fosters meanings of connection to and care of the earth, as well as to each other.

Open Grave in the Prairie, Foxfield Preserve, Wilmot, Ohio. Courtesy of Sara Brink.

Shroud Burial, Ramsey Creek Preserve, Westminster, South Carolina. Courtesy of Billy Campbell.

Wicker Burial, Ramsey Creek Preserve, Westminster, South Carolina. Courtesy of Billy Campbell.

Shroud Burial, The Meadow, Bellingham, Washington. Courtesy of Brian Flowers.

Pine Box Burial, Ramsey Creek Preserve, Westminster, South Carolina. Courtesy of Billy Campbell.

Shroud Burial, Eloise Woods Community Natural Burial Park, Cedar Creek, Texas. Courtesy of Ellen Macdonald.

Burial Mound, Pine Forest Memorial Gardens, Wake Forest, North Carolina. Courtesy of Dyanne Miller Matzkevich.

Burial Mound, Greensprings Natural Cemetery Preserve, Newfield, New York. Courtesy of Suzanne Kelly.

Tree Planting over Burial Mound (Magnolia), Prairie Creek Conservation Cemetery, Gainesville, Florida. Courtesy of Freddie Johnson.

Prairie Grass, Foxfield Preserve, Wilmot, Ohio. Courtesy of Sara Brink.

Meadow, Greensprings Natural Cemetery Preserve, Newfield, New York. Courtesy of Suzanne Kelly.

Steelmantown Cemetery, Steelmantown, New Jersey. Courtesy of Amy Cunningham.

6

Restoring Our Relationship to the Land

In 2011, I finally made my way north to Greensprings Natural Cemetery Preserve, a pioneer green burial ground in Newfield, New York. There was no burial scheduled and dense cloud cover threatened rain, but we walked anyway, stopping at gravesites poured-over with love, some mounds populated with uncommon native perennials, others completely grown over with goldenrod and ragweed. Gently swelling hills with patches of mixed forest spread way beyond our field of vision.

Greensprings's executive director, Joel Rabinowitz, retold tales of loss and the labors of ritual, of families torn by suicide, disease, and accident. Burials had taken place in all manner of weather—mud and snow, wet and wind, on frozen February days and in spite of August swelter. Down a trail of scents freed through gentle weed rustle and the crunch of dried grass beneath our feet, it was obvious the journey to the earthen grave had been a process of remaking the chaos of death into renewed meanings of connection for the living.

Perhaps, most fundamentally, that's because "land is not merely soil," as Leopold reckoned, but "a fountain of energy flowing through a circuit of soils, plants and animals."[1] Though Leopold didn't speak directly of human death, his "round river" concept and praise song to the biotic community was rich with this vision of interdependence, of the necessity of interplay among the living and dead organisms that inhabit the natural world. Out of this energetic interchange "a land community" is born. And humans are part of it.

Our dominant *strange* view of nature, however, has long pushed this knowing to the margins. One of the more common ways this continues to happen—in our thoughts, our words, our dreams, and our deeds—is by reducing the land to mere "landscape." Drawing from her Pueblo roots, Leslie Marmon Silko has reasoned that thinking about the land as mere "landscape" can be "misleading," as it often summons up an image of a person looking at the land "in a single view," parsing out one piece from the whole. "This does not," she insists, "correctly describe the relationship between the human being and his or her surroundings."[2]

While green burial grounds like Greensprings are fostering connection between the human and the more-than-human, conventional burial grounds haven't done much to contribute to thinking dead bodies matter to the land community. In lawn-park cemeteries, the land is viewed as both resource and landscape. Land is simply *used* to bury the dead. The relationship between bodies, trees, bees, blossoms, birds, soil—between the parts of specific ecosystems—is consistently *instrumentalized* and *backgrounded* to the purpose of a landscape of the dead. The land, it seems, is imagined only in terms of what it can offer to the human world.

This meaning of the land is not exactly specific to the lawn-park. If anything, how we came to define our cemeteries was only an extension of emerging American ideas about the land, ones anchored in that *strange* view of nature and fanned through the manifest destiny driving rampant colonization. Spreading with great fervor, Europeans not only settled communities in North America and never left, but also went about inculcating nature—the land itself—with its notion of separateness.

Silko has hardly been the only critic of this view of the land. Plumwood worried that it privileged sight over other embodied ways of experiencing the land. How smell and touch are ignored, for instance. How listening or conversing with the land is rendered odd. "Can you talk or speak to the landscape," Plumwood wondered, "as you can to the land?" Perhaps the worst part of thinking about the land in this way is that it robs it of any agency, positioning the more-than-human as passive receptors of human doings.[3] And yet, a concept of the land as a landscape to be looked at, to be merely used and enjoyed, and that requires the viewer be situated outside of it to see, feel, and know anything about it at all, is what's come to prevail.[4]

It's been more than half a century since Leopold first lamented our inability to lead with an ethic of the land rooted in interdependence, to make the shift in thinking necessary to fuel an environmental commitment with no end. Living for fifteen years in the Southwest United States, Leopold was most surely influenced by local North American understandings of the land as a living, changing, and breathing web of relations. He never said whether his encounter with native people might have shaped his ideas, but his land ethic unambiguously reflects a relationship to the land that runs counter to mainstream European influence.[5]

Prior to Leopold, American nature writers, such as Henry David Thoreau and John Burroughs, also went about trying to undo this distant gazing upon the land—grasping the particularities around us, discovering how our being in and among the more-than-human shapes what we can and cannot know. Since then, a whole tradition of nature writers has flourished with just that resonance. The unyielding works of Terry Tempest Williams and Wendell Berry, for instance, have greatly influenced my own sense of the land. As the green burial movement embraces a concept of the land community, of that quality of interdependence we're still so lacking, GBAs are hardly reaching in the dark. Which is to say that seeing counter to a view of the land, as mere landscape, is rich in our bones, too.

But that richness also requires some tempering. A criticism often made against Leopold's land ethic—*A thing is right when it tends to preserve the integrity, beauty and stability of the biotic community. It is wrong when it tends otherwise*—is that the biotic community is always and forever privileged over any particular part within the whole. What happens when some part of that whole is in need more than the others? How are the different exigencies of the land community addressed, weighed, honored?

Unfortunately, talking about the land community has sometimes devolved into curtailing human needs all together. As can sometimes happen with ideas, Leopold's have been deployed in ways that have not always served all parts of the biotic community well. This has been especially true in terms of deep ecology approaches that have ignored the people most affected by environmental degradation (e.g., the urban poor) in favor of protecting lands that often support the privileged few; where environmental protection has been reduced to defending pure wilderness, ignoring how the land is also tied up with the well-being of the humans who inhabit it. Of course, Leopold also believed humans must "use" the land, that in order for us to truly understand the nature that is not ourselves we must live, enjoy, and draw from it. And we must do so despite knowing that our doings, conscious or not, may threaten to destroy some of those parts in our midst.[6]

To avoid such traps, some thinkers have tried to reframe Leopold's land dynamic. Carolyn Merchant, for instance, has said we'd do better to think in terms of "partnership,"[7] a relationship in which we're all allies in one biotic whole. "A partnership ethic," she said, "holds that the greatest good for the human and nonhuman communities is in their mutual, living interdependence." Perhaps it's *only* by way of foregrounding these partnerships that both connection and sustainability will flourish.

As we partner with other aspects of the land community, renewed meanings of connection to the earth are given steam. If such meaning is wrought through an ethic of the land, the question remains: To what extent is the green burial movement succeeding? In order to answer that question we must turn to face the land, to look at emerging green burial grounds themselves.

Though not the *only* aspect of the movement, they're unequivocally the heart of it. Without them, not only would there would be no place for funeral directors and other caretakers of the dead to implement green practices, but there would also be no place for those human meanings of connection to grow.

Over the last decade, the Green Burial Council (GBC) has surfaced as the standard bearer of green burial terrain, identifying and certifying burial grounds at three levels—Conservation, Natural, and Hybrid. Either because they haven't pursued it or because they've been denied it, not all burial grounds are certified by the GBC. Still, their categories and criteria give much-needed shape to the differing goals of green cemeteries as they've been slowly emerging throughout the states. Surely, as the movement expands and new questions and concerns come to the surface, the GBC's standards are likely to change, too. Regardless, their current terms are becoming commonplace lingo among GBAs and, in varying ways, within the growing public discourse around greening death more generally.

I'll say more about the value of GBC certification in the next chapter. But for now, I wander through a range of green cemeteries that have grown up over the last decade and a half, using the GBC's framework to help make sense of what's happening on the ground. How green burials grounds are imagined, established, and maintained can tell us a lot about the promise, or the lack thereof, of an earth-based ethic of human death.

CONSERVATION BURIAL GROUNDS

When Dr. Billy and Kimberley Campbell opened Ramsey Creek in 1998, their goal wasn't singular. While the green burial pioneers wanted to offer greener forms of death care, they also had a broader mission—to use the fact of human death to fund wildlife preservation and land conservation efforts. "What we're doing is basically land conservation. By setting aside woods for natural burials we preserve it from development."[8] Kimberley Campbell told me that what they're doing is "CPR for the land—conservation, preservation, restoration. That's always been our main focus."[9]

From the start, Campbell's vision was far-reaching—dreaming of "saving a million acres." Not solo. But by engaging with others to build what's come to be called *Conservation burial grounds* throughout the United States.[10]

Though a fresh and radical concept at the time, budding ideas are often scattered about the margins of movements. Billy wasn't alone in his zeal to combine death care and land conservation. Former Jesuit lay minister and media consultant Joe Sehee was living as a new transplant in the Mojave Desert and was also thinking along these lines. He and his wife, Juliette, had come out to the land in the hope of beginning an eco retreat for the grieving. But all that would change when he and Campbell would meet and combine efforts toward a green burial ground project outside the Bay Area. That project would ultimately go on without Campbell and Sehee, but the idea of Conservation burial would not fail in its wake. The dream would remain very much alive.[11]

For Campbell, this translated into continuing to steward the thirty-three acres he was already burying on in Westminster, South Carolina, while restoring the remaining land for burial somewhere down the road.[12] It also meant trying to build that million-acre dream through consulting work.[13] Sehee's sights were set on building Conservation burial as well, but he also saw the pressing need for certifiable standards for the burgeoning field. Concern over potential greenwashing, and the belief that green standards for funerary care providers and products would be the only way to make burial grounds accountable to the public, Sehee founded the not-for-profit Green Burial Council (GBC) in 2005, a third-party eco certifier of green burial providers. Campbell has made his own contributions to the GBC, collaborating on the first standards committee and serving in an advisory capacity ever since.[14]

Every movement has its origin stories, and, in the United States, green burial's is steeped in conservation. Land conservation, to be exact. Like the mainstream U.S. environmental movement that's long been bound to land protection, green burial emerged with a similar aim. Since the 1960s, there's been a growing sense that human burial was somehow anathema to environmental aims. As cremation was thought to not take up precious resources or unnecessarily use up land, it appeared to be the only eco death care choice. Conservation burial turned this thinking on its head. Do human bodies use up land? It's all a matter of how you look at it. The dead are buried and, in turn, land is protected from other uses. By preserving habitat, air, soil, and water are healthier, and, of course, the living only benefit from that. In Conservation burial, human death is understood to be a path to environmental protection.

What does the GBC say makes a Conservation burial ground? What standards do cemeteries have to meet to be granted their top-tier status? I break it down here to its most salient aspects.

First, the burial ground must fulfill the most basic requirement of any green burial ground, which means bodies must be buried "green"—no chemical embalming, no burial vault, and with the use of a biodegradable burial container. Scattering and burial of cremated remains may also be accommodated at the site, although those are not requirements.

Second, they must make a commitment to landscape-level conservation, which means that they must create a long-term endowment fund for the land

and commit to conservation practices, such as being mindful of more sensitive areas where burial, perhaps, should not take place, protecting vegetation and native diversity, using native plants in restoration, and rescuing rare plants whenever possible.

Third, the land that makes up the burial ground must be conserved in perpetuity, which means that there must be some kind of memorialization, like an easement or deed restriction, to ensure that the land won't one day turn into a conventional cemetery. What's more, this easement must be held by a third-party conservation entity, like a land trust, that keeps the land in conservation forever.[15] In other words, the burial ground must establish an abiding and legal agreement with a conservation partner. By holding an easement on the property, the conservation entity provides a strong guarantee of long-term stewardship, as well as third-party monitoring and reporting of the area.

It's tough to say precisely how many green burial grounds are operating in the United States right now. The NHFA maintains a list—of certified and uncertified providers—that's crested above the one hundred mark. To date, a little over half of those are certified by the GBC. Of all of them, however, only seven have emerged with such conservation partnerships: Ramsey Creek Preserve in Westminster, South Carolina; Foxfield Preserve in Wilmot, Ohio; Honey Creek Woodlands in Conyers, Georgia; Prairie Creek Conservation Cemetery in Gainesville, Florida; White Eagle Memorial Preserve in Goldendale, Washington; Preble Memory Gardens Cemetery in West Alexandria, Ohio; and Herland Forest Natural Burial Cemetery in Wahkiacus, Washington. (Only the first six listed here are currently certified by the GBC).[16]

These conservation partnerships have formed in varying ways. For example, Ramsey Creek was open and burying for seven years before they joined with Upstate Forever, a land trust whose mission is to "promote sensible growth and protect special places in the upstate region of South Carolina."[17] Alternatively, Prairie Creek partnered with Alachua Conservation Trust from the get-go, building the model for the cemetery in conversation with the land trust. Foxfield and White Eagle also grew from initial partnerships, except the land trusts that hold their easements were hardly outsiders to their operation. Gordon Maupin was executive director of The Wilderness Center, a not-for-profit nature center and land trust in Wilmot, Ohio, when he started exploring establishing a green burial ground as a way to fuel their conservation efforts. Out of that, Foxfield was born. White Eagle emerged from an existing conservation entity, too,—Sacred Earth Foundation—that was already expert at stewarding over one thousand acres of land in south central Washington. It wasn't until their founder died quite unexpectedly, and they sought to bury him on the land he'd lived and tended for decades, that they began to think about Conservation burial in the first place.[18]

Joining with an established conservation entity has proven to be one of the trickiest parts of building the Conservation burial dream. But if such pairings have been rare and difficult to make, it's not because the land trust community has somehow been kept in the dark. In 2005, Joe Sehee introduced the concept of Conservation burial at the Land Trust Alliance National Rally. Two years later, Stephen Christy made a compelling case for Conservation burial grounds in an article he wrote for the Land Trust Alliance (LTA) newsletter, *Exchange*. As a landscape architect and former long-time executive director of a land trust outside of Chicago, Christy was well positioned to argue for his and Sehee's early vision and to get fellow land trust folks thinking about future partnerships. "Doesn't it behoove the land trust community," Christy said, "to look at death as, in Hannah Arendt's words, 'the final stage of growth?'"[19]

Even though a majority of the land trusts in the United States belong to the LTA, Sehee's and Christy's urgings were slow to take root. "It's not a subject people want to confront head on," Christy said. However, he was fortunate to become part of a project that did. Christy serves on the board of the Philander Chase Corporation (PCC), the land trust established by his alma mater Kenyon College in 2000 to preserve the college's rural surroundings. After several years' discussion, and with the urging of PCC's new chairman Peter White and managing director Lisa Schott, in October of 2013 the PCC board approved the creation of a green burial cemetery. They purchased a nearby fifty-two-acre golf course threatened with development and retained Christy to design a green burial cemetery on twenty-three acres of that property. PCC named this project the Kokosing Nature Preserve (KNP) (after the local state scenic river). It expects the cemetery to be "open for business" in the summer of 2015.

Despite this effort, the fact remains that less than one half of one percent of the more than 1,700 land trusts in the United States have joined the growing green burial fray—and understandably, from Christy's viewpoint. "The learning curve is daunting, especially if you're a land trust just starting out with one of these projects." Regulations, financing, planning, construction: all are complex. PCC had the kind of reinforcements it needed to work through these complexities—a dedicated project coordinator, Amy Henricksen, a committee devoted solely to the project, and the experience and support of the folks at nearby Foxfield.[20]

Some land trusts may be slow to get on board for other reasons. For instance, there's the matter of public perception. Will their supporters approve? There also may be the concern that a partnership with a green burial ground might amount to a kind of "mission creep," and, most likely, they won't want to be seen as getting into the death care business. Some may simply not see it in their purview. And indeed, for some land trusts that have a very narrow scope in terms of the kinds of lands they can protect, green burial might present as a real barrier. There's also the money factor. Will green burial bring in enough of it to compensate them for their work? In the end, some land trusts may just not "get" the concept at all.

But from the movement's perspective, land trusts are a natural fit. Long after a cemetery's been filled, long after the people who initiated it are dead, who will be there to care for the land? Given that land trusts are all about conserving and protecting land *forever*, there seem to be few better partners positioned to assist the movement with its conservation goals. Moreover, land trusts can often offer expertise in restoring soil quality and wildlife and plant habitat to lands harmed through the likes of industrial farming, mining, sprawl, oil spills, mountain top removal, clear cutting, and any other number of polluting and depleting practices. Ecological restoration is one of the places where a conservation entity can really shine in terms of aiding the stewardship of green burial grounds.

For example, the land at Foxfield Preserve was farmed "for quite a long time" and with not very "environmentally minded practices," its steward, Sara Brink, told me. "It's not pristine land, it's land we're in the process of restoring." In the six years since they opened, soil health has improved dramatically. "Today," she said, "we've generated about two and a half new inches of topsoil." With trained naturalists on staff, experienced wetland mitigators, and eco foresters, Foxfield makes such restoration efforts look easy. Experience helps. Stewarding over 3,500 acres of "forest, streams, prairies and farmland," the forty-three acres of Foxfield must surely seem like a piece of cake.

Those forty-three acres are comprised of the recovery of two different ecosystems—prairie and mixed hardwood forest. In the latter, a big push to replant happened about a decade ago. "Right now," she said, "trees are about seven or eight feet. Some of the white oaks are still very small." The preserve is in the process of adding additional trees, mostly "for people who want a living memorial," Brink explained. "Planting a tree can often bring great comfort." The other two sections of the preserve are focused on bringing back prairie.[21] Former executive director Gordon Maupin observed the success of some of their efforts back in 2012 "black-eyed Susan growing . . . big bluestem sticking up above other things, tall coreopsis, tall sunflower . . . butterfly weed . . . milkweed, and [many other species native to the] tallgrass prairie."[22]

Talking about the return of tallgrass prairie can bring a spark to even the most dispirited environmentalist. For over eight thousand years the ecosystem stretched, uninterrupted, over 150 million acres east of the Rocky Mountains to the Missouri River. By 1900, the farm plow had all but wiped it out and, today, only about 2 percent of it remains.[23] Spawned by Leopold's initial observations, protecting what's left of this highly endangered ecosystem is a top priority for many Midwestern conservationists. While the prairie was mostly lost, even Leopold saw a faint light in a far corner of the cornfield. Each summer, passing by a small nineteenth-century graveyard, giant yellow asters bloomed—*Silphiums*, a prairie flower that had vanished just about everywhere else. Safe from the plow blade, and later the lawnmower, Midwestern pioneer cemeteries remain mini reminders of what once was. As Foxfield works to reestablish lost ecosystems, these historic and "green" cemeteries offer both lessons and hope.[24]

Restoration efforts have also been underway at Prairie Creek. Under the direction of the Alachua Conservation Trust, nearly half of the five-hundred-acre property is undergoing changes. A former pine plantation has been thinned and fire has been reintroduced in order to "help restore the structure of natural pinelands."[25] Some four hundred miles north, Ramsey Creek has also been eradicating pine as part of their restoration efforts, at least on the thirty-eight acres they've not yet begun to bury on. Billy Campbell told me that over twenty years ago that land "was the cooler, older growth section, but some local forester yahoo recommended clear cutting and bulldozing it in order to get the pines to grow back." The pines did grow back, only that particular pine species is not native to the area. "Loblolly pine," Campbell said. "I hope to make caskets out of them one day."[26]

Not all Conservation burial grounds are in need of such restoration, however, or even all parts of them. The other thirty-three acres at Ramsey Creek are rich with biodiversity and soil health. Campbell knows this firsthand, as he completed the initial biological survey himself. "I'm a pretty good field botanist," he told me with well-earned satisfaction, though the survey was later improved upon with the help of Southeastern field-trained naturalist L. L. "Chick" Gaddy. The splendor, solace, and sanctuary of the woods may be what visitors walk away with, but the value of that survey cannot be understated. Over three hundred species were identified. Such biodiversity may be a mere matter of geography. "We're at the crossroads of the Piedmont and the mountains. We have some Central Plains species. We also have this weird circumneutral soil with a lot of magnesium, iron, and calcium in it," Campbell explained. And there are microhabitats, too. "We have species that are not normally found below 2,000 feet," Campbell went on to say with great enthusiasm. And for good reason. The highest point at Ramsey Creek is at about one thousand feet.

But whether the land that makes up a Conservation burial ground is in need of rehab or is relatively unspoiled, not all will be conserved in precisely the same way. That is, the GBC provides no input on style, form, or layout. For instance, White Eagle calls itself a "wilderness cemetery." And indeed, if we're thinking about wilderness in the way Leopold did as "a wild, roadless area where those who are so inclined may enjoy primitive modes of travel and subsistence,"[27] then parts of White Eagle are surely wild. Moreover, if we're abiding by these definitions, White Eagle and other Conservation burial grounds that steward larger tracts of land, much of which are not accessible by roads, would be considered wilderness cemeteries too—like its neighbor, Herland Forest Natural Cemetery (although Herland refers to itself as "a forest cemetery"). The "wild" quality of these burial grounds is often not only a matter of an inaccessible nature but also of a "wild" aesthetic, one that resists the orderliness of cemetery design.

In many ways, KNP represents a blending of this "wild" style with a more traditional approach to cemetery planning. KNP has a fairly rigid structure to it—long, straight turf allees and elevated gathering areas. Stephen Christy explained it to me this way: "Our board liked the concept of honoring the departed with some cues from the Rural Cemetery Movement, giving people a sense of order and place. But it also wanted the property to be a true nature preserve, so the entire landscape has been converted to native vegetation." While every grave will have path access, burial areas will be cloaked in native shortgrass prairie and savanna.[28]

Just as styles vary, the terms and arrangements of partnerships vary, too. Alachua Conservation Trust directs, even oversees, the restoration of Prairie Creek, while Ramsey Creek does most of it on their own. "We have a very simple easement," Campbell told me, calling it more "process based." It specifies burial density and where burials can take place. It also spells out what native plants are to be used for restoration, "like local cultivars of pine," he said. Upstate Forever holds an easement on the land and visits twice a year to observe compliance. Still, there's no doubt that Campbell along with his wife, Kimberley, act as their best stewards. Long before the land trust partnered with Ramsey Creek, the Campbells had an obvious and enduring commitment to understanding and caring for the land.[29]

Not unlike Ray Mitchell, founder of Sacred Earth Foundation. In 1974, Mitchell came out to south central Washington and, along with some friends, began buying parcels—land holdings that would eventually be held by the foundation. "Ray built a strong, sacred connection to the land," Jodie Buller said, tending the earth and connecting people to it through summer horse camps for kids, teaching off-grid, back-to-the-land skills, and practicing sustainable forestry.

When Ray suddenly died in 2007, his friends and family knew he wanted to be buried on the land he loved. White Eagle Memorial Preserve Cemetery was created in Ray's honor, a twenty-acre, GBC-certified Conservation burial ground that's a subsidiary of Sacred Earth Foundation, now a bona fide land trust in the arid hills of the Klickitat Valley.[30] Like Campbell, Ray didn't need the foundation to tell him to care for the land. And yet, without it, who exactly would be doing so now that Ray had died? Ray's death is a reminder that the land will outlive us all. Partnering with a conservation entity is one way to provide continuity of care long after Ray or Campbell, long after you or I, are gone.

Not too far from White Eagle is Herland Forest Natural Burial Cemetery. Herland is overseen by Windward, an intentional community comprised of stewards who've been living on that particular piece of land since 1988. Windward's not just a community, however, it's also a 501c3 foundation supporting a research center to aid in moving toward a more sustainable future. "Stewardship," the Windward website reads, "at its heart, is the ongoing hands-on search for harmony with other people, with other forms of life, and ultimately, with the entire biosphere."[31]

As far as eco certification goes, Herland and the GBC are now in conversation. When I talked to the cemetery steward, Andrew Schreiber, he told me that they're "looking into Conservation level status." Windward's established commitment to the land as a community to be cared for and its partnership with Herland certainly positions it as a formidable long-term caretaker of the cemetery.

Schreiber said that stewards of Windward focus "on a combination of elements necessary to create a sustainable rural village." The land-stewardship members, of which there are currently five, actually live, work, and play on the land, although there are other people involved at various levels who come to apprentice and learn. On the 131 acres, the elements of sustainability are pretty basic—food, fuel, clothing, shelter. Added to that, now, is caring for the dead. The community's elder member, Walt Patrick, brought the idea of sustainable burial back to the community after he'd attended a green burial lecture given by Cynthia Beal in Portland, Oregon, mulled over the possibility for some time, and then said, "hey, let's try and explore this potential for the community." Cemetery plot sales in the twenty-acre cemetery are open and available to the public at large, broadening the parameters of the land community once more.

But it's not only the dead that are aiding in its expansion. As Schreiber told me, "We very much want the land-based human culture to be integrated into the cemetery. We're looking to love the land and nurture it. Not leave it alone."[32] All the Conservation burial ground owners and operators I talked to have, in one way or another, said the same thing—that green burial is as much about the living's relationship to the land as it is the dead's. Despite design, and the varied ecosystems that make them. Conservation burial grounds invite the living in.

This has certainly been one of the foundational ideas behind the development of KNP. Included right in the center of its design is a grass amphitheater meant for college events and functions. "It's not meant to be a somber gathering area," Stephen Christy noted. After all, "The site had been a place of pure fun and recreation—a golf course—for the past half-century. The departed enjoyed themselves in life too."[33]

Echoing Christy, at nearby Foxfield Sara Brink told me that one of her fondest memories is of a butterfly walk they held one summer day when her son was about two and a half. Joining about twenty-five other kids and their parents, they followed the naturalists through a haze of milkweed and monarchs. Some family members of folks who'd been buried at Foxfield in the past were also there that day. In the midst of kids racing around with butterfly nets and learning about the land, one woman turned to Sara and said, "It's just so beautiful. My husband would have loved to see how people are enjoying his gravesite."[34]

As people are summoned to spend time in these conservation areas, the land community swells. A land trust can do a good job in expanding these parameters. So, too, can an individual or a community, those who know the land most intimately. But established partnerships between the two provide the best assurance the land will be cared for forever. Today, however, the majority of green burial grounds do not have such partnerships.

How's the land community faring without them?

NATURAL BURIAL GROUNDS

Much like the thirty-three acres at Ramsey Creek, Steelmantown Cemetery is set amid a vibrant and diverse ecosystem. Its sandy and acidic soil spared it the way of agriculture, and the forest remains nearly as unspoiled as it was in the late seventeenth century when Ed Bixby's family first settled in the area.

When people talk about enchanted forests, Steelmantown is surely what they have in mind. Sensitive and globally rare, the Pine Barrens is magical terrain. Purple mushrooms surge through sand and downed leaves. Verdant moss and royal ferns animate the blush of lady slippers and other rare orchids. Bladderwort, a carnivorous plant, threatens mosquito larvae and young tadpoles with their swelling traps. And then there are the ghost mushrooms that only last for a day. As I was on the lookout for native blueberry and huckleberry bushes, Ed Bixby told me about box turtles searching out toxic mushrooms, black bear on the trail, and coyote scat on burial mounds.

Like Campbell, Ed Bixby cares for the woods himself. He has a team of men helping him in trail making and grave digging, and a nature educator from a nearby park who assists with plant identification. But he's the sole proprietor of the cemetery, and his stewardship runs deep. Ed's ties to the land stretch back through several centuries, both in terms of the cemetery and the surrounding forest.

Part of the land of what is now Steelmantown includes a one-acre cemetery that dates back to the 1700s. Before the cemetery was sold in 1956 to a funeral director who'd won a contract to bury children from a nearby residential facility, it was owned and operated by a long-standing church congregation. As Bixby's family belonged to that church, many of them were buried in the cemetery. "My family came here in 1680," Bixby told me. Indeed, his ancestors were no strangers to the land.

The last member of his family to be buried in the cemetery was his baby brother, just a year after the church sold it. The church congregation still convened at the cemetery chapel (Bixby's grandmother actually taught Sunday school there), but eventually the members didn't like the way the new owner was maintaining the cemetery and moved on. Over the years, the lack of upkeep was like an open wound for Bixby's mother. At one point she even considered moving her son's remains to another location.

In 2007, when Bixby was inspecting a parcel adjacent to the cemetery for a potential building lot (he's a contractor and developer by trade), he noticed the lack of upkeep firsthand. Overgrown and filled with garbage, Ed called the owner, Jack Langley, and asked him to clean up the land. Langley was long retired by then, and without the money or the energy to care for the cemetery he offered it to Bixby for free. Bixby eventually did take it over, reopening it as a green burial ground, though, in many ways, it had always been one. No vaults, for instance, had ever been used in any of the burials at Steelmantown, before or after the funeral director took possession. After Bixby obtained the property, he began buying adjacent parcels to grow the size of the cemetery.[35]

Bixby would be the first to tell you that his decision to take over the cemetery was rooted in sound business principles. But he would also tell you that his ties to the historic cemetery section, as well as the forest, played pivotal roles, too. "I grew up playing in these woods," he said, as we strolled the rugged paths beyond the cemetery and into the neighboring twenty-one-thousand-acre Belleplain State Forest. Passing by a deep and wide ravine, he talked about the past of that particular spot, how "there used to be a big giant lake here, a giant cranberry bog." But the cranberry industry withered and "the state eventually took the dam out." Staring down at that wide chasm in the earth, I tried to imagine what it might have looked like then, and what it means to hold these stories—these memories of the land—and how their retelling is part of being a steward, too.[36]

While on the face of things there appear to be few real differences between Steelmantown and a Conservation burial ground like Ramsey Creek, Steelmantown is certified by the GBC as a Natural burial ground, their second-tier-level certification. Like Conservation burial grounds, Natural burial grounds must inter bodies "green," eschew pesticides and insecticides, create an endowment fund for long-term care of the land, and in some way memorialize the parcel to ensure that the cemetery will not one day turn conventional. This is most often done in the form of a deed restriction that runs with the land; that, in essence, limits the use of the land through a legally enforceable covenant.

But these certification levels also differ in some crucial ways. Though the current standards do not say so, Conservation burial grounds are typically larger in terms of acreage. According to GBC board member Katey Bean, however, the soon-to-be-passed new standards *will* require that Conservation burial grounds be at least ten acres, or at least five acres that are also contiguous to other protected lands.[37] Steelmantown (which is fifteen acres and also buffered by twenty-one thousand acres of protected state park) certainly fits that criteria. However, for a certified Natural burial ground there is nothing apart from the deed restriction that runs with the land to enforce long-term environmental protection. That is, Steelmantown, unlike a Conservation burial ground like Ramsey Creek, has no formal partnership with a third-party conservation entity. And for the GBC, that's a crucial distinction.

For Bixby, such a partnership remains a future goal. "Right now," he said, "I have the freedom to make good choices for the cemetery. Maybe someday when all the pieces are in place." His hope is that when green burial becomes "more recognized," the state, rather than a land trust, might have some interest. "Being located next to a state park makes it a good fit," he told me. As of yet, however, no states have collaborated with any operating green burial ground.

For some Natural burial grounds, partnership with a land trust is an enduring quest. That's certainly been true for Greensprings Natural Cemetery Preserve, which, at one hundred acres, all but functions like a Conservation burial ground sans partnership. Off grid and sandwiched between two large conserved parcels, Greensprings had once been a working potato farm, but now acts as a kind of open space between those two conservation areas, creating over eight thousand acres of uninterrupted natural habitat. For them, having a conservation entity oversee this link is critical.[38] For some other Natural burial grounds, like Eloise Woods Community Natural Burial Park outside Austin, Texas, there seems to be less pressing concern. Because the deed restriction must run with the land, there's a sense of security that the acreage will be cared for down the road. Whoever takes over the cemetery in

Still, not all Natural burial grounds, like Steelmantown, are freestanding, nor does the GBC require that they must be. Their presumably stand-alone status also does not require that they be freestanding in terms of the business side of things, which means that the same for-profit or not-for-profit entity that owns and operates a conventional cemetery can also own and operate a green burial ground. To make matters even more complicated, there's actually nothing in the GBC guidelines that requires a Conservation burial ground, like Ramsey Creek, be freestanding either, though at least right now all but one of them are. The Conservation burial ground at Preble Memory Gardens Cemetery, in West Alexandria, Ohio, is connected to a conventional ground, both in terms of the view (if you're standing in the burial ground you can see the conventional cemetery) and in terms of being owned and operated by the same entity.

Even though some Natural burial grounds have been manifesting as free standing, most of them are taking shape in one of two ways. Either the green burial section is separate and simply linked in terms of the corporation (for-profit or not-for-profit) or the green burial ground is actually some cordoned-off section of the conventional space that utilizes green practices eschewed in the rest of the cemetery. Regardless of how things might appear, all of these parcels of land, large or small, must, as I said earlier, be designated forever green. Wholly separate or visually more integrated, both must make a legal declaration, as in the form of a deed restriction that runs with the land.

Examples of the former include Pine Forest Memorial Gardens' the "Garden of Renewal," a Natural burial ground established in 2011 in Wake Forest, North Carolina, and quickly certified by the GBC.[42] Though a separate and distinct designated area, not mixed in with conventional practice in any way, the "Garden" is under one corporate entity. Moreover, access to the "Garden" is made through the conventional cemetery area.[43] The green burial ground in my community of Rhinebeck, New York, is sited in a similar way. Behind the open lawn-park-style conventional cemetery, which belongs to The Town of Rhinebeck, sits nearly eight acres of wooded land, of which about two-and-a-half have been surveyed for green burial. Like Pine Forest, one accesses the trail to the burial ground by way of the conventional section.

About an hour-and-a-half drive north of Rhinebeck is Vale Cemetery, in Schenectady, New York. The curvilinear roads, trees, and shrubs harken to the Rural Cemetery Movement style, and, indeed, like other rural cemeteries that were created on the outskirts of town in the mid-1800s, Vale grew to respond to the need for more "sanitary" burial space. Over the next century, Schenectady would grow up around the rural cemetery, positioning Vale deep within the heart of the inner city. Vale's green burial ground, a meadow called "The Dell at Vale," is certified by the GBC at the Natural level. But unlike Pine Forest and the Natural burial ground in Rhinebeck, "The Dell" is sited within the framework of the conventional burial ground, flanked by both historic and recent burials as well as a crematorium. It's only a small portion of the one-hundred-acres cemetery—less than three acres with about 190 burial sites, where mowing is shunned and goats are brought in twice a year to keep down saplings.[44]

Understanding how Conservation and Natural burial grounds are different in terms of certification criteria, and how they actually come to manifest in the land, seems rather crucial to the movement's success. First of all, these varied dimensions ought to be clear to consumers. Indeed, that's one of the reasons the GBC emerged in the first place. As green burial grounds are growing in number, the GBC works to refine their standards to meet the needs of consumers, as well as the land. Beyond that, making sense of these differences reveals the extent to which an earth-based ethic of human death is actively being forged on the ground.

But consensus on these matters is not always easy. For example, Billy Campbell still serves in an advisory capacity to the GBC and feels that free-standing Natural burial grounds, especially ones that are making a commitment to landscape-level conservation, and ones tied to conventional burial grounds ought to have different statuses. For him, green burial grounds bearing some relationship to a conventional burial ground are benefitting from the infrastructure and revenue stream that comes from conventional practices. "It's not clear competition," Campbell argues. "And if consumers can't tell the difference, then that's a problem."[45]

Other GBAs worry that green burial sites within already existing cemeteries threaten the overall spirit of green burial, as the traditions and mechanisms of conventional cemeteries might limit not only environmental goals but community ones, too. An active member of Green Burial Massachusetts, Judith Lorei told me that one of the reasons they've been pursuing the development of a green burial model that doesn't include an already existing cemetery is because conventional cemeteries more often than not have their own culture; for instance, "their own rules about using machinery, or about who can and cannot dig the grave"—basically about who and at what level families can be involved. Green Burial Massachusetts is a small grassroots group working to establish a Conservation burial ground somewhere in the state.[46] "The idea for us," Lorei said, "is about trying to create an opportunity for people to take much more of an active role,"[47] something that's also been important to the GBC. One of the requirements for all certified burial grounds, regardless of level, is that family must be given the chance to be involved in the burial process.[48]

Of course, just because a green burial ground is tied to a conventional one doesn't mean the cemetery culture can't change. Likewise, as GBC programs coordinator, Kate Kalanick, told me, just because a green burial ground is "tied to a conventional one in some way, doesn't mean they can't do good conservation work."[49] It's not that Campbell disagrees. "They can do a good job," he said. "You can have a cemetery that has 300 acres off the back and they could have a separate entrance and everything else. And they can provide excellent habitat. But I still think it should have an asterisk on it." Even at its best, Campbell believes a distinction should be made that bears reflection in certification levels. "I liken them to restaurants that have both meat and vegetarian fare on the same menu,"[50] he explained. His point: We wouldn't call them vegetarian restaurants.

Some of the tension around the precise formulation of standards criteria for Natural burial grounds might stem from a gap over just what certifiable standards are meant to do. Landscape architect Kim Sorvig, who also served on the original standards committee, told me that though standards are the best portal for a consumer to come through they're also a tough tightrope act.[51] The GBC has just recently revised their standards, although these concerns are not echoed in any of the changes. I'll say more about the challenge of establishing certifiable standards in the next chapter. But in the end, Kalanick reminded me that standards are a living, breathing tool and that as burial grounds take shape, the standards will surely shift and change too. Joe Sehee agrees. "It's not a perfect thing," he said. "You can have standards in 2015 that in 2023 make less sense. Eco standards have to be raised as the industry grows."[52]

Whatever concerns linger about green burial grounds that are tied to conventional ones, it remains that far more of them exist than freestanding ones. The majority of these are not actually certified at the GBC's Natural burial ground level, however. Most green burial grounds are certified at their lowest tier, Hybrid.

HYBRID BURIAL GROUNDS

The word *hybrid* denotes the cross between two different species or varieties. To hear it in this context, the mind wanders, wondering just what is being crossed with what? Billy Campbell told me when he "first spoke of Hybrids it was in reference to those types of operations" that combined conventional and green burial.[53] To his mind, any human burial ground that harbors these two approaches to interment—whether they're owned by the same entity, take up the same land, or not, or whether they further conservation goals and are tied to a land trust—are technically some kind a Hybrid. But this isn't how the GBC sees it. As I already pointed out, there is one example of a GBC-certified Conservation burial ground and several examples of GBC-certified Natural burial grounds that are in some way tied to a conventional cemetery. Right now, the standards allow for that.

By the GBC's standards, Hybrid burial grounds are conventionally run cemeteries that offer whole-body "green" burial (no chemical embalming, no vaults, and with the use of biodegradable burial containers).[54] Plots interspersed within a conventional cemetery or, like some Natural burial grounds, an entire section set within an existing conventional cemetery, may be designated "green." In fact, in situations where a section is set aside "green," a Hybrid might look much like Vale or Pine Forest, both certified at the Natural level.

This Hybrid "section" approach mirrors what is happening not too far from where I live at Sleepy Hollow Cemetery, another historic New York Rural Cemetery and, now, GBC-certified Hybrid. The twisted roads and shaded vistas at Sleepy Hollow take me through iron gates, past Andrew Carnegie's family plot and over to a small hillside meadow, less than half an acre, where green-only interment takes place. Many other examples of these are now peppered throughout the United States, including—Brooksville Cemetery, in Brooksville, Florida; Estacada Cemetery District, in Estacada, Oregon; both of which are certified by the GBC; and Bellefontaine Cemetery, in St, Louis, Missouri, and Most Holy Redeemer Cemetery in Niskayuna, New York, both of which are not certified.

Unlike Natural burial grounds, however, and regardless of whether there is a designated section or not, Hybrids do not have to manage pests with natural methods. Above ground, business can go on as usual, whether that means using insecticides, herbicides, or synthetic fertilizers. The other key difference is that no deed restriction is required for Hybrids. Of course, without one, there's always the threat that at some point down the road those unsold designated plots, or the segregated land space, could revert to conventional practice. It also leaves green plots already sold vulnerable to the weight of those conventional practices. Some Hybrids, however, are already set up this way, like Mount Auburn Cemetery—the first rural cemetery in the United States—that now offers green burial plots that are interspersed among conventional ones. In order to create some assurances among purchasers that their plot will be a forever-green, Mount Auburn writes a restriction into the deed of every green grave sold.[55]

Today, Hybrid burial grounds dominate the movement. That's mainly due to one reason and one reason alone—they're much easier to establish than either Conservation or Natural burial grounds. With no state or federal laws requiring bodies be embalmed or that vaults be used, conventional cemeteries can alter their rules with little effort or expense to accommodate whole-body green burial, or cremation burial with a biodegradable urn. With experienced caretakers on hand, and the institutional foundations to support it, offering these services within an already existing conventional cemetery can often just be a matter of paperwork.

Given its conservation origins, it might come as some surprise that the movement is shaping up in this way. Much of this has been a matter of business. Greening up death care for the already initiated can be simple, as well as advantageous. Established cemeteries can diversify their interment options with little expenditure or extra work. And as many cemeteries around the United States struggle to survive, blossoming interest in green burial gives them one more way to stay afloat.

But there's more to this story of the rise in Hybrids than business opportunity. Lack of access to land and money, and land trusts too, make Conservation or even freestanding Natural burial grounds difficult to launch. I'll say more about that challenge in the next chapter. But there is no doubt that it remains one of the main reasons why Hybrids have been emerging in greater numbers.

With more Hybrid options available, especially ones that are closer to home, people are more likely to choose them. There are a number of reasons for this, but one of them is surely environmental. If one of the goals of green burial is to leave this world "a little lighter," as GBA Stephen Christy said to me, dying in Vermont and being buried in California might not be the way to go. To those ends, in 2011 the GBC completed some preliminary research that showed just how much a green grave could lighten our death load, specifically one's carbon footprint.

The GBC's researcher, Samuel Bar, told me that they were looking to compare how much CO_2 green burial was able to pull from the air into the ground versus conventional burial. (Putting it into the ground, by the way, is a good thing. It's called *sequestration*, and it aids in photosynthesis.) For each green grave it was estimated that about ten pounds of CO_2 was removed from the atmosphere, while for each conventional grave there was about 380 pounds of CO_2 added. This was estimated over a twenty-year period. That's the equivalent, Bar said, "of driving about 500 miles."[56] But with only seven Conservation burial ground choices in the United States at this juncture, this could mean a lot of travel for most folks. That being said, I've had several Conservation burial ground operators tell me that they have had bodies, as well as the bereaved, flown in from as far away as 2,500 miles.[57]

There are undoubtedly reasons beyond carbon footprint concern that folks might want to be buried closer to home. Expense is one of them. What will it cost to fly a body to its final destination? Family is another. Although Americans are increasingly portrayed as nomads, void of roots, statistics show that "nearly four in ten . . . have never left the place in which they were born." And though economic opportunity is often cited as the catalyst for why people stay or go, the other looming reason is "the tug of family and connections."[58] If people are tied to their families, to their communities, might this not also come to be reflected in our death practices, no matter how green they are?

Only time will tell. But GBC board member Katey Bean told me that in all her conversations with green burial providers most of them cite proximity as a key factor in why people end up choosing the burial ground they do. In the end, people want a place their kids can easily travel to.[59] There's also the matter of wanting to be buried near other family. Whatever the reason, Hybrids touch people where they live.

Perhaps in a much more essential way, this tug back to our communities is really all about our ties to the land itself. After all, in breaking down the human/nature dualism we are reminded that the land is made up of human culture, too.[60] As environmental justice advocates have implored us to see, the land is shaped by the people who "live, work and play" on it, and those people are inversely shaped by the land.

In the 1990s this view was finally heard by the mainstream environmental movement, most notably in the SouthWest Organizing Project's letter, a statement signed by a range of influential community members in New Mexico, all people of color, charging "the Big 10 groups . . . with a history of racist and exclusionary practices . . . and an all-around failure to support environmental justice efforts."[61] That letter posed a strong challenge to conservation goals that have often been criticized as privileging land over people, biotic communities over human needs, and ignoring how environmental degradation, especially in air, soil, and water, disproportionally affects the most disenfranchised and oppressed.

Not only has conservation often been deployed in the service of privilege, it's also sometimes had the effect of pushing the land into too small a corner of life. Is only what's wild worth saving? Leopold, like other early American naturalists, urged people to spend time in the wild so that they could learn to love it. More than a hundred years before I was born, the Hudson River School painters worked their canvases toward this goal, too, illuminating the untouched beauty of the earth space I've long called home as a way to get people to care for it. But what about what's profoundly broken and contaminated? And what about the human bodies that are often victims of both because that's the terrain they call home?

It's not as though Conservation burial is somehow rooted in a vision void of the presence of people—quite the opposite. As I've demonstrated through many examples, the living's engagement with the land is key. Even Billy

Campbell's been resolute about this, saying that his "million acres" dream is fundamentally all about changing our relationship to the land.[62]

Still, a history of conservation in the United States carries a great deal of historical baggage. But if conservation is key to the movement's goals—and I for one believe it is—how can we begin to incorporate the principles of conservation within the most tame, polluted, and marginal terrain like those in urban areas, where biodiversity is sparse, where open lands are few? More-over, how might we apply those principles to the poisoned and sanitized lands of conventional burial grounds? If we're really talking about a movement built in restoration and care of the land, what more than a lawn-park cemetery could be in need of it?

What lands—what nature—are worth the time, care, and attention of the green burial movement? And where does this leave green burial grounds that pair up with already existing conventional cemeteries? Do Hybrids count? Do they contribute to building an ethic of death rooted in the land?

Billy Campbell has said that he worries Hybrids "could deflate market demand for larger projects of greater total acreage and much greater conser-vation value."[63] And he's probably right. But in tying our past to our present, Hybrids still hold out some unique potential.

If the movement is looking to change consciousness, what better venue than a green burial in a sea of conventional ones? Such pairings can have the effect of doing more good than harm, that by having a green burial ground in the midst of toxic practices, a reversal of sorts might be at work. With conventional practices rubbing up against green ones, the fact of the rotting body—the "ick" of decay itself—might soon "make good sense," just as the chemicals and waste of the lawn garden might alight upon the mind with disgust.

Though there may be GBAs who worry that conventional cemeteries will greenwash the natural aspects of these new greener burial sites (and there's always that risk), it just may be that Hybrids will come to achieve the oppo-site effect, bending the rules the other way, in favor of the biotic community. Who knows? What now looks like a Hybrid could one day become a land teeming with biodiversity.[64]

TOWARD AN EARTH-BASED ETHIC OF HUMAN DEATH

A human community that lives in a mutually beneficial relation with the surrounding earth is a community, we might say, that lives in truth.

—David Abram

Not all green burial grounds share the same level of environmental commitment, and working toward restoring our biotic community has so far been
anything but a uniform project. But by not allowing chemical embalming,
nonbiodegradable caskets, and vaults or liners, all green burial grounds are,
at a bare minimum, fulfilling a guiding principle of interdependence. After
all, even a bona fide Hybrid like Mount Auburn draws from the wisdom of
its original founder, Jacob Bigelow, who called upon the value of decomposition in the name of those emerging nineteenth-century rural cemeteries:
"The elements which have once moved and circulated in living frames do not
become extinct nor useless after death: they offer themselves as the materials from which other living frames are to be constructed."[65] No matter which
type of burial ground we might look at, even those that meet the lowest GBC
standards, human decay is left do its own thing. In all of them, the matter of
human death matters once more to nature.

But in challenging our *strange* view of nature that says that humans are
somehow separate and apart from it, green burial grounds are enabling us to
do something more, something "ecologists have been telling us" for a long
time is necessary. Green burial provides a way to acknowledge "our debt to
the sustaining others of the world."[66] While all green burial grounds embody
this potential, some of them directly recognize it. For example, Herland Forest Natural Burial Cemetery named their burial ground in honor of Charlotte
Perkins Gilman's 1915 novel, *Herland*. Gilman's utopian tale depicts an
isolated all-women society free of enforced gender roles and, thus, the domi-
nation and injustice that grows from it. Herland cemetery steward Andrew
Schreiber told me the book inspired the possibility "of a different way of
life," of living in community with each other and the land. "We live well and
die well in that forest." And one of the ways that happens is by "honoring the
way that death nourishes new life."[67]

We may be humbled before a nature that will always succeed in doing
more than we could ever return in favor, but we "acknowledge our debt"
because that's how healthy, equitable, mutually respectful relationships are
built. Anthropologists Davies and Rumble have already made the case for
understanding the act of green burial as a way of gifting back to the earth, an
exchange both symbolic and real.[68] The reason why gift giving is so powerful
in building such relationships is because, as Davies and Rumble remind us,
when we give "part of the giver is [always] retained in the gift."[69] So, whether
it's a Conservation burial ground or a Hybrid whose goals might never be as
lofty as Ramsey Creek's or Foxfield's or White Eagle's, they all at once contribute to building a bond with the land. And not simply because they all have
some potential to do conservation work—like bringing back natives, fortifying soil ecology, and eradicating invasive species—of giving the land a real

opportunity to thrive. But, more simply, because the primary gift circulated in any green burial ground is human.

Green Burial Council (GBC) founder Joe Sehee has often said, "Nothing connects people to the land like being buried on it."[70] But for too long now, our cemeteries have functioned under a prevailing concept of land as outsider, as other, making our ability to reclaim it only a matter of how best the arbiters of social definition and power could bend it toward their own ends. Indeed, there is a long history of land reclamation like that in the United States. No matter the cemetery model, green burial grounds offer up another kind of reclamation. They give us another way of laying claim to a vision of the land as a community. Indeed, we're in need of more ways to manifest such a vision of interdependence, of partnership. These burial grounds, in their varying capacities, offer that possibility—of restoring our lost relationship to the land.

7

Obstacles and Other Challenges

Aldo Leopold was certain that "when we see land as a community to which we belong, we may begin to use it with love and respect."[1] But sometimes seeing is not enough. We're in need of practices that give us more direction on how best to act in partnership with the more-than-human world. As green burial grounds are manifesting death care practices and rituals that are honoring dead bodies that matter to nature, they're also offering us immediate and intimate contact with the land community, an anchor from which we can better understand that we are, in fact, *in* community. It's only from there that all green burial's other goods—deeper care of the land and deeper connection to each other—are made a living possibility.

But barriers block the way to these goods. The movement has been struggling with obstacles from the get-go, some of which have been chipped away at a bit, and others that only seem to be growing insurmountably. Like any movement building, getting past fierce opposition requires naming these obstacles and other challenges for what they are. Here, I've pared them down to five (not listed in order of importance): 1) adherence to certifiable standards; 2) the death care industry; 3) laws, land, and money; 4) environmental injustice; and 5) the language of "choice."

ADHERENCE TO CERTIFIABLE STANDARDS

In 2003, Joe Sehee and Billy Campbell joined forces with Tyler Cassity, a young and dynamic cemeterian, who'd recently purchased a thirty-two-acre cemetery named Fernwood in the heart of Marin County, California. Fernwood had been around since the 1800s, but, in more recent years, had fallen into terrible disrepair. Rooted in a family of cemetery owners who'd built up something of a death kingdom of their own, Tyler Cassity bought the property and then spent over a million dollars fixing the place up.[2]

Sehee was Cassity's communications consultant in the years leading up to the purchase. Their conversations about future green burial at Fernwood would eventually lead to bringing in Campbell, with his expertise in developing what was at the time one of the only green burial grounds in the nation. With the Golden Gate National Forest as its neighbor, and sited within a progressive area not far from San Francisco, the project seemed destined for collaborative success. After working together for a couple of years, however, their partnership would dissolve, and Cassity would go on to establish green burial at Fernwood solo. In a 2005 *New Yorker* article, Tad Friend would tell of this collaboration breakdown without ever really getting to the bottom of what happened. And yet, one catalyst for their disbandment shines through Friend's telling—the plan for Fernwood lacked a shared vision.[3] Indeed, by all accounts, Sehee agrees.[4]

Lessons are often the best fuel for innovation. Sehee and Campbell longed to see the movement grow, but not in ways that would denigrate its purpose. Billy Campbell had already written his own "management guidelines and classification system" for green burial grounds prior to the Cassity collaboration.[5] They were "'meta-rules,'" Campbell told me, "to ensure that projects did not degrade landscape-level diversity elements." He also thought they could "help the public understand whether the project was designed to protect and restore significant landscape diversity."[6] From Sehee's and Campell's perspectives, the collaboration with Cassity, and ultimately the dissolution that followed, might have been avoided had there been some codified language they could have drawn from to adequately explain what they were planning to do.[7]

In part, setting up standards was about "putting a fence around [the concept] so people could talk about it," Sehee told me. It was about providing a language that could be called upon to move the idea forward. But it was also, he said, about preventing "green burial from getting co-opted by those unwilling to commit to the kind of transparency, accountability and ecological responsibility the concept required."[8] For all of those reasons, Sehee established the Green Burial Council in 2005. Standards, as he saw it, could prevent providers from "making false claims." They could also "enforce promises at higher levels" should a green burial ground fail to keep its word. With certification, there'd be some recourse. At the very least, providers who fell short of their commitment could be decertified.[9]

With no eco certification experience of his own, Sehee would call together a talented team of professionals. Campbell's framework served as ground zero for their conversations. In addition to Sehee and Campbell, the first standards committee was made up of William Jordan[10] III, a leader in the field of restoration ecology; University of New Mexico research professor and landscape architect, Kim Sorvig, who consulted on the Green Building Council's Leadership in Energy and Environmental Design (LEEDS) and Sustainable Sites Initiative Program (SITES) standards as well as several municipal codes; The Trust for Public Lands' Ernest Cook; and executive director of the Funeral Consumers Alliance (FCA), Josh Slocum. Working with a group of attorneys, the newly formed GBC came up with three levels of certification—Conservation, Natural, and Hybrid.

The committee toyed with establishing four levels of certification, rather than three. Environmentally low impact (ELI) would have been situated between the Hybrid and Natural levels. Sehee explained that compliance for that level looked a lot like a Hybrid, only ELIs would have been required to have a separate and distinct green section and not simply intersperse green graves among conventional ones. But if making providers accountable and creating a common language were important goals from the gate, cultivating information where consumers were "less, and not more confused in the marketplace" was crucial. In the end, settling on three levels, rather than four, just seemed better for the public.

Although the standards have been set for the consumer's benefit, there's really no telling whether or not these certification distinctions make any substantive difference in people's decision making. GBC board member Katey Bean said one provider told her "that what consumers are looking for is a green cemetery that's certified by the GBC and that their friends and family can visit."[11] They might not always be looking for the best model of burial ground or who's doing the best job. In fact, people may choose green burial for any number of reasons, like cost, location, or aesthetic. New Jersey funeral director Bob Fertig told me most people who come to him and are interested in the idea of green burial often seem less concerned about environmental impact and more concerned about the simplicity of the process, like "the fact that they don't have to use a casket," he said.[12] The degree to which the land is being cared for might have little to nothing to do with why they're choosing one burial ground over another. At this point, the choices of green burial grounds for most folks, in most communities, still remain far and few between anyway.

But whether these certification levels matter to the average consumer or not, they still matter to the land community—another reason why certification is essential. Yes, consumers should have the highest quality of green death care to choose from, but it ought to be the certifier's job to see that the land ethic is consistently heeded. "That's where the GBC should be leading the way,"[13] Bean said. And indeed, it has, claiming from the start that we need "to embrace a new ethic for a new era," and emerging as the standard bearer of green burial ground certification in the United States.[14]

Eco certification is hardly a uniform project across the nation. For example, "certified organic" foods are produced in keeping with federal standards that are set forth by a national government program. If a farmer wants her food to bear the label "certified organic," she must comply with the terms of the standards by meeting the set requirements. She must apply to be certified, which includes paying a variable fee.[15] Not all eco-certification programs, however, are governmentally operated. Many independent third-party eco certifiers are functioning in the United States too, such as the Green Building Council that's now well known for its LEED standards for green construction. This is just how the GBC would ultimately come to set themselves up. Like the Green Building Council, the GBC, and not the federal government, would monitor compliance. And just as a certified LEED-level building would be read as an expression of environmental commitment, so, too, would the burial grounds that came to be certified under the standards of the GBC.[16]

Compliance basically works on a point system. Criteria are established, and if the facility meets them then certification is granted. If compliance continues to be met, certification continues to be granted. If compliance falters, the facility is decertified.

A good example is Mount Carmel Cemetery, in Wyandotte, Michigan, that was once certified by the GBC but has since been decertified. As I mentioned in chapter 4, this Hybrid cemetery was born from the passionate work of Father Charles Morris, the church's pastor. Though Father Charles's heart and soul was in the cemetery, things changed when he left the congregation. "I got transferred, and the priest that took over the cemetery administration did not see the value in a special green section. Nor was he even interested in the continuing administration of the cemetery," he said. "So he gave over care of Mount Carmel to the diocese." Father Charles is not sure how Mount Carmel is doing these days. "They've honored a few more green burials there, but they've not kept up their affiliation with the Green Burial Council, and they don't mark it as a green burial ground."[17]

But standards do even more than simply weed out the compliers from the violators. Setting up criteria also frames the priorities of the field. Kim Sorvig told me that the original GBC standards committee spent a good amount of time hashing out just what those priorities were, distilling the primary purposes and goals of green burial grounds.[18] This is part of what Sehee meant when he said that before standards there was no public language to make sense of what was beginning to take shape on the ground. In many ways, the committee's work was to essentially write that language, one that's always in need of revisiting, rethinking, and, of course, revision.[19]

And yet, for all the good standards do, they also have their limits. When you make everything a bullet or a point to be satisfied, absolutely everything can't be covered and accounted for, and so you might end up with facilities that look different on the surface even though they're certified at the same level. "The major problem with most eco certification," Sorvig told me, "is that you're taking something holistic and chopping it up into parts." This may explain at least some of the visual differences in the green burial grounds that have come to be in recent years (as I discussed in chapter 6). But these kinds of contrasts in burial grounds might never be rectified through better or higher standards. "When you're applying specific human purposes to a landscape that's really variable," Sorvig explained, "you're not going to get the same outcomes. That can often be conceptually really difficult." He also said that such uniformity ought not to be the aim anyway. Because if green burial grounds become all about the standards, "we can often miss something quite essential" about the particular cemetery we're looking at.[20]

In Sorvig's opinion, what standards are really meant to do is provide consumers with information in the form of questions, of what to ask for when seeking greener death care. That list of questions helps them to think through their options in an objective way "without having to do all the research from scratch." Although the point system is necessary for compliance on the provider side of things, "it's most useful and respectful and conducive to people making a good decision if you give them questions," he said. Indeed, the GBC has such a list on their website.[21]

All third-party eco certifiers face another challenge—certification is voluntary. Right now, only about half of the green burial grounds in the United States are certified by the GBC. (Fernwood, by the way, is not one of them).[22] How does the GBC, or the larger green burial movement for that matter, convince providers that meeting verifiable standards is reasonable and necessary in the first place? That the nominal annual fee is worth the expense?[23] How might providers be better incentivized to think about their facilities in terms of standards, and, moreover, to step up and apply for certification?

Sehee says that eventually the competition between burial grounds will become so great that certification will set them apart from one another, although he also thinks it may take something worse yet to get providers to see the value in adhering to certifiable standards. Some problem might come to the surface in which an uncertified or decertified burial ground made promises it didn't keep, like saying they eschewed embalming or vaults when they actually allowed one or the other. When the media gets hold of such a fact, wariness will set in. Such public awareness is likely to alert consumers to the potential downside of burial grounds that are not certified. And sooner or later, he said, "All providers will want in."[24]

After Fernwood, Billy Campbell remarked to Sehee that "we can't just tell the time, we have to build the clock."[25] What Campbell meant was building more burial grounds and protecting land at the same time—"a million acres." Notwithstanding the desire to see the movement grow in that way, the need for scaffolding that could both protect and inform the public also seemed a logical next step. Despite some of the drawbacks inherent to certification, Joe Sehee feels just as passionately as ever that they're key to fomenting a strong movement. As he said to me, "How does a green economy emerge if we can't legitimately certify whether what's being offered furthers ecological aims?"[26] Perfect or not, creating standards is about rising above the skepticism in order to help build a movement with integrity and teeth.

THE DEATH CARE INDUSTRY

A more than $15 billion machine, the death care industry is made up of funeral homes and their directors, product companies—caskets, chemicals, vaults—insurance companies that manage prepaid funerals, and cemeteries. The NFDA has a long and storied history of advocating for the robust industry. Their first meeting in Rochester, New York, in 1882, in which new embalming methods were demoed to fledgling morticians, has given way to a nearly twenty-thousand-person trade organization whose sole purpose is to support the big business of death.[27]

By the 1930s some folks started to fight back against the business, most notably in the formation of regional memorial societies that confronted the growing cost of funerals in the midst of the Great Depression. Still, the largely unregulated and unchallenged funeral industry wouldn't begin to feel strong resistance until Mitford published *The American Way of Death* in 1963. Despite the economic expansion of the 1960s, Mitford's smear of the funeral industry tapped into simmering feelings of distrust and repulsion at the excess that was our mourning. Death care was just too much—too much money, too many products, and too much interference. Post-Mitford, memorial societies spread across the states, educating people, keeping the funeral industry on their toes, and pressing for reform. U.S. citizens began to think of themselves as consumers of death care who should have more of a say in what happens to them when they die.

In 1984, after more than two decades of activism, the Federal Trade Commission (FTC) came down on the funeral industry, implementing the Funeral Rule that finally made it possible for consumers to pick and choose only those funerary services they wanted and to leave the rest at the door. The Funeral

Rule took at least some of the wind out of the sails of an unregulated industry with no competition. But rules must be monitored, and the FTC hasn't always done such a great job with enforcement.

For example, although the Funeral Rule requires that all services be itemized, some funeral providers, with the help of the NFDA, have found ways to skirt it.[28] This has been especially true for the larger publicly traded providers such as Service Corporation International (SCI), which owns nearly two thousand funeral homes, more than five hundred cemeteries, and one hundred crematories throughout the United States, Canada, and Puerto Rico.[29] These big conglomerates have often proven to be bigger and stronger than any laws or regulation. Over the years, the FCA (which was the former memorial societies) has been doing the important work of challenging an industry that, time and again, struts its power and resources despite the public good. In fact, today there are about ninety FCA affiliates around the country.[30]

Although there are some funeral directors who are enthusiastically engaged with green burial, the industry as a whole has long been focused on the bottom line. Products—caskets and vaults in particular—make up a good portion of their profit margin. But with green burial requiring neither, there may be no incentive to offer it as an option at all. The FCA has warned that the industry will work to get around greener options costing less by offering "greener" coffins with a higher price tag. But as FCA crusaders Josh Slocum and Lisa Carlson have said, "You shouldn't have to spend more in order to waste less." Indeed, "The greenest casket you can buy is the one you *don't* buy."[31]

If Slocum and Carlson are concerned with industry greenwashing, it's for good reason. The NFDA does its best to stay on top of "funerary trends," as they like to call them.[32] As green burial replaces cremation as the funeral industry's illegitimate spawn, the industry waits it out. Will green burial's time come, or will it fizzle away as a funerary fad?

Preempting outcome, the NFDA has set up their own Green Funeral Practices Certificate Program, telling their members that "there's no downside to going green!"[33] About two years before this offering, the NFDA tried another angle—scare tactics. In 2008, the NFDA published "a green indemnification form" forewarning potential consumers of faulty green burial containers, diseased corpses, and sinking graves, a form they hoped to get funeral directors to get customers to sign. The FCA soon enough exposed these lies on their website, and the NFDA swiftly responded by taking it down from theirs.[34]

In keeping with the industry's past, some movers and shakers have begun to seize the opportunity to come up with new products for the industry. While some seem useful in streamlining the green burial process, others seem to be just another way of maintaining the reigns of control. Biodegradable burial cooling blankets, in which dry ice can be inserted and then positioned around the body, are a good example of the former, while plant-based embalming fluids are a most egregious example of the latter.[35]

Champion, a leader in the production and sale of embalming fluids since 1878, has come out with a fluid made of essential oils that poses no risk to worker health. Champion surely has a sense of humor, as they named the fluid "Enigma." As I talked about in chapter 3, the practice of temporary corpse preservation formalized funerary work, delegitimizing the informal care of families and other community members, mostly women, who were once called upon to prepare the dead for final disposition. Enigma may be greener, but the practice of embalming since the middle of the nineteenth century has been deployed as a tool of authority over a living public that has slowly, but surely, come to believe that embalming is necessary. Of course, the real enigma of embalming—beyond its pollution and its thwarting of decay—is why the corpse must be preserved through such invasive and authoritarian methods at all?

Funeral directors will tell you that nothing works to firm up a body like formaldehyde, making many industry workers resistant to using greener fluids as an alternative anyway, despite the health risks.[36] Some industry-trained workers who see the enigma in embalming are embracing less invasive practices that work to slow down decay, especially for those families who still want a viewing. Green-friendly funeral director Amy Cunningham will tell you that old-fashioned refrigeration works very well. That followed with dry ice "cut in slender slabs, wrapped in terry cloth toweling and placed beneath the torso or sometimes over the abdomen is often an excellent way to slow decomposition and allow for a viewing."[37] In light of these more basic practices, many that DIY (Do It Yourself) home funeral advocates are bringing back to the fore, the need for greener embalming fluid appears questionable at best. Besides, if funeral directors aren't interested in using it for their own protection, what purpose, exactly, do these new fluids serve?

Rick Touchette told me that one of the reasons they have not pursued certification by the GBC for their green burial ground at Most Holy Redeemer Cemetery in Niskayuna, New York, is because they wanted to allow families the possibility of embalming if need be. "We don't want to create a situation that would prohibit a family from celebrating the full course of the order of a Christian funeral—the vigil, the funeral mass or liturgy, and the right of committal." And yet, he also told me that in all the green burials they've had so far, not one body had been embalmed.[38]

Having seen to hundreds of burials at Ramsey Creek, Kimberley Campbell can attest that those choosing green burial don't seem interested in any kind of embalming, toxic or green. For the industry, "it's just another product to sell, something they just can't seem to get away from." Taking into account all the encounters she's had with people seeking greener disposition over the last fifteen years, she told me, "[green embalming fluid] just seems to go against the whole idea."[39]

And yet, even in the face of this kind of industry resistance, the green burial movement still needs the involvement of funerary professionals to move the cause forward. When the GBC first began certifying burial grounds, they hadn't thought to include standards for funeral providers, crematories, and products. But within no time it became clear that certification of burial grounds was only one piece of the puzzle.[40] For folks seeking greener disposition, finding a provider who will fulfill the needs and wishes of both the deceased and the family is crucial. This is especially true in the nine states where consumers are required to hire a funeral director to deal with final disposition—Connecticut, Illinois, Iowa, Indiana, Louisiana, New York, Michigan, Nebraska, and New Jersey.[41]

If the strength of the growing NHFA is any sign, DIY death care is growing along with the home funeral movement in the United States. By and large, however, most folks still rely on funeral professionals for death care, whether they're required to or not. Whether you're of the mind that the whole industry ought to be dismantled and families should take back care of their dead, or you want no part in that care at all, the industry remains the key player in that care.

At both the national and the state levels, the FCA is doing the much-needed hard work of facing down greenwashing in the midst of a bona fide green burial movement struggling to take shape. But their watchdog combative approach is sometimes not always best suited to the goals of green burial. Lobbying to change laws and licensing schemes, like the ones that still exist in Oklahoma and Virginia that require consumers only purchase caskets from a licensed funeral director, is crucial. Indeed, such laws might have a direct impact on someone planning for a green burial. But we also need to be working to get funeral providers to *offer* the services required of a green burial, to prepare bodies in ways that their mortuary training never asked them to take up.

Because many Jewish and Muslim burial societies often take care of their own dead, there are, in fact, some funeral directors who have no experience with preparing an unembalmed body for burial, or even, perhaps, for a viewing, which some green burial folks actually want. The use of refrigeration and dry ice, prepping a body for burial in a shroud, and transporting it to the burial location all pose new challenges to a funeral industry that's grown accustomed to their sanitizing and smoke-and-mirrors methods.

In the end, people have a right to know which funeral directors are willing to take on this work with care and respect and which ones are not. Indeed, this explains at least some of the reasons why the GBC eventually began certifying

funeral homes. While the FCA has been facing down the industry and fighting for our rights for decades, as National Home Funeral Alliance (NHFA)
president and GBC board member Lee Webster attests, "We also need to build
bridges with the industry."[42]

LAWS, LAND, AND MONEY

Interested in starting a green burial ground?

Many folks may hear about green burial, become advocates, and think to
themselves—"there's no green burial in my community, wouldn't it be great
to start one?" Somewhere along the way that enthusiasm will probably be
tempered with hard facts. Judith Lorei of Green Burial Massachusetts said
one of the difficulties in getting a burial ground going is that "there's no
template, no one size fits all." Over the years, their "spirited grassroots group
of educators and activists" talked about different models. "At one point we
considered a co-op model," she said, "but we settled on partnering with a land
trust instead.[43]

Amazingly, despite everything I said earlier about the uneasiness of land
trusts to get on board, Green Burial Massachusetts now has the interest of
one. But if you're lucky enough to have all that figured out—overcoming the
hurdle of standards and structure, of how to put it all together, and have even
secured a land trust as a partner—there are other looming barriers. Laws, for
one. States have different rules for how cemeteries can be set up, with some
more strict than others. But even if you're able to come that far and sort
through the arcane language of regulations, two other obstacles rise up on the
horizon—access to land and the money to make it all happen.

Once Ellen Macdonald set her sights on providing greener death care, she did
some preliminary research in order to hatch a plan. She found out that a 1992
Texas statute required that all new cemeteries be sited a certain distance from
a major city. She also found out that community cemeteries in Texas under ten
acres are exempt from state laws that require an endowment fund of $50,000
be established prior to opening. "In Texas, I'm considered a community cemetery," she told me, "like a church cemetery, so I don't need to set up the fund."
She borrowed some money from her parents, purchased a little over nine acres
not far from Austin, set up a limited liability company (LLC) to protect herself
from any personal legal responsibility (the cemetery basically leases the land
from the LLC), and then opened Eloise Woods Community Natural Burial
Park. Later, she filed a deed restriction with the county that limits the property
to green burial in perpetuity, a restriction that runs with the land.[44]

All things considered, Macdonald had it easy. In some states, such as New York, New Jersey, Washington, Ohio, and Virginia, the endowment trust fund required to establish a not-for-profit or an LLC cemetery can drive even the most well-intentioned GBAs away from the green burial dream. "Yes, we had to do a trust fund," Kenneth Kyger told me about his experience opening Duck Run Natural Cemetery. "In Virginia, if it's a commercial cemetery then the trust fund is required. We're an LLC, so we had to come up with $50,000 before we could open." But even once you've come come up with the money, the funds will need to be set up in an account. And not just any account. "What people don't realize," Kyger told me, "is that only your large banks meet the requirement for these trust funds," he said, "and the state tells you how you can invest the money. Their minimal fee is $4,500."[45]

If the endowment fund seems prohibitive, as well as prohibiting, there are still good reasons states have come to mandate them. The fund is for cemetery care in perpetuity. In other words, it's the state's way of taking the long view. The cemetery will outlive owners and caretakers and eventually will fill to capacity. The money is kept in trust for future maintenance. The fund isn't static, however. A certain percentage of every plot sale must also go into the pot, building it up while the cemetery is in operation.

More often than not, church, family, and municipal cemeteries are exempt from the endowment requirement, which basically makes it easier for such entities to set up a cemetery from the start. Although there are few examples of green municipal cemeteries right now (the one we developed in my town of Rhinebeck, New York is one), there are quite a few that have emerged from religious groups, though at this point most of those are Hybrid or Natural models. The only religious-based Conservation burial ground is Honey Creek Woodlands, in Conyers, Georgia. It's owned and operated by the Monastery of the Holy Spirit, a Catholic order of monks.[46]

Of course, some states, like Texas, have laxer laws that enable cemeteries to operate without the endowment fund if they meet certain criteria. Just like Ellen Macdonald was able to do. And then there are some states, such as South Carolina, that lack oversight all together. The stars surely aligned in the Campbells' favor when they went to the state to find out what rules they would need to follow in order to begin burial at Ramsey Creek. To their surprise, the state board had recently fallen apart, which meant they could pretty much do whatever they wanted.[47] This in comparison to a state like New Jersey, which according to Ed Bixby "has made it so stringent to make a cemetery there've been only six applications since 1971." And only three of them were accepted. That's because "they want $250,000 in preservation of maintenance funds before you bury the first person," Bixby explained to me. "It's such a major investment."[48]

Sometimes cemeteries can get around this endowment fund if they forgo the licensing that enables them to presell plots. This is true in Florida, for instance, where a stipulation in the cemetery law enabled Prairie Creek Conservation Cemetery to commence their partnership with Alachua Conservation Trust sooner than later. "We're regulated less," Executive Director Freddie Johnson said. In exchange, "We can't take people's money before death. It does mean you get your money slower. But we've found a way to work without doing that."[49] Even so, Prairie Creek invests ten percent of all burial revenue in a "care and maintenance fund," a requirement of the GBC for certification at the Conservation burial ground level.

If setting up the cemetery and securing the funds is more or less a challenge depending upon where you live, there's also the matter of the land. No matter how you look at it, land is expensive, and depending upon where in the United States you're trying to do burial, securing the right property for a green burial ground can be daunting. This often leaves GBAs looking for land donors.

Green Burial Massachusetts has been doing as much. Although they have the interest of a local and well-established conservation entity, Mount Grace Land Conservation Trust, there's still the matter of procuring the land. That's because Mount Grace won't be pulling from any of their in-house land holdings to make the green burial ground happen. This—in contrast to a place like Prairie Creek that had the good fortune to draw from land that Alachua Conservation Trust had recently acquired. Mount Grace Land Conservation Trust is, however, in the process of pursuing land. They announced their Green Cemetery Initiative in 2014. Right now they're looking for an appropriate site—someplace "at least fifty acres, with land not steeper than a 15 percent grade, relatively dry and with access to a road."[50]

If such parameters are crucial, that's because not all properties are perfectly sited for green burial. The land can't be too wet or too close to natural water sources, too rocky or too steep, or too far from public access. And there's the matter of trails. Can they be easily added without affecting sensitive habitat? There's also the matter of economic viability. Is it somewhere green burial is likely to be popular, where the cemetery will thrive financially? Municipal regulations and zoning ordinances must also be dealt with.

But even if the land trust could help in securing the right land, properties that are typically held in easement through a land trust must be funded in some way to fulfill the work of long-term stewardship. Ramsey Creek paid Upstate Forever $15,000 for their easement.[51] Other cemeteries have been paying as they go, making it a bit easier on their budgets. For instance, Preble Memory Gardens pays Three Valley Conservation Trust $750 annually.[52] Of course, there are tax benefits that come along with property easements, but it's still an expense a burial ground seeking a partnership with a conservation entity will need to consider into its plan.

For all of these reasons, the easiest way to establish green burial in just about any community—to get it in the most basic of ways—is through being connected to an already existing cemetery. First of all, there's no finding the land and no endowment fund to set up from scratch. Setting aside plots or even a separate section can cost very little. And even in cases where the setting up of green burial does accrue some cost—say if they needed to get a land survey for the new green section, clear trees for access, or create paths for walking—the cemetery would most likely have some funds to draw from to make that happen.

Some GBAs, however, do not want to go this route. Judith Lorei and the members of Green Burial Massachusetts are holding strong to their vision of a free-standing green burial ground that's tied to a land trust. But with the capital it takes to set up a new green burial ground, especially a free-standing Conservation burial ground, the feasibility of this model in terms of widespread success is slow going.

It also makes for a very privileged project. If only those who have access to land and money are able to get free-standing Conservation burial off the ground, who will be included in this green burial vision, and who might be left out? When looked at this way, perhaps the most promising aspect of green burial grounds that are tied to conventional ones, is that they potentially make green burial accessible to everyone.

ENVIRONMENTAL INJUSTICE

No doubt, access is an issue the movement needs to contend with. Green burial grounds may dissolve the human/nature split that leads to human distancing from nature, and at their best, eschew a conservation agenda dismissive of people's place on the land. While green burial holds out great potential to connect people with the land and to restore our ties to nature, one look at the barriers that land and money present necessitates an examination of privilege. Which people? Which lands? Who exactly is green burial touching? And who's not being reached?

Lack of access has practical as well as philosophical foundations. Our cultural ideas about nature have been largely shaped by race, sex, and class privilege. For instance, popular ideas about a wilderness from which white men are able to secure their masculinity and power saturate the American imagination. (Just think about the characters of Ernest Hemingway or those played by the likes of John Wayne.) Though women and all those other bodies feminized in the culture (e.g., the poor, people of color, LGBTQ people,

people with disabilities) are considered to be closer to nature, the lived reality for those bodies is more often one of restricted access to the wilds of nature.

Environmental justice advocate Mei Mei Evans has said that, "One of the ways of understanding the culturally dominant conception of what constitutes 'nature' in the United States is to ask ourselves, who gets to go there?"[53] Not only that, but who feels safe there? Although I've lived for most of my life in rural places and know the woods of local conservation areas like my own backyard, I can say for sure I've never once walked them alone.

"Nature" on its own may be offering such wild and renewing possibilities, but the overlay of what's historically been done to certain bodies within those wild spaces may summon the most dreadful notions of nature. A history of racist, classist, and sexist practices have made the wild, for many women and people of color, places of fear and trepidation, not places of restoration, comfort, health, or wholeness. Indeed, one of the goals of environmental justice is "equal access to natural resources that sustain life and culture . . . for the right of all people to share equally in the benefits bestowed by a healthy environment."[54] But if access to the so-called wilds of nature is limited, can the benefits of green burial ever be equally shared?

That's one matter. Here's another—

In making the connections between environmental degradation and people, environmental justice is also largely about righting the reality that the poor and people of color have been unduly burdened by environmental contamination. How can an earth-based ethic of human death touch people in their disparate communities? On lands in need of restoration that they call home?

And, more specifically, what about the polluted, small, and tame lands that are increasingly everywhere in the United States, especially in urban areas where population is high and environmental quality low? While environmental injustice is happening on both rural and urban fronts, many more people live in urban areas than rural ones. The 2010 census estimates that just over 80 percent of the U.S. population is now urban. In 1850, when the Rural Cemetery Movement was calling both the dead and the living out to the land, those percentages were nearly reversed.[55]

There's a promising contemporary corollary to be found in this question of urban life and greening death—urban farming. Not only white, middle-class Brooklynites are taking part in planting seeds in the midst of asphalt. For the disenfranchised living in food deserts who never dreamed of growing anything out of the earth where they live, urban farming is proving to be not only a way of changing the face of food production but also a means of healing urban communities, as well as urban land.[56] And so, in the quest to build an earth-based ethic of human death that emerges from a diversity of human communities, particularly ones urban and wounded, we may need to think more innovatively—and more *urbanly*—about this project of greening death.

To begin with, this might mean the establishment of more green burial grounds that are within city limits. A good example is Vale Cemetery that's sited right in the middle of Schenectady, New York. Interestingly, Vale's not only added a green burial section to its historic 100 acres, but it also boasts an urban farm! And yet, it might take more than making natural burial plots geographically accessible to link disenfranchised communities to new green burial spaces. According to Vale's president, Dr. Bernard McEvoy, the changing demographics of that part of Schenectady has saddled Vale with something of an identity crisis. "Some white folks think it's a black cemetery and some black folks think it's a white cemetery."[57] While burial grounds like Vale may seem to answer the fundamental question of access, the movement's still faced with matters of cultural identity as they're tied to histories of racism and exclusion. Which open spaces—especially those that are also human places of remembrance—belong to whom, living and dead?

Still, no matter how you look at it, there's only so much open space available, which means that at the most practical of levels thinking in terms of an "urban nature"[58] will likely require something more than considerations of access and identity. To these ends, and beyond the promise of green burial grounds within or close to urban centers, other green methods of final disposition have been making landfall. The use of recycled graves, as they do in parts of Europe, is now being offered at one green burial ground in the United States, Duck Run Natural Cemetery in Penn Laird, Virginia. Duck Run's president, Kenneth Kyger, told me the idea is that "at the end of seventy-five years the plots will revert back to the ownership of the cemetery," at which point any markers would be moved and incorporated into a common area of the burial ground.[59]

There is, of course, the matter of the bones, too, which depending upon soil conditions can take many years to decompose. In places like Germany where burial plots are basically rented, the bones are removed from the plot and placed in a common ossuary when a family decides to no longer lease it.[60] Bob Jenkins's company, Let Your Love Grow, has spent four years working with forensic entomologist Dr. Neal Haskell using pigs to develop "the correct product to organically advance decomposition." They hope to start research on human burial in the summer of 2015.[61] "Our goal," he told me, "is to eliminate the body, bones and all, in twenty-four months." Jenkins would not reveal the makeup of his product, but said that it was composed of items you'd find in just about any household yard.[62]

Greening cremation is yet another avenue to including "urban nature" in an earth-based ethic of death. Reducing mercury emissions by 100 percent, which is Europe's goal by 2020, and employing renewable and more energy-efficient methods of running crematories could certainly add to the greening of death care.[63] Scattering cremated remains in city spaces, with memorializing possibilities, might also be a consideration. With cremation rates expected to surpass conventional burial in 2015, this avenue to greener death ways certainly faces fewer barriers. Crematories still typically incinerate the body out of view of family and friends, however, a fact that continues to make modern cremation a hard sell for some.[64]

This "out of view" disposition is no longer confined to incineration. Two new methods, alkaline hydrolysis (a.k.a. biocremation, resomation, or bioliquifaction) and Promession have in recent years been presented as a green answer to conventional funerary pollution and growing populations. Alkaline hydrolysis includes placing the corpse in a steel chamber with a mixture of water and potassium chloride. With increased pressure and temperature, the dead body is eventually reduced to both bones and liquid. Proponents say the bones can be crushed up and given to families, the liquid put down the drain.[65] There's also a process called Promession, developed in Sweden, which effectively freeze-dries the body. Through a combination of liquid nitrogen and vibration, the body is reduced to a dry powder. Promession is not, as of yet, available in the United States.

The jury is out on what, if any, positive environmental impact these practices might hold. Moreover, will the bodily remnants wrought through these distancing practices find their way back into the land community in the same way, for instance, that cremated remains have through scattering in natural areas, or burial in green cemeteries?[66] Can these practices fulfill an earth-based ethic of human death? And will Americans seeking greener death ways come to embrace them?

In many ways, Katrina Spade's Urban Death Project is a more deliberate attempt to insert a wedge in a movement that's not really thinking about "urban nature." Spade is working on a prototype for what can only be described as "a human composting machine." Her design includes a circular walkway that leads to "The Core," an apparatus that facilitates in the corpse's final transformation. The walkway, which echoes Frank Lloyd Wright's famously elegant Guggenheim Museum staircase, ushers family and friends along to the site.

Inside "The Core," a human body is expected to turn to compost in a matter of weeks. Ritual and family involvement are important to Spade's design, generating meanings around death that tie us back to the value of decomposition. "We tend to think of nature as growth—trees, flowers, plants," Spade said to me. "But half of nature's cycle is decomposition—death and decay. The Urban Death Project is a way of bringing nature to the city."[67]

Her prototype design is based on something already being used to dispose of livestock. Unlike a composting bin you might have in your backyard, however, the body will not be turned and churned throughout the decomposition process. Instead, the body will lie flat for somewhere between two and six weeks. That's phase one. In phase two, after the body's been broken down into something that no longer resembles a human body, it will be moved to another container of sorts and mixed with the remains of other composted bodies. This "mixing" is key to her design. For Spade, the project is as much about bringing meaning to the living as it is about a shift in thinking—of the one returning to the all.

Once the composting process is complete, Spade imagines that families could take some of the compost back home with them. "One body," she told me, "will make somewhere around a cubic yard of compost," which might be too much for any one family to manage, especially if they have no yard of their own. "They'd be welcome to take less, of course." The details of where the compost will end up is still being worked out, but Spade imagines that some of it might be used in and around the Urban Death Project itself and/or folded back into designated open spaces within the city limits. She sees memorializing possibilities at these sites too, ways of commemorating the dead. One of her greatest hopes is that city parks will want to partner with Urban Death Projects to make that happen.

Spade envisions Urban Death Projects in every city, ones that reflect particular geographies and cultures.[68] Time will tell how the public will respond to the idea of human remains as "compost," as well as to the collective nature of the "compost" itself. Whatever comes to be, Spade's design is pushing the movement from the outside in, getting us to think more about our ideas of nature, and the parameters of greening death.

How do we begin to tie the goals of environmental justice to the movement? How do we build an earth-based ethic of human death in which those who are most disenfranchised from nature are included? Right now, the nature that green burial grounds are offering may not be speaking to every community identity. This includes, of course, not just urban populations as I've talked about them here, but disenfranchised communities in rural spaces, too. While these other greening death possibilities (urban Hybrids, recycled graves, greener cremation, alkaline hydrolysis, Promession, and the Urban Death Project) might hold out some hope for meeting people where they are, how various communities come to make sense of them, in terms of their own social and political priorities, and the histories that inform them, remains to be seen.

But whatever greener practices come to be embraced in the places most of us call home, we still ought to be doing more to empty nature of its meanings of privilege. After all, the answer to injustice isn't accommodation, it's inclusion. The fact that much of nature remains off limits to many marginalized groups is a challenge yet unmet by a movement that's still, in many ways, finding its legs. While it's a problem that extends far beyond green burial, our work is not done until nature is open to everyone.

THE LANGUAGE OF "CHOICE"

In 2010, the *New York Times* ran a story, the opening of which read "At the end of an eco-conscious life, there is a final choice a person can make to limit his or her impact on the planet: a green funeral."[69] It was not one of a kind. Public discourse around green burial has mostly devolved into giving people more "green" choices (baby boomers in particular). Those voices also fairly well sum up the market-driven, consumer voice of the movement that has focused on the living's individual preference for a certain kind of green experience. Hybrid cars, backyard composters, and household rain barrels have much in common with green burial these days—just one more "green" option among many Americans now have in the midst of overwhelming environmental problems. Even if the choice of a green burial is not an environmental one, the choice itself is what seems to count the most.

Certainly, what we each individually do matters, and dissenting from practices that continue to violate the environment is key for prefiguring a more sustainable way of living with the earth. But as the rhetoric of "green" choice surrounds us at every turn, it never cuts below the surface, giving well-intentioned individuals the possibility of feeling good at the cost of corporate controls enacting ruin on the natural world. It also provides the illusion that individual acts amount to profound cultural shifts. Individual consciousness and conscience are necessary and precious, but we should know by now that they do not by themselves change the world.

Funeral directors are encouraged to appeal to the choice makers in all of us, rising to the challenge of "personalized funerals,"[70] a narrow approach that also hasn't been all that effective in expanding and/or changing our practices. For all the focus on personalization and choice, funerary rites have little to show for it. Jews may say no to embalming and yes to pine coffins, and the length of time between death and burial may be shorter than for Catholics. But regardless of the differences that run the gamut of folks' social locations and identities, the fact remains that not unlike fashion or, up until more recently, food in the United States, funerary patterns remain quite uniform and our choices rather slim.

Our role as funeral consumers who have more or less choices is shaped not only by the funeral industry, but also by the folks who would ideally like to take it down—the funeral consumer movement. Lisa Carlson's *Caring for the Dead* (1998)—a consumer guide to death care—is a bold, grassroots if not radical DIY example of that movement's response to a powerful funeral industry that often disarms the bereaved at every turn. Obviously, consumer choices matter with respect to all kinds of things we purchase in the marketplace, including death care. We need information about products and services so we can make informed decisions about what we buy. Cost is also an important component of this. Consumers shouldn't have to pay through the nose for death care or to go into debt in order to bury their family and friends. And to these ends, the FCA has been invaluable. But even in this good work and helpful approach, human death has not been spared the ontological shift Americans have suffered from being citizens, neighbors, and community members to mere consumers. The perfunctory influence of culture and religion may be waning, but the sway of a secular society that values personal consumer choice has gone viral.

Another problem with grounding a movement in the language of choice is that it puts us in that all-too-comfortable place of pointing the finger at those who are not making the "right choices" without ever having to question the forces that have shaped those choices to begin with. For environmentalists concerned with other issues, such as water, agriculture, or energy, the critique of choice is plain. If taking shorter showers won't save our global water problems, then choosing green over conventional burial will not be the end-all solution to our environmental death problems, either.[71] Besides, building an earth-based ethic of human death ought not be about using coercive arguments to move people to choose greener death practices in the way some environmentalists have been apt to do with other green practices—the kind that at their worst have been exercised in the form of shaming or cleverly persuading others to do right by choosing greener lifestyle habits—like not drinking coffee out of a Styrofoam cup, or driving an SUV, or idling one's car, or using an air conditioner, clothes dryer, or a lawn mower, consuming factory-farmed meat, or even eating meat at all.

Of course, the language of individual choice can't be left at the movement's door either. Our choices still frame the narrative arcs of our lives and meaning grows out of our most heartfelt decisions around death, reminding us to the core what it is to mortal. Without a doubt, having greater consumer choices in death care goods and services in the marketplace is primary for reclaiming rites, and rights, that have for too long now felt foreign and prescribed. The work of the GBC, for instance, has been crucial to these ends. And yet, we're more than mere consumers with purchasing power. Ideas inform the meanings of lives, individual and shared. They also drive our death care options that come to be rendered as goods and services in the marketplace.

To the extent that our choices are made with compassion and in the spirit of love and with sustainable and meaningful outcomes for the living, the dead, and the land, there's no disputing that our choices matter. In fact, securing the choice of green burial ought to continue as a movement goal. But the language of choice remains a risky guiding philosophy to bank on for change as it mistakenly places the path to social transformation in the hands of each individual quest. Besides, in a culture like ours, so steeped in social inequalities, to have a choice at all is often a condition of access and privilege.

No, the green burial movement can't be reduced to something as easy as having another choice in a sea of American choices. And that's because green burial is about something greater and more elemental than "choice," It's about stretching the parameters of the land community that Leopold so fervently believed in. It's about recognizing human death in the circuit of life.

8

Mobilizing the Ethic

"It's really ironic," green burial pioneer Kimberley Campbell said to me, "that what we're calling a movement is what people have done for thousands of years,"[1] though maybe there's a bit of irony—in the sense of the absurd—in every social movement. It's nothing new—having to rally around something that *ought to be* but that was made unthinkable through social and philosophical forces seemingly beyond our control. But as any movement can teach us, such forces are not, in fact, beyond our control. If anything, this might be one of irony's more hidden gifts, alerting us to social and cultural shifts—being a harbinger of change.

Like other social movements, the green burial movement has many telltale signs that it is a bona fide movement, however informal it may sometimes appear. One of those signs is the recovery of lost knowledge, of ways of caring for our dead that have been forced to go underground to survive. Examples of knowledge recovery abound in other movements, too. Perhaps the most obvious within the second wave of feminism is the rise of birthing midwives, home births, and less clinical ways of approaching childbirth. When medicine took the reigns of birthing from the bodies of women, that seizing wasn't just a matter of economics, bodily integrity, or labor, it was also a matter of wisdom. Whose knowledge about bringing human life into the world became primary in that transfer? And whose became shunned?[2]

I already spelled out much of this in chapter 4, but it bears repeating: The green burial movement is not only about securing death care rights we've been stripped of, it's about recouping ways of caring for our dead that bespeak a different way of knowing death, and, ultimately, a different way of knowing nature.

What other signs mark green burial as a real movement? According to longtime activist and organizer Marshall Ganz, movements do something more than take back rights and knowledge. They also tell stories. And that's because movements aren't "just about rearranging economics and politics. They also rearrange meaning. . . . (T)hey're not just about redistributing the goods. They're about figuring out what is good."[3]

That's why stories like the ones retold to me by so many other GBAs, especially those providing firsthand care for the dead, are likely to take hold of us in ways that not only fill us with knowing but also move us to action. While Mark Harris's *Grave Matters* (2007) didn't exactly lay waste to conventional death care in the United States, it did contribute to a new conversation about pursuing greener death care. And it did so through story. Like Ganz has said, "It's through the particular experience that I'm able then to communicate the emotional content of the value that is moving me."[4] The kind that's on fire in Harris's tales of people offering and opting for greener death care and, more recently, in *A Will for the Woods* (2013)—a documentary that follows one dying man's quest for a greener way of death in North Carolina.[5] In figuring out a "good" way of death care, these stories create a kind of magic space for seeing what the movement is all about.

If more robust mobilization is what the movement needs right now, then story is one of the vehicles that can take us there. As a shared and tangible entry point of understanding, we can do our part in telling and retelling the stories of these renewed death practices. But equally important, however, is doing our best to pay attention to what those stories are saying to us about what the movement is all about. What stories are rising to the surface from our greener practices? What messages do providers send? Do the media spin? What meanings find their way into the public? Are they largely stories of cost, choice, and the market? Of products and services? Or are they stories of connection to a planetary order we've lost sight of? Of mending the gaping rift shorn between the living and the dead, the dead and nature, of healing a relation of the dead body's tie to the land?

While stories have great promise in catalyzing what sometimes seems stuck, there's yet a more basic driver of all social movements—collective action. It's no wonder the word *social* is derived from the Latin *socius*—meaning "ally." The "social" in social movement isn't only a reference to the societal change that the movement is rallying around, but to the interdependent relationships inherent to human communities.[6] If by definition social movements are group actions, it's essentially because our very coexistence lies at the heart of them.

It should come as no surprise that the necessity of this coexistence is all too often thwarted by the same damaging form of rationality Plumwood claimed was responsible for our imagined separation from nature (as I described in chapter 1). The separate, self-contained, ego-driven individual often overshadows the whole organism, the "context," as Evernden talked about it, within which we are situated.[7] Focused so much on the individual quest and vision, we all too easily *background* all of the living energy that gives rise to the work we set out to do. Indeed, this is what second-wave feminists said many decades ago about the state of domestic life—an invisible private realm that enabled the public domain to carry on and do the "real" work of the world.

Which is to say that this hardening of the self that denies its context and its dependency on others not only disables our ability to see the interdependence of our relationships with the more-than-human, but also, it seems, with each other. All movements, in one way or another, eventually come around to reminding us of this truth. Only by noting, and then leading, with such interdependence will the green burial movement truly flourish.

One of the quotes most popularly cited by Charles Darwin is one he actually never said—not in print anyway, that "the long history of humankind (and animal kind, too) those who learned to collaborate and improvise most effectively have prevailed."[8] It's a curious thing, this quote appearing with such vigor throughout the Internet, mentioned as motivational food for corporate executives, budding activists, and even for family politics. While American culture's love affair with the myth of the individual's solitary quest toward success goes on, a counter-public mythology is being rewritten in our midst. How best to buttress such a contradictory view of human nature? Remind people that it was the father of evolution himself—he whose ideas paved the way for the inglorious places some have come to take the survival of the fittest—who underneath it all really believed that the path to social good looks a lot more like hand holding than sword fighting. The misquoting of Darwin may wound the stickler in me, but read as resistance for a wounded planet it gives me hope.

There's been no way for me to capture the voices of even a fraction of those GBAs working in communities large and small, and their efforts to forge a path with others toward reclaimed death ways. But collective action in the form of coalitions, partnerships, and other found affinities abound in the movement. Still, we'd do well to highlight them, to pay homage when we see them, and to see in them greater potential than the myth of going it alone. The movement is pregnant with the chemistry of interesting couplings, and yet we still need more of them—more alliances, more promising networks, more solidarity. We need more folks banding together, in communities large and small, to make this movement happen with fire, openness, and integrity.

COLLABORATIONS

In 2000, two environmentalists—science writer Mary Woodsen and Cornell University plant physiologist and son of Aldo Leopold, Carl Leopold—came together to figure out how they might create a nature preserve for cremation scattering somewhere near their community of Ithaca, New York. Within no time, they would hear stirrings from two women from nearby Corning, New York—Jennifer Johnson and Susan Thomas—who, having read about dust to dust burial in South Carolina, wanted to create the same where they lived. Johnson and Thomas would eventually sway Woodsen and Leopold away from the commemorative scattering idea. Referring to themselves as "the pre-posthumous society," the four would come together to push the green burial project forward. It would take six years to realize their dream of green burial in the Finger Lakes region of the state.[9]

When it opened in 2006, Greensprings Natural Cemetery Preserve was still only one of a handful of green burial grounds in the United States. About a year later, Carl Leopold made this remark: "I believe in the environmentalism that is generated by real work out in the real world"[10]—the kind that eventually manifested in Greensprings. Almost a decade later now, the cemetery is going strong, the land is being actively stewarded, and the community is, slowly but surely, making use of this former hilltop farm turned resting place for the human dead.

Though there will always be examples in any movement of folks going it alone—Kenneth Kyger at Duck Run Natural Cemetery and Ellen Mac-donald of Eloise Woods Community Natural Burial Park immediately come to mind—the number of success stories in the movement seem to increase exponentially with stories of collaboration. Even Kyger worked closely with the GBC to adhere to their standards criteria and hired an architectural firm recommended by Joe Sehee to come up with the cemetery design. And Mac-donald, herself, has said that connections with others in the movement have made her enduring work at Eloise Woods possible. She may have opened the burial ground on her own, but she's since found herself "surrounded by compassionate women in the field of death and dying." Each month she cohosts a "green burial/home funeral meet-up," joining with either a local home funeral consultant or a green-friendly funeral director. She's also linked up with the president of her local FCA, working together to give presentations that join end-of-life planning to green burial. Talking about these connections, there's an ebullience that can't be matched even by the satisfaction of having opened the burial park alone. "They bouy me up when I feel like I'm about to sink in my ventures," she told me—encouragement born from solidarity. "We are all pioneer women on the modern plains exploring a new way to accomplish old customs."[11]

Macdonald has not been alone in the kinds of connections she's made over the years. That's because as the green burial movement has been taking shape in disparate parts of the United States, other moves to reclaim lost knowledge and meaning around death have also been taking shape. Kimberley Campbell summed it up well when she called these other aspects of death reclamation "moving parts" of a larger and growing movement to reclaim death rites in an age of disaffection. There's "the illness [if there is one]," she said. "Then there are the dead themselves and the caring of the body, and then there's the burial. Sometimes those pieces work well together and sometimes they don't. But they're all intertwined."[12]

There's also one more part to this moving advancement of death knowledge, one that's gaining a bit more traction these days—planning for death. Ann-Ellice Parker explained it to me this way, "We're living longer, but we're dying harder," she said. And so, like other death educators, "I'm trying to draw people closer to end-of-life matters. And that starts with advanced care planning for everyone, not just the elderly."[13] While she's engaged in many of these other "moving parts," she's finding advanced care planning to be the least threatening in her community, the place where she's getting the most traction.

Licensed funeral director Adriana Corral's been motivated to reach out to communities, too, especially those that are often sidelined by the death care industry. And, like Parker, she offers education that meets people where they are. For example, she told me about two workshops she recently developed, one that combined issues around grief, crocheting, and sign language and one that was geared toward the LGBTQ community. Although she's been working primarily in African American funeral homes, she told me that from her perspective most funeral homes in Miami, no matter the ethnic makeup, do not generally offer workshops around death and dying issues.[14]

Parker and Corral are also what's known as home funeral guides, death midwives, or funeral rights educators, providing guidance to families in caring for their own dead. Since the late 1990s the home funeral movement's been growing, mostly with the leadership of women who are educating the public on their rights to their dead while recovering lost wisdoms on just how to do it. Pioneer in the field, Jerrigrace Lyons, has been giving home funeral workshops for over fifteen years now.[15] As interest in reclaiming death care apart from the industry increased, there became enough home funeral guides trained by the likes of Lyons, and others, to come together in common cause. Out of that the National Home Funeral Alliance (NHFA) was founded.[16]

Still, long before home funeral guides began growing with a kind of fresh avidity around the United States, there were other moves to take death back from the reigns of the industry. Perhaps more than any other entity prior to what's happening with green burial and home funerals today, the FCA has been on the front lines fighting both laws and perfunctory practices people believe are law, dispelling the mistruths of the death care industry while fighting for families to take back rights to their dead. For them, educating the public on their rights as consumers, particularly around the soaring costs of making final arrangements, has been priority number one.[17]

In a culture where anything death related is spoken in hushed tones, having FCA affiliates sprinkled throughout the United States has given people a place to turn. In fact, for many interested in greener or more family-directed funerals, the FCA is sometimes the first place they look. But as consumer rights are only one aspect of the green burial movement and the home funeral movement, folks interested in both have often been left searching for more. The creation of both the GBC and the NHFA have been crucial to these ends.

As I already mentioned in chapter 4, there's often been great overlap in those affiliated with these organizations, marginal as they are to the main-stream cog of death care. The grassroots Green Burial Massachusetts, for instance, grew out of their local FCA affiliate, where one member started a green burial committee and then attracted other volunteers. Judith Lorei was part of this initial group. But Lorei's also strategized with those doing home funeral workshops and with people holding Death Cafés throughout the state, too. Ultimately, the fundamental focus of all of these "moving parts," as NHFA president and GBC board member Lee Webster sees it, is to get people more "fully participating in the death experience," whether that means knowing our rights, how to care for our dead, being more empowered in end-of-life matters, or seeking greener death practices. Which is to say that all of these are about "deindustrializing death," dismantling an industry that's for too long complicated death care and created the kind of distance that has left Americans both void of knowledge as well as meaning.[18]

Of course, the organizational green burial corollary to the NHFA and the FCA has been the GBC. But as I pointed out in the previous chapter, the GBC initially formed with one specific purpose—to create standards for the burgeoning field of green burial. It's mission was to reign in providers and serve the needs of consumers. In becoming an eco certifier, the IRS would require the GBC to obtain 501c6 status, which is different from the status of a 501c3 in that a c3's focus is largely educational. Joe Sehee did, in fact, envision the GBC as a hub of green burial education; however, he told me that if they wanted to eco certify, the IRS offered them no other option. For some naysayers, this c6 status has been a sticking point. And that's because trade organizations, not unlike the National Funeral Director's Association (NFDA), are also classified as c6s.[19] But the GBC is far from a trade organization. As Sehee says, "The GBC was organized and operates as a 'public' benefit corporation, rather than a 'mutual' benefit corporation."[20] Several years into certification, the GBC did establish a c3 arm of the organization to do what a c3 does best—educate, although they've long worked toward educating the public anyway.

There's no disputing that green burial had a much lower profile before the GBC came into existence. In fact, of the many things Joe Sehee is most proud it's his outreach work on behalf of the GBC. "From 2006 to 2012," he told me, he led "seminars for more than fifty different trade associations including every national organization and most state organizations." He also wrote many articles in support of the idea, many of them for trade publications. "I strongly believe that had the GBC not invested in laying a foundation of receptivity for green burial, it's likely the movement could have had any number of roadblocks thrown in our way," he said. The GBC has been driving forward the importance of education in other ways, too. For instance, they were instrumental is helping the filmmakers of *A Will for the Woods* get their project off the ground and into theaters, all in an effort to inform and surge the movement forward.[21]

But the GBC has been more than a strong public voice of the movement. Before Sehee resigned from the organization in 2012,[22] he was always available by phone for any movement talk. Indeed, he has been a resource unto himself. Before its founding, in 2005, there was essentially nowhere for the public to turn for information about green burial. News stories tended to churn out the same old narrative of "greener choices," all the while ignoring the impediments to those choices. And with the choices not yet available to most people anyway (and still not available to most people), those interested in green burial had few resources from which to draw. The few providers who were on the ground at the time were already inundated with calls from green burial enthusiasts who wanted to know more, especially about how they might establish green burial in their own communities.[23]

For many of us, this meant a lot of self-education. It also meant a lot of reinventing the wheel. Whether it was in their c6 purview, or not, the GBC answered this call. But they also answered another—connecting players big and small in the movement. In this way, the GBC became both a visible and an invisible hub, cultivating not only knowledge but also much-needed relationships. Still, the GBC senses it needs to do more. Changes are now underway in the organization, with education a main priority for the future.[24]

If there's one thing GBAs all seem to agree on, it's that the movement needs to do more educating, not only in terms of outreach, but internally as well—among GBAs themselves. Prairie Creek's Freddie Johnson sees a real need for "regional or national collaboration," he told me. "Particularly among Conservation burial grounds, if not more natural burial areas." He imagines that there could be regional hubs, and sharing through scheduled skyping sessions. "Identifying things that are common across the board can be valuable for everyone," he said.[25]

Lee Webster's vision is an "integrated national movement," perhaps under one organization, that's all about information sharing and knowledge building. Kimberley Campbell agrees, especially when it comes to joining forces organizationally. "I think rather than going to the International Cemetery, Cremation and Funeral Association (ICCFA) Conferences, we should have an entirely separate thing with the GBC, the FCA, and the NHFA, those three groups working together, having their own association and their own conference."[26]

PROMISING CONNECTIONS

Collaboration among GBAs is key, especially in terms of educating the public and each other. But even that's not enough—mainly because green burial grounds need to be built. Overcoming the barriers, many of which I talked about in the previous chapter, will require inventiveness and nerve. Pursuing the commitment of land trusts, as I talked about in chapter 6, is one of these hopeful avenues. But more possible paths must be imagined, especially in terms of making green burial accessible to everyone.

Here are three examples of promising connections in the movement, a reminder of the yet untapped ways we might move an earth-based ethic of human death forward.

Public Parks

The oldest FCA affiliate in the country, People's Memorial (PM), in Seattle, Washington, has been collaborating in many ways toward the greening of death. First, PM is all about its members, providing reduced rates on all kinds of death care, one of which is green funeral services. This is something they're able to offer through their Cooperative Funeral Home, which is certified by the GBC. Second, through investment in wind and solar their funeral home was "one of the first in the nation to provide carbon offsets" for both cremation and conventional burial services. Third, they've also long partnered with American Forests, an organization that plants trees in depleted areas. For each funeral they arrange, a tree is planted in memory of the person who died. Fourth, PM contracts out with nearby green cemeteries in Bellingham and Bremerton, Washington, in order to offer their members the lowest prices on services.

As PM is all about serving its members, they're now exploring ways of bringing green burial closer to the populations they serve (the green burial grounds in Bellingham and Bremerton are more than an hour's drive from the city center). Former PM executive director John Eric Rolfstad told me they've been in conversation with the King County Parks Department in the hope of partnering with some of their lands. "We now have the blessings of the County Executive and support of the county council," he said. "So we're hoping we can make this a reality in the next few years."

The way he explained it is that PM would form a separate not-for-profit cemetery association that would manage and operate the burial ground "on undeveloped park land in some of the more rural areas of the county." This partnering with the parks would be much like a green burial ground partnering with a land trust, except that the county parks, and not a land trust, would hold title to the land and steward it in perpetuity. In keeping with this Conservation burial ground model, the area would be open to visitors for hiking and other natural recreational uses while preserving the land as green space.[27]

What's also important to note about this budding partnership is that it may not have come to be had the GBC not been in existence. A call into Joe Sehee from a program manager at the King County Parks Department eventually led to a connection with People's Memorial—yet another example of how building networks is crucial to the fate of the movement.[28]

Even before that call from the King County Parks Department, however, Sehee saw great promise in partnering with parks, county or otherwise, for leveraging interest in green burial into larger-scale conservation. In 2006, he got a call from a woman in Texas whose father operated a cemetery adjacent to a Texas state park near Corpus Christi. "The woman was inquiring to see if Texas Parks and Wildlife (TPWD) might be willing to take over the cemetery and operate it as a green burial ground." And so he put in a call to TPWD. Turns out, TPWD wasn't interested in the cemetery, but it opened up a conversation about using green burial as a way to acquire more land for Texas state parks. "Five years later," Sehee said, "the agency decided to move forward with the idea of testing a cremation scattering program in four state parks where the proceeds would fund conservation." But complications associated with the kinds of memorial features and ritual space parks might be willing to accommodate stalled the launch of the program.[29]

Still, the delay in that project gave them an opportunity to revisit the original idea of using burial as a means of facilitating landscape-level conservation. TPWD Land Conservation director Ted Hollingsworth told me that one of the models he and Sehee have been talking about would include

TPWD collaborating with private landowners. "The idea," he said, "is that someone would see enough conservation or economic value in acquiring a significant piece of land adjacent to a state park or wildlife management area to carve out a portion for green burial." Then, at some point down the road, most likely after the cemetery had sold all of its plots, some or all of the land would be donated to TPWD and managed by them in perpetuity. Cemetery management and operations would not fall to TPWD, however. Hollingsworth was clear on this point—TPWD's business is in conservation, not death care. Just who this potential partner might be remains wide open. "It could be a family or a funeral home," he said. "From my perspective it doesn't really matter who the partner is as long as everything we do is transparent, legal and tasteful."[30]

As I said earlier, the potential for this model already exists in the state of New Jersey. Ed Bixby's Steelmantown Cemetery is sited next to the Belleplain State Forest, twenty-one thousand acres of protected land. Perhaps when more parks systems get on board, others will begin to open up to the possibility.

There are many promising aspects of future public parks partnerships. First of all, they're already in the business of long-term stewardship of the land. Second, in not being privately owned, they essentially already belong to the people. Third, they also often have some type of infrastructure, with trails and road access and integrated care. But engaging this dream's full potential also has limits in a culture where cemeteries are thought of as separate from other human doings. We have, of course, evidence to the contrary in the Rural Cemetery Movement—a movement that, in fact, gave rise to the parks movement in the United States.[31] Of course, with the potential of these partnerships on the horizon we might just be witnessing history in reverse.

Lastly, public parks exist in rural and urban areas alike, although environmental justice activists are quick to point out that those with class and race privilege enjoy better access to green space than others. In fact, studies show that the location of parks is key to accessibility.[32] The Olmstead brothers (sons of the renowned landscape architect, Frederick Law Olmstead, designer of Central Park) knew all too well the centrality of siting parks in a way that distributed green space equally among people. But more often than not, the bottom line has come to be the determining factor in creating such spaces. In more recent years, the work of Majora Carter, in the South Bronx of New York, and Van Jones too, has been about bringing justice to this disparity by building private and public partnerships that work to "green the ghetto."[33] Of the many promises green burial and public park partnerships have to offer, beginning to sort through these questions in a new way is undoubtedly one of them.

Audubon International

As Hybrids grow in number, addressing landscape-level conservation ought to become more, and not less, of a priority for the movement. Cynthia Beal teaches an online course on Sustainable Cemetery Management at Oregon State University, while also urging cemeterians to get to know the flora and fauna of the cemeteries they care for, mostly through spending time in them. Through observation, and possibly even hooking up with a local extension office for more direction, cemeterians can enhance the biological health of their conventional facilities.[34]

But getting conventional cemeteries, especially the ones now offering green burial, to commit to that kind of change can be a hard sell. Joe Sehee told me that he "used to think it was worth trying to encourage conventional operators to consider ideas like prairie restoration, xeriscaping with native plants, and reducing their use of fertilizers, pesticides and herbicides." But the resistance was always there. Anything that might get in the way of the "overall aesthetic" wasn't considered worth doing. He said this was true even when it meant that conservation practices might save them money.

For a while, the GBC had been in discussions with Audubon International, an educational and eco-certification organization that helps businesses protect the environment without compromising, and sometimes even enhancing, their bottom line. One of Audubon's most successful programs has been for golf courses. With over two thousand members across the globe, Audubon certifies courses with a commitment to maximizing wildlife habitat minimizing the impact of on-the-ground operations.

Former Audubon International Sanctuaries program director, Joellen Lampman, told me that what's made the program so successful is working closely with the industry. "We really want to tailor our programs to the issues of each [industry], to meet those needs and address their challenges. The partnership is what's made it work." Lampman imagined bridging such a partnership with U.S. cemeteries, another place turf use is traditionally high. In 2001 she was slated to give a talk on the promise of eco certification for cemeteries at the ICCFA's annual meeting. "But then 9/11 hit," she said. After that, interest dwindled until she was contacted by Joe Sehee and learned what the GBC was doing for burgeoning green burial. "It seemed like the perfect way in, and it was a much more comfortable fit."

Even though the GBC provides its own certification for cemeteries, the way Lampman saw it was that much of what the GBC is focused on is happening below ground while Audubon International's focus is all above. "Of course that's an overgeneralization," she said, mostly because Conservation burial grounds and to a lesser degree Natural burial grounds certified by the

GBC must make a commitment to landscape-level conservation.[35] Hybrids, however, do not. Given the amount of mowing and water that goes into keeping many conventional cemeteries looking green and trim, Sehee told me that "he had always wanted the GBC do more with Hybrids than just requiring them to accommodate shrouds and not force people into burial vaults"[36] Despite such palpable resistance to change, from what Sehee could see, Audubon International was making some inroads.

Although Audubon International has not yet developed a program specifically geared toward cemeteries, or Hybrids, for that matter, right now about two-dozen cemeteries are members of Audubon International, with four of them officially designated as "certified" in their Audubon Cooperative Sanctuaries Program (ACSP). One of them—White Haven Memorial Park, in Rochester, New York—also happens to offer green burial in a separate section of the cemetery,[37] and is certified as a Natural burial ground by the GBC. So, the potential is there. Among other things, certified properties must demonstrate that eighty percent of plant life is native, and fifty percent of any shorelines naturalized. With ACSP already focused on areas like water conservation and quality management, and energy and wildlife conservation, the effect on Hybrids could be profound.[38]

ACSP provides guidance as well as help in goal setting, while also being a resource to their member properties—something invaluable to the success of greening Hybrids. In fact, without such guidelines, what looks like good management practices could actually end up being the opposite. For example, while memorial trees provide solace to the living, cleanse the air we breathe, provide habitat for wildlife, and offer shade on hot summer days, tree plantings may not always be warranted for every site. And in the places where they are, having a long-term plan for planting is crucial. Though the landscape level conservation that's in practice at Conservation burial grounds may not seem in keeping with conventional cemetery operations, there's still much to draw from. At Foxfield Preserve, for instance, families do have a choice of a living memorial, at least in their hardwood section. Indeed, it's about more than reforesting that space about offering something to the living. And yet, Foxfield only works from a list of approved species, and all requests for tree planting are made on a case-by-case basis."[39]

Billy Campbell's been critical of many of the Woodland Burial grounds in the United Kingdom that have sometimes moved forward without such foresight. For instance, he's said that in the quest to green cemeteries, some of them might actually be doing more harm than good by planting trees in spite of other eco-systems, like ancient meadow. He also worries about over-planting. "The first UK Woodland Burial project in Carlisle was planting a tree over each grave," Campbell told me. "With a density of 800/acre many of the trees would [eventually] have to be culled."[40] The point here is that the ecological needs of all Hybrids are not the same.

Of course, the GBC could consider setting up these guidelines themselves. But given that an eco-certifier like Audubon International has a staff of professionals with the expertise to guide cemeterians toward the particular ecological needs and health of the land they're caring for, a partnership with the GBC seems just like what Lampman said of it—"a comfortable fit." Both Lampman and Sehee remain hopeful that talks between the two organizations will pick up sometime in the near future.

Faith-Based Cemeteries

When Fr. Charles Morris set out to create a green burial ground at his church in Wyandotte, Michigan, the desire to do so was tied up with his interest in putting eco-theology into action, something he'd already been doing for a long time. "I became involved in faith-based environmental groups in the 1990s, did an energy audit at St. Elizabeth's and then in 2001 installed solar panels on the church," he told me. Way back in 1992 he tried to bring some churches together around energy efficiency, but the organizing of that meeting wasn't so successful. "No one showed up." He'd read about the work of Sally Bingham, who was trying to bridge connections between faith and environmental concerns. She eventually started the Interfaith Power and Light movement. He was inspired. On a yearlong sabbatical in 2003, Michigan Interfaith Power and Light was born. Which is to say, that by the time he helped to carve out a section for green burial at his church in 2009, he'd already undertaken a number of environmental projects.[41]

Faith-based communities already thinking about environmental concerns seem a logical connection for the development of green burial grounds throughout the United States. And if the growing number of Christian green burial grounds is any indication, building coalitions with faith communities certainly seems to be in the movement's future. Not to mention that churches own a lot of cemeteries, and a lot of other lands.[42] But as these cemeteries are often only open to members of the faith, the capacity to further the goals of the movement through these burial grounds, beyond the communities they serve, prove challenging.

As someone who teaches fledgling pastors, Professor Benjamin Stewart hopes to have more practitioners like Father Charles on the ground who want to cultivate Christianity "as an earth-rooted experience of life and death."[43] That hope, he told me, is tied up into "leveraging church cemeteries for the good of the world." Unfortunately, he's witnessed barriers to this potential firsthand. He told me about a church cemetery in Chicago that was thinking about offering green burial, but in the end, decided against it because some of its board members worried there would be people outside the faith wanting to be buried there, especially if it was the only game in town. While he understands the need to maintain Christian distinctiveness, he also sees promise in having those "cemeteries wide open to everybody who wants to be part of a healed earth."

Stewart's not discouraged, however. The pastors coming out of his program are energized by the possibilities inherent to the green burial movement, ones that resonate with both Christian liturgy as well as the common good. He sees only great promise in what they can bring to the lived experience of the bereaved through the rekindling of greener forms of disposition.[44]

As green burial offers us the possibility of reconnecting to an earth from which we've been separated, it reminds us that our connections to each other are part of that biotic whole, too. And so, more bridges must be built—in the movement, around the movement, and, even what sometimes seems to be outside of the movement.

Between the living and the dead.

No doubt, Carl Leopold's hand in the making of Greensprings was a kind of synchronicity. While neither father nor son ever exactly called for an earth-based ethic of human death, integral to Aldo Leopold's "land ethic" was the understanding that "(m)an or mouse, oak or orchid . . . ultimately we give ourselves"[45] to the land. Carl Leopold sealed his conviction through his own death, put into the ground at Greensprings in 2009.

And so hearts and minds can be changed. Perhaps because we feel there is no good side to death it's difficult to find the bond that makes us feel the fight is worth it. Grief can be the great equalizer, but those same feelings, often as individual as they are shared, can also be powerful inhibitors to collaboration. If we are ever to live in community, our attention must turn toward common ground. "Our primary connection is to the earth,"[46] Alice Walker reminds us. Let that light the way.

Epilogue

Heeding the Light, "Feeding the Green"[1]

Land in the Hudson Valley is golden. No matter the season, hidden hangouts and remote open hollows are touched with an equal kind of glimmer. For those of us who hail from this region, and pay even the slightest attention to the land, this play of light can be felt in nearly everything—in rock and seed, in wet and wind, in fire and flesh. In all the markers of what we call home.

In 1836, Hudson River School painter Thomas Cole rhapsodized this light, calling it a "liquid gold [that] breathes over the earth,"[2] though he needn't have said anything. His paintings spoke for themselves. Since then, critics have come to call his work quixotic and exaggerated, and even problematic in its view of nature as a landscape to be enjoyed rather than a home to be lived in. And yet, I'm still bewitched by his use of light. Despite his romanticism, I can't help but see his paintings as offerings—a way of reminding us of our tie to the land.

School, work, and adventure have at one time or another taken me away from this place, but it's always been the light's play on the land that's lured me back. I was a child of the 1970s, perhaps the last generation of children to spend their days scouring the corners and contours of the great outdoors, to sense through our own developing bodies that terrestrial bond to something outside of the human-made stuff that's now all around us. Over time, this geography has rendered out a mapping of my own life, a path steeped in a particular place and time. Living in the Hudson Valley has been an ongoing process of exchange and change. As the terrain shifts I move along with it, never fixed or finished, never completed, and never just simply myself. Having found my way back years ago now, I've come to know what so many others who've gone before did, that all things begin and end with the land.

But this interplay could have just as well been derailed upon my death. In 2010, the small Hudson Valley town I call home joined with others around the United States in challenging the taboo of mingling the dead directly with the earth, embarking on a project to ensure that a life spent tied to the land could continue in death. Over the last several years I've been fortunate to be a part of that project.

As Cole was doing his own kind of illuminating of the land, our death practices hadn't yet begun their slow creep away from nature. I wonder what he might have thought, paintbrush in hand, gazing through the haze of dusk as he watched the river flow south. When Cole died in 1848 he likely had no idea the tide was about to turn, or that a century and a half later, it would turn once more.

I came to be the committee chair of the Town of Rhinebeck Cemetery in 2010. We're an all-volunteer group appointed by a hardworking, but poorly paid, part-time town board swamped with other responsibilities. I'd served on the committee for about a year before that, working with a group of long-dedicated community members, advising the town on all cemetery matters and making recommendations for improvements. Some of my fellow members had been on the committee for decades.

What's now called the Town of Rhinebeck Cemetery was once the Rhinebeck Cemetery Association. In New York State, cemeteries can be owned and operated by families, by religious institutions, by municipalities, or by not-for-profit associations. The State of New York's Division of Cemeteries regulates only the last type, the association cemetery. All the others must abide by general state laws that apply to all human burial, including minimal maintenance standards and other laws that have to do with contracts between consenting parties. In 2002, the Rhinebeck Cemetery Association found it could no longer meet the fiscal standards set forth through Albany and was faced with having to turn the cemetery over to the town. Such is the law in New York State, as in many others, that when an association cemetery can no longer operate on its own it falls to the municipality to care for it.

By law, a town or city can opt to no longer sell plots, and many do, with its only ownership duty to provide minimal maintenance to the site, like mowing twice a year. But given that church cemeteries within the Village of Rhinebeck were forced to close during the mid-1800s, the nonsectarian Rhinebeck Cemetery Association that lay on the outskirts of town had become a repository of many, if not most, of the community's dead. For these reasons, the town saw in the transfer from association to municipal ownership a community responsibility to keep it open and running.

It was admirable, on the town's part, to have taken on the operations of the cemetery. As the Association's downward spiral indicates, small-town cemeteries are not moneymakers. The town could have closed the cemetery's doors and moved on. Or they could have outsourced responsibility to a third party, like a funeral director. But the leaders of the town saw the cemetery as a communal good, and that ethic, at least in my tenure, has traversed political party lines and largely skirted the kinds of philosophical scuffles that have become the heart of small-town politics.

The Rhinebeck Cemetery Association was founded in 1883, although burial had begun there at least thirty years prior. As the village churches could no longer bury in their own yards, most of them purchased land at the newly growing site for their congregations. Eventually, those church sections would become part of one nonsectarian cemetery—open to all. Traces of the Rural Cemetery Movement style are still everywhere in this "old" section. Black locusts guard the cemetery gate but grant you entrance all the same. Obelisks catch the sunlight at dusk. Narrow dirt roadways skirt past trees and knolls, around worn-out paths and time-worn markers of families now long forgotten. But like the history of cemeteries in the United States, the garden style of that "old" section soon fell away. When a tree's life came to an end, another would not be planted in its place. Eventually, the cemetery's varied areas would become more gridded, uniform, and open.

By the 1970s the twenty-four acres that made up the "old" part of the cemetery was reaching capacity. The Rhinebeck Cemetery Association acquired seventeen acres of land for new burials nearly across the street from that original "old" part of the cemetery, although they didn't start burying on it until about a decade later. Less than half of that newly acquired land, some of which was once old growth forest turned open cornfield, was surveyed for conventional burial. That area is called "Grasmere," named after the large Hudson Valley estate that still borders it. That "new" part of the cemetery is a flat and largely treeless plot of land that fulfills the look of your standard lawn park—a barren space, now populated by machine-cut polished granite and a few mausoleums. But the other portion of that land would remain wooded and untouched. When the committee set out to think about a green burial ground, they knew just where to site it.

In 2009, several community members came to the town asking whether they might consider opening up some plots to natural burial. And so, the town board charged the cemetery committee with coming up with a plan. I came onto the committee soon after that.

For nearly a decade I'd been researching, writing, talking, and teaching about green burial, while also trying to find a way to start a green cemetery in my area. My fantasy burial ground was more in line with a Conservation burial ground model. Time and again, however, the barriers to building something like that proved insurmountable (just as I spelled out in chapter 7).

Before the Rhinebeck project, much of my time was spent in the same way that others, like Judith Lorei from Green Burial Massachusetts, had been spending it. Trying to secure those three necessary corners—the money, the land, and, ultimately, the land trust. Finding the right folks to collaborate with who could help me build capital, finding the right piece of land that would draw folks to buy plots and, ideally, finding a land trust to partner with to hold the easement in order to further other conservation goals was ongoing grassroots work. Like anything else, all that hard work needed was to run into a little bit of luck.

But that luck didn't end up coming in the way I imagined. For many years, I thought the burial ground would come together more like Greensprings did, both in terms of the landowner or conservation entity that would agree to donate their land for the green burial vision and also in the actual lay of the land. The sweeping farmland of Greensprings paralleled my green burial ground fantasy in other ways, a vision, no doubt, born from my own worn-in land aesthetic—one that's reflected even in my own small homestead.

My house is situated on the edge of a nearly one-hundred-acre open hay field. After living away for years, the light in the land had drawn me back precisely for these kinds of vistas. I'd grown up on a small farm, the context of which at the time I could have done without, but the birth, death, and muck memories of which, as I grew older, remained in my bones. When I first set eyes on what would become my home, a small 1930s farmhouse in complete and utter disrepair, I hardly noticed. Just beyond the house, past the rusting shed and the towering silver maples, were the rolling hills and round bales of my childhood. The birds I thought I might miss for lack of tree cover were soon made up for in harriers and hawks, bobolinks and meadowlarks, and lunging swallows. Long before I'd seen Greensprings, before Greensprings was even formed, long before I saw what's now my home, my vision of a green burial ground looked a lot like this.

But like John Burroughs, who left the view of the Hudson River because he longed for the close contours of the nearby woods, once I began to live in my house—in the wide-open vast wind tunnel of the hay field—I started to pine for the forest. (Such is human nature, I suppose, and the art of desiring.) When I first saw the woods where the Town of Rhinebeck Natural Burial Ground would be, not even a half of a mile down the road from my home, it was like the backyard of my new daydreams. And all things considered, I suppose it is.

Though my green burial work landed me on that committee, my interest in the cemetery, more generally, was only deepened by a love of history and hauntings, by my own experiences with death and the fact that the cemetery was just a stone's throw from my home. It was more than an "ask and thee shall receive." It seemed meant to be.

The possibility of the Rhinebeck project was more than exciting. There was no having to find the land, because the town already owned it. There was no having to set up a $50,000 trust fund to establish a new association cemetery. But there were also limits to all this newfound ease. Because the municipality owned the natural burial ground, a land trust could never hold an easement on the property. And because the town only agreed to survey two-and-a-half acres to start, the conservation potential would be minimal (at least on the front end of the project).

Though it's true that the burial ground is small in terms of acreage, the woods themselves have no borders, and so the land is actually part of a much larger tract that extends down toward the Hudson River. To the east is the more than two hundred acres of Grasmere estate, still privately owned. The location of the cemetery is critical, sited in a highly regulated zoning area with strict wetlands laws. It's a double gateway—to the south end of town and to a matchless undergirding of habitats supporting a rich variety of species, both regular and rare. Within a few miles of each other meadow and shrubland give way to forest and marsh, rare clay bluff, and ravine. In short, the natural burial ground was in a beautiful spot.

With the parameters drawn, our committee set out to make sense of the land and come up with a plan for burial. As luck would have it, one of the long-standing members of the committee, who also served on the Association board before the town acquired the cemetery, was also a skilled professional engineer and licensed land surveyor. He not only understood the finer contours of land but also what it would take to lay out burial plots in a forest. His plan for the survey was based on a conventional grid system that some might say defies the logic of the woods. But the plotting of gravesites within such a dense canopy is, despite the grid, dependent upon the location of trees. In the end, the final layout of actual saleable plots looks much more scattered. Of course, we knew burying in the woods would be a different project than in the existing open gridded system of the conventional cemetery. As a government entity, we're fortunate to have a well-trained in-residence caretaker.

Getting the natural burial ground up and running required establishing rules and regulations and completing the land survey. The pace of town government is notoriously slow, and so the survey took some time. Planning out the specs, bidding out the job, doing the survey, and then the final filing of the map took about two years. Our committee was in agreement that we wanted the burial ground to adhere to the highest standards of green burial and that it made no sense to reinvent the wheel. To these ends, we looked to other established green burial grounds for guidance—when we could get it—as well as to the GBC for standards.

It took many discussions, but our committee finally voted to pursue certification by the GBC. One of the requirements for this level of certification is obtaining a biological assessment of the surveyed area. I'd been a member of the town's Conservation Advisory Board for several years and knew that Hudsonia, a local not-for-profit environmental science research and education organization, had come into some grant monies for municipal projects. Their assessment by a conservation biologist confirmed the woods as a suitable place for human burial while also noting species population and diversity, and making recommendations for dealing with invasives, deer browsing, and forest restoration. As former pastureland to the Grasmere Estate, the woods are quite young. Evidence of past human disturbance is everywhere. The understory canopy is made up of largely locusts and cherries, and the forest floor is covered with invasive non-native herbs like mustard and wild garlic. Massive deer grazing has been inhibiting tulips, elms, and oaks. Moving forward, the Hudsonia report remains a valuable tool as we care for the land.

During the summer of 2013, all along the northeastern seaboard of the United States, cicada nymphs journeyed from the underworld place they called home for the last seventeen years and into the light of day. *Magicicada septendecim* ascended by the billions per acre throughout Rhinebeck and beyond. For weeks, the fervor of their mating calls, as they shed their skins and prepared to morph into what they were destined to become, seemed prophetic. Cicadas have long inspired prescience, their periodic life cycle and liminal qualities potent reminders of the fragility of life, the necessity of change, and the unseen movers of transformation.

Several months after the cicadas had come and gone, our work on the burial ground would be complete. And by the spring of 2014 we would begin to sell plots. As I write this, we've sold more than a dozen and have already had our first burial. We're also in the process of preparing our application for certification with the GBC, hoping to be approved at the Natural level.

In all, I come away from this project with many lessons learned.

Working collaboratively at the municipal level made it easy for us to act as citizens first, and consumers second. Although we understood offering the "choice" was necessary and that community members, as consumers, ought to have it, our work was really just an extension of the municipality's other responsibilities, like safe roads, clean water, and good planning.

I've been continually surprised by my own feelings for this burial ground, attached as it is to a conventional cemetery with all its distancing of decay and lack of attention to the land as community. There's something both energizing and humbling about turning toward the truth of human decomposition and embracing our partnership with the more-than-human in the face of our past.

But what I've learned most from this experience is the value of collaboration at an entirely fresh level—in this case, the kind that can build community through caring for the living, the land, and the dead. For those of us who team up with others, for no pay, no personal gain, no anything except the satisfaction of building a movement that ties us to the more-than-human, this is our way of "feeding of the green"—offerings to an injured earth.

Suzanne Kelly
December 30, 2014

Notes

INTRODUCTION

1. Sandra Gilbert, *Death's Door: Modern Dying and the Ways We Grieve* (New York: W. W. Norton, 2007), xvii.

2. Marcel Proust, *In Search of Lost Time, Volume 6: Time Regained* (New York: Random House, 1993), 315.

3. Online Etymology Dictionary, http://www.etymonline.com/index.php?term=wake, accessed January 30, 2015.

4. CDC.NCHS, National Vital Statistics System, Mortality, http://www.cdc.gov/nchs/data/dvs/Mortfinal2005_worktable_309.pdf.

5. Ramsey Creek, however, was not influenced by the woodland burials that began taking place in the United Kingdom during the 1990s. In fact, according to Billy Campbell, he and his wife, Kimberley, were wholly unaware of what was emerging across the Atlantic when they started Ramsey Creek in 1996 and opened up for burial two years later. Email exchange with Billy Campbell, January 19, 2015.

6. Mark Harris, *Grave Matters: A Journey through the Modern Funeral Industry to a Natural Way of Burial* (New York: Scribner, 2007), 157–58.

7. National Home Funeral Alliance, "Green Burials in the U.S. and Canada," http://www.homefuneralalliance.org/Resources/Documents/Green Cemeteries List.pdf, retrieved December 6, 2014.

8. There's only one place in the United States that offers open-air pyre burning, in Crestone, Colorado. The projected cremation rate for 2020 is 55.8% http://nfda.org/about-funeral-service-/trends-and-statistics.html. The NFDA projects that in 2015 cremations will surpass conventional burial by 2 points. Burial projected at 45.8% and cremation at 48.2%. http://nfda.org/news-a-events/all-press-releases/4046-consumer-preference-for-cremation-expected-to-surpass-burial-in-2015.html.

9. "Cremation Continues to Expand," Cremation Association of North America, http://www.cremationassociation.org/?CremationContinues, accessed December 9, 2014.

10. Interview with Bob Fertig, January 14, 2015.

11. Email exchange with Joe Sehee, January 29, 2015.

12. Bill McKibben, "Movements without Leaders: What to Make of Change on an Overheating Planet," Tomdispatch.com, August 18, 2013, http://www.tomdispatch .com/blog/175737/, accessed December 6, 2014.

13. Jane Caputi, "Feeding Green Fire," *Journal for the Study of Religion, Nature, and Culture* 5, no. 4 (2011): 410–36. Also, Jane Caputi explains, "The word *greening* came into prominence with the publication of Charles Reich's 1970 book, *The Greening of America*, which heralded the birth of a new consciousness, one that had evolved beyond greed, mechanistic models of humanity, violence, and fragmentation. *Greening*, which previously, in the vernacular, had meant only the ripening of green apples, began in the 1970s to take on a new (if not ancient) meaning of rejuvenation, the return of vitality or freshness after decay or destruction. Not insignificantly, *green* also became the color most aligned with the ideals and practices of the environmental movement." Jane Caputi, "Introduction," *Journal of American Culture* 35, no. 1 (2012): 1–3. See also Jane Caputi, "Green Consciousness: Earth-Based Myth and Meaning in Shrek, *Ethics & Environment*, 12.2 (2007), 23–24.

14. Aldo Leopold, *A Sand County Almanac* (New York: Oxford, 1949), 130.

15. Vandana Shiva, *Biopiracy: The Plunder of Nature and Knowledge* (Boston: South End Press, 1999).

16. Film interview with Jane Caputi, September 20, 2014, appearing in the forthcoming film *Feed the Green: Feminist Voices for the Earth*, (Caputi, 2015)

17. Neil Evernden. *The Social Creation of Nature* (Baltimore: The John Hopkins University Press, 1992), xi. Evernden actually distinguishes between this nature, with a lowercase *n*, and the nature that is dominated with a capital *N*.

18. Merriam-Webster, http://www.merriam-webster.com/dictionary/conventional, accessed January 12, 2014.

19. Janice Gibbs, "Green Funerals See Jump in Popularity," *Killeen Daily Herald*, http://kdhnews.com/news/green-funerals-see-jump-in-popularity/article_601ac430-3b92-11e4-a3f6-001a4bcf6878.html?mode=jqm, accessed December 15, 2014.

CHAPTER 1

1. Neil Evernden, *The Natural Alien: Humankind and Environment*, 2nd edition, (Toronto: University of Toronto Press, 1993), 18.

2. Rachel Carson, *Silent Spring* (New York: Houghton Mifflin, 1962).

3. Ibid.

4. Thomas Berry, *The Great Work: Our Way into the Future* (New York: Bell Tower, 1999), 15.

5. This is the argument Evernden makes in *The Natural Alien: Humankind and the Environment*.

6. I borrow this term from David Abram, who coined the phrase in the 1990s. See *The Spell of the Sensuous: Perception and Language in a More-Than-Human World* (New York: Vintage Books, 1996).

7. Leopold, *A Sand County Almanac*, viii.

8. Leopold, *A Sand County Almanac*, 203.

9. Leopold, *A Sand County Almanac*, 204.

10. Val Plumwood, *Feminism and the Mastery of Nature* (London: Routledge, 1993), 102.

11. Interview with Freddie Johnson, May 23, 2014.

12. "Foxfield Preserve," Marge Thomas, Wooster, Ohio, http://www.foxfield preserve.org/home/visit/, accessed August 3, 2014.

13. Interview with Kimberley Campbell, May 18, 2014, interview with Brian Flowers with Jodie Buller, November 27, 2013, "Speak Up, Speak Out," Skagit Valley College Radio http://24.113.141.253/mp3/suso-2013-11-27-NaturalBurialWithBrian Flowers.mp3, accessed August 4, 2014.

14. John Campanelli, "Ohio's Only 'Green' Cemetery Lets You Rest in Peace, in Nature," *Plain Dealer*, March 20, 2011, http://www.cleveland.com/pdq/index. ssf/2011/03/ohios_only_green_cemetery_lets.html, accessed November 14, 2014.

15. In trying to understand rationality's hierarchical opposition to the more-than-human, there's much to be gleaned from the feminist movement, both locally and globally, because where there are hierarchies harm is quick to follow. On the academic front, environmental feminism has amassed a long litany of complaints against this normalized concept of rationality, the problem of human exceptionalism, and the underlying dualism that makes it all possible.

16. See Mary Wollstonecraft's *A Vindication of the Rights of Woman* (1792) and Jean-Jacques Rousseau's *Emile* (1762).

17. Plumwood, *Feminism and the Mastery of Nature*, 48.

18. See Benjamin Stewart's "The Place of Earth in Lutheran Funeral Rites: Mapping the Current Terrain," *Dialog: A Journal of Theology* 53, no. 2 (2014), and Benjamin Stewart, "Committed to the Earth: Ecotheological Dimensions of Christian Burial Practices," *Liturgy* 27, no. 2 (February 2012), 70. See also Caroline Walker Bynum, *Fragmentation and Redemption: Essays on Gender and the Human Body in Medieval Religion* (New York: Zone Books, 1991), 183–84.

19. Nancy Tuana, *The Less Noble Sex: Scientific, Religious, and Philosophical Conceptions of Woman's Nature* (Bloomington: Indiana University Press, 1993), 58.

20. Vandana Shiva, *Staying Alive: Women, Ecology and Development* (London: Zed Books, 1989), 16.

21. Carolyn Merchant, *The Death of Nature: Women, Ecology and the Scientific Revolution* (New York: Harper and Row, 1983).

22. Plumwood, *Feminism and the Mastery of Nature*, 70. Also see Shiva, *Staying Alive* and Carolyn Merchant's *The Death of Nature*.

23. Martin Buber, *I and Thou* (New York: Scribner and Sons, 1958). Early second-wave feminists such as Mary Daly, for instance, have looked to Buber's *I and Thou* to make sense of a patriarchal culture that posits women as objects, where, like our relationship to nature, the "I-It" relationship prevails. See Mary Daly, *Beyond God the Father: Toward a Philosophy of Women's Liberation* (Boston: Beacon Books, 1973).

24. Neil Evernden talks about "relationship as context" in *The Natural Alien: Humankind and Environment*, 133–44.

25. Abram, *The Spell of the Sensuous*, 22.

26. Plumwood, *Feminism and the Mastery of Nature*, 48–51.

27. Val Plumwood, *Environmental Culture: The Ecological Crisis of Reason* (London: Routledge, 2002), 5.

28. Suzanne Kelly, "Dead Bodies That Matter: Toward a New Ecology of Human Death," *Journal of American Culture* 35, no. 1 (2012): 37–51.

29. Plumwood, *Feminism and the Mastery of Nature*, 102.

30. See Val Plumwood, "Tasteless: Towards a Food-Based Approach to Death" in *The Eye of the Crocodile*, edited by Lorraine Shannon (Canberra: ANU E Press, 2012), and Val Plumwood, "The Cemetery Wars: Cemeteries, Biodiversity and the Sacred," *Local-Global: Identity, Security, Community* 3 (2007): 54–71.

31. Herbert Marcuse, *One-Dimensional Man*, 2nd ed. (Boston: Beacon Press, 1991), 6–7.

32. Leopold, *A Sand County Almanac*, 203.

33. Leopold, *A Sand County Almanac*, 224–25.

CHAPTER 2

1. Joy Lukachick Smith, "10th Anniversary of Bodies Discovered at Tri-State Crematory in Noble, Georgia," *Times Free Press*, Sunday, February 12, 2012, http://www.timesfreepress.com/news/2012/feb/12/horror-in-noble/, accessed July 25, 2014.

2. Sam Knight, "Bodysnatchers Steal Alistair Cooke's Bones," *Times Online*, December 22, 2005, http://www.thetimes.co.uk/tto/news/world/americas/article2002922.ece, accessed October 25, 2011; Robert D. McFadden, "Scores of Bodies Strewn at Site of Crematory," *New York Times*, February 17, 2002, http://www.nytimes.com/2002/02/17/national/17CREM.html, accessed November 22, 2011; Brad A. Greenberg, "Jewish Cemetery Accused of Desecrating 500 Graves," Jewishjournal.com, December 12, 2009, http://www.jewishjournal.com/thegodblog/item/jewish_cemetery_accused_of_desecrating_500_graves_20090912/, accessed November 22, 2014; also see Mary Roach's *Stiff: The Curious Lives of Human Cadavers* (New York: W. W. Norton and Company, 2003). See also Hollywood films such as *Weekend at Bernie's* (1989) and *Little Miss Sunshine* (2006).

3. Randall Patterson, "The Organ Grinder," *New York Magazine*, October 16, 2006, http://nymag.com/news/features/22326/, accessed August 10, 2014.

4. Associated Press, "Three Philadelphia-Area Funeral Directors Nabbed in Scheme Selling Body Parts," Foxnews.com, October 4, 2007, http://www.foxnews.com/story/2007/10/04/three-philadelphia-area-funeral-directors-nabbed-in-scheme-selling-body-parts/, accessed August 13, 2014.

5. Daniel E. Slotnik, "Michael Mastromarino, Dentist Guilty in Organ Scheme, Dies at 49," *New York Times,* July 8, 2013, http://www.nytimes.com/2013/07/09/nyregion/michael-mastromarino-dentist-guilty-in-organ-scheme-dies-at-49.html?_r=0, accessed August 13, 2014.

6. Paul M. Barrett, "Huge Funeral Chain Settles Graveyard Desecration Suit, Buries Financial Details," *Bloomberg Business Week*, February 28, 2014, http://www.businessweek.com/articles/2014-02-28/huge-funeral-chain-settles-graveyard-desecration-suit-buries-financial-details, accessed November 22, 2014.

7. Joy Lukachick Smith, "Walker County Still Working to Memorialize Tragedy at Tri-State Crematory," *Times Free Press*, February 12, 2012, http://www.timesfree-press.com/news/2012/feb/12/walker-county-still-working-memorialize-tragedy-tr/, accessed August 14, 2014.

8. Thomas Lynch, *The Undertaking: Life Studies from the Dismal Trade* (New York: W. W. Norton, 1997), 25.

9. Émile Durkheim, *The Elementary Forms of the Religious Life* (London: G. Allen & Unwin, 1915), 390.

10. This polarity marked what would be for Durkheim the foundations of all religious thinking, one based not on morality but, rather, epistemology. Because what Durkheim sought to uncover was not how the profane was bad and the sacred was good, but how it is that societies organize themselves around what's knowable and what's not. Durkheim would later be criticized for his foreclosure of subjective awareness and intuition in what we can know, but in his observations of the dead he has not been alone.

11. Ruth Richardson, *Death, Dissection and the Destitute* (Chicago: University of Chicago Press, 2001), 17. Also see Peter Metcalf and Richard Huntington, *Celebrations of Death: The Anthropology of Mortuary Ritual*, 2nd ed. (Cambridge: Cambridge University Press, 1991).

12. R. W. Habenstein and W. M. Lamers, *Funeral Customs the World Over* (Milwaukee: Bulfin, 1960).

13. Mike Parker Pearson, *The Archeology of Death and Burial* (College Station: Texas A&M University, 2000).

14. Jean-Pierre Vernant, *Mortals and Immortals: Collected Essays* (Princeton: Princeton University Press, 1991).

15. David Jackson, "Obama: We Treated bin Laden Better Than He Treated 9/11 Victims," *USA Today*, May 5, 2011.

16. Filmmaker A. Keala Kelly's addresses the desecration of native burial grounds and resistance to it in her documentary *Noho Hewa: The Wrongful Occupation of Hawai'i*.

17. John Ahni Schertow, "Police Arrest Hawaiian Activists Protesting the Desecration of Sacred Site," *IC Magazine*, May 5, 2011, https://intercontinentalcry.org/police-arrest-hawaiian-activists-protesting-the-desecration-of-sacred-site/, accessed July 12, 2014.

18. Opening Plenary, Q&A with independent filmmaker/artist A. Keala Kelly, April 11, 2014, "Ecology, Spirituality, Sustainability: Feminist and Indigenous Interventions."

19. Julie Bosman and Joseph Goldstein, "Timeline for a Body: 4 Hours in the Middle of a Ferguson Street," *New York Times*, August 23, 2014, http://www.nytimes.com/2014/08/24/us/michael-brown-a-bodys-timeline-4-hours-on-a-ferguson-street.html. See also Isabel Wilkerson, "Michael Brown's Shooting and Jim Crow Lynchings Have Too Much in Common. It's Time for America to Own Up," *The Guardian*, August 25, 2015, http://www.theguardian.com/commentisfree/2014/aug/25/mike-brown-shooting-jim-crow-lynchings-in-common, accessed September 10, 2014. Thank you to Jane Caputi for pointing this out.

20. Adam Rosenblatt, "Sacred Graves and Human Rights," in *Human Rights at the Crossroads*, edited by Mark Goodale (Oxford: Oxford University Press, 2012).

21. Rosenblatt, "Sacred Graves and Human Rights," 129 [italics mine].

22. James Farrell, *Inventing the American Way of Death, 1830–1920* (Philadelphia: Temple University Press, 1980), 163.

23. Ruth Richardson, *Death, Dissection and the Destitute* (Chicago: University of Chicago Press, 2000), 32. Iserson, *Dust to Dust*, 216.

24. A most well-known example of this pursuit is the case of Saartjie Baartman—a Khoi woman who was owned by the Dutch, sold to the British, and displayed in "freak" shows around London until her death in 1815. Until 1974, and without consent, Baartman's dissected skeleton, preserved genitals, and brain were displayed in the Musée de l'Homme in Paris. Outcries to remove the display began in 1940, with formal requests of repatriation led by Nelson Mandela in the 1990s. Her remains were finally returned to South African soil in 2002.

25. Richardson, *Death, Dissection and the Destitute*, 419.

26. Richardson, *Death, Dissection and the Destitute*, 30.

27. Richardson, *Death, Dissection and the Destitute*, 31.

28. Caroline Walker Bynum, *Fragmentation and Redemption: Essays on Gender and the Human Body in Medieval Religion* (New York: Zone Books, 1991), 183–84. In that context, Bynum suggests that it was "a way of emphasiz[ing] body as the locus of the sacred."

29. This was 2006.

30. Thrasy Petropoulos, "Seat at the Autopsy Sideshow," BBC News, November 21, 2002, http://news.bbc.co.uk/2/hi/health/2497889.stm, accessed August 10, 2014.

31. http://www.bodyworlds.com/en.html, accessed June 25, 2014.

32. Alhough the allegations have never officially amounted to wrongdoing. Neda Ulaby, "Origins of Exhibited Cadavers Questioned," NPR, August 11, 2006, http://www.npr.org/templates/story/story.php?storyId=5637687, accessed July 9, 2014.

33. Thomas Laqueur, "The Deep Time of the Dead," *Social Research: An International Quarterly* 78, no. 3 (2011).

34. Conversation with elder law attorney Michel P. Haggerty, Esq., August 17, 2005.

35. Laqueur's point may be problematic for other reasons, as there's evidence that some more-than-human animals, like elephants, for instance, also care for their dead. See Shaoni Battacharya, "Elephants May Pay Homage to Dead Relatives," *New Scientist*, October 26, 2005, http://www.newscientist.com/article/dn8209-elephants-may-pay-homage-to-dead-relatives.html#.VLvfCGTF8mc, accessed June 5, 2014. Thomas Laqueur, "Why Do We Care for the Dead?" presented at Radcliffe Institute for Advanced Study, Harvard University, April 29, 2014.

36. Jessica Mitford, *The American Way of Death* (New York: Simon and Schuster, 1963), 50.

37. Alkaline hydrolysis is a process now legal in a handful of states in the United States, a process that uses lye and heat to dissolve a body within a chamber. The liquefied remnants are then returned to sewer systems or used as fertilizer. The EATR is a flesh-eating robot created by Robotic Technologies and funded by the U.S. Department of Defense (John Scott Lewinski, "Military Researchers Develop Corpse-Eating Robots," *Wired*, July 15, 2009). Promession was developed by a Swedish biologist, a process that essentially freeze-dries the dead and turns it into particles in minutes.

38. Leslie Marmon Silko, "Landscape, History and the Pueblo Imagination: From a High Arid Plateau in New Mexico," in *On Nature: Nature, Landscape and Natural History*, edited by Daniel Halpern (San Francisco: North Point Press, 1987), 83.

39. Val Plumwood, "Tasteless: Toward a Food-Based Approach to Death," *Environmental Values* 17 (2008): 323–30.

40. Val Plumwood, "Being Prey," *Utne Reader*, July/August 2000.

41. Kenneth V. Iserson, *Death to Dust: What Happens to Dead Bodies?* 2nd edition (New York: Galen Press), 387.

42. Iserson, *Death to Dust*, 50.

43. Richard Selzer, *The Exact Location of the Soul: New and Selected Essays* (New York: Picador, 2001), 194–95.

44. Monica Raymunt, "Down on the Body Farm: Inside the Dirty World of Forensic Science," *The Atlantic*, December 2, 2010, http://www.theatlantic.com/technology/archive/2010/12/down-on-the-body-farm-inside-the-dirty-world-of-forensic-science/67241/, accessed November 20, 2011. The five body farms are at the University of Tennessee at Knoxville; Western Carolina University in Cullowhee, Texas; State University in San Marcos; Sam Houston State University in Huntsville, Texas; and California University of Pennsylvania.

45. William D. Haglund and Marcella H. Sorg, eds., *Forensic Taphonomy: The Postmortem Fate of Human Remains* (Boca Raton: CRC Press, 1997), 1–12.

46. David O. Carter and Mark Tibbett, "Does Repeated Burial of Skeletal Muscle Tissue (*Ovis aries*) in Soil Affect Subsequent Decomposition?" *Applied Soil Ecology* 40 (2008): 529–35.

47. Plumwood, *Feminism and the Mastery of Nature* (London: Routledge, 1993), 101. Plumwood says this about modern Western culture more generally.

48. Jacob C. Eggert, "Life Cycle Impact Analysis of the Average Death in the United States: Inputs, Residuals, and Opinions of Primary Disposition Methods," master's thesis, University of Wisconsin-Green Bay, Environmental Science and Policy.

49. Richardson, *Death, Dissection and the Destitute*, 14–17.

50. World Health Organization, Flooding and Communicable Diseases Fact Sheet, http://www.who.int/hac/techguidance/ems/flood_cds/en/; Centers for Disease Control and Prevention, Information on Creutzfeldt-Jacob Disease for Funeral Home, Cemetery, and Crematory Practitioners, http://www.cdc.gov/ncidod/dvrd/cjd/funeral_directors.htm, accessed June 4, 2014.

51. Richardson, *Death Dissection and the Destitute*, 17.

52. Mary Douglas, *Purity and Danger: An Analysis of Concepts of Pollution and Taboo* (New York: Routledge, 1966), 2–3.

53. Thomas Laqueur, "Spaces of the Dead," *Ideas: The National Humanities Center* 8, no. 2 (2001): 10. Laqueur details this shift in nineteenth-century Europe, a history that parallels much of what was taking place in the United States.

54. For example, *CSI: Crime Scene Investigation* (2000–present), *Ghost Whisperer* (2005–2010), *True Blood* (2008–2014), *The Walking Dead* (2010–present), *The Returned* (2012–present).

55. Barbara Creed, "Horror and the Monstrous-Feminine: An Imaginary Abjection," *Screen* 27, no. 1 (1986): 44–71.

56. Julia Kristeva, *Powers of Horror: An Essay on Abjection* (New York: Columbia University Press, 1982), 3.

57. Plumwood, "Tasteless," 2008.

58. Evernden, *The Natural Alien*, 11–12.

CHAPTER 3

1. Not all indigenous peoples of North America practiced whole-body earth burial. For example, the Lakota, practiced scaffold burial, whereby the dead were placed in a box and elevated in a tree or scaffold seven to ten feet high. Once the body had been there for some time, the remains were taken down and buried. For many Lakota, scaffold burial is not a thing of the past.

2. See Donald P. Irish, Kathleen F. Lundquist, and Vivian Jenkins Nelsen, eds., *Ethnic Variations in Dying, Death and Grief: Diversity in Universality* (Philadelphia: Taylor & Francis, 1990). Also see Peter Metcalf and Richard Huntington, *Celebrations of Death: The Anthropology of Mortuary Ritual*, 2nd ed. (Cambridge: Cambridge University Press, 1991), 194.

3. Cremations and conventional burial numbers are neck and neck. A recent report from the NFDA predicts that in 2015 cremation rates will actually surpass conventional burial by two points. http://nfda.org/news-a-events/all-press-releases/4046-consumer-preference-for-cremation-expected-to-surpass-burial-in-2015.html.

4. This is commonly found in news and other popular stories about green burial.

5. Stephen Prothero, *Purified by Fire: A History of Cremation in America* (Berkeley: University of California Press, 2001), 46–47, and James J. Farrell, *Inventing the American Way of Death, 1830–1920* (Philadelphia: Temple University Press, 1980), 103.

6. See John Duffy, *A History of Public Health in New York, 1625–1866* (New York: Russell Sage, 1968); Sarah Hoglund, "Hidden Agendas: The Secret to Early Nineteenth-Century British Burial Reform," in *Victorian Secrecy: Economies of Knowledge and Concealment*, edited by Albert D. Pionke and Denise Tischler Millstein (Surrey: Ashgate, 2010); Prothero, *Purified by Fire*, 46–66; James J. Farrell, *Inventing the American Way of Death, 1830–1920* (Philadelphia: Temple University Press, 1980), 103; Gary Laderman, *The Sacred Remains: American Attitudes toward Death, 1799–1883* (New Haven: Yale, 1996), 69–70.

7. *New York Daily Times*, July 13, 1852, 2.

8. Prothero, *Purified by Fire*, 58.

9. Farrell, *Inventing the American Way of Death*, 102–3.

10. Duffy, *A History of Public Health in New York*, 220–22; Gary Laderman talks about it as "exile," *The Sacred Remains*, 69.

11. Prothero, *Purified by Fire*, 56.

12. Laderman, *The Sacred Remains*, 42, 48.

13. Mary Douglas, *Purity and Danger: An Analysis of Concept of Pollution and Taboo* (New York: Routledge, 1966), 50.

14. The ban on burials began in 1843 and in total force by 1858. Village of Rhinebeck Minutes, March 1, 843, April 30, 1844, November 12, 1858. Village of Rhinebeck Archive, Rhinebeck, New York.

15. United States Census, 1850. Index. *Family Search*. http://FamilySearch.org: accessed January 1, 2015. Citing NARA microfilm publication M432. Washington, D.C. Thank you to Beverly Kane for providing me with this statistic.

16. John Duffy, *The Sanitarians: A History of American Public Health* (Chicago: University of Illinois Press, 1992), 274.

17. Laderman, *The Sacred Remains*, 70.

18. Laderman, *The Sacred Remains*, 71. Also see M. G. Blanche Linden, *Silent City on a Hill: Picturesque Landscapes of Memory and Boston's Mount Auburn Cemetery* (Amherst: University of Massachusetts Press, 2007).

19. Laderman, *The Sacred Remains*, 44; Farrell, *Inventing the American Way of Death*, 106.

20. Farrell, *Inventing the American Way of Death*, 109.

21. Laderman, *The Sacred Remains*, 70.

22. David Charles Sloane, *The Last Great Necessity: Cemeteries in American History* (Baltimore: Johns Hopkins University Press, 1995), 2.

23. Farrell, *Inventing the American Way of Death*, 116.

24. Quoted from Farrell, *Inventing the American Way of Death*, 136. Also Alfred Farmar, "The Modern Cemetery: The Perpetual Care Lawn Plan," *Overland Monthly* 29 (April 1897): 440–47.

25. Farrell, *Inventing the American Way of Death*, 127.

26. Laderman, *The Sacred Remains*, 102.

27. Kenneth V. Iserson, MD, *Death to Dust: What Happens to Dead Bodies?* (New York: Galen Press, 2001), 240.

28. Laderman, *The Sacred Remains*, 152.

29. Gary Laderman, *Rest in Peace: A Cultural History of Death and the Funeral Home in Twentieth-Century America* (New York: Oxford University Press, 2003), 14–15.

30. Laderman, *The Sacred Remains*, 162.

31. Laderman, *The Sacred Remains*, 162–63.

32. Farrell, *Inventing the American Way of Death*, 160–62.

33. Laderman, *The Sacred Remains*, 160–61.

34. Jessica Mitford, *The American Way of Death* (New York: Simon and Schuster, 1963), 84.

35. Iserson, *Death to Dust*, 239.

36. Farrell, *Inventing the American Way of Death*, 163.

37. Iserson, *Death to Dust*, 232.

38. World Health Organization, Disposal of Dead Bodies in Emergency Conditions, http://www.who.int/water_sanitation_health/hygiene/envsan/tn08/en/, accessed January 23, 2015.

39. Lisa Carlson, *Caring for the Dead: Your Final Act of Love* (Hinesburg: Upper Access, 1987), 136–37.

40. Marsh, Tanya D. "Ebola, Embalming and the Dead: The Spread of Infectious Diseases," Wake Forest Law Review, Volume 2, 2014, 113–123.

41. Oliver Morgan and Claude de Ville de Goyet, "Dispelling Disaster Myths about Dead Bodies and Disease: The Role of Scientific Evidence and the Media," Special Report, *Pan American Journal of Public Health* 18, no. 1 (2005): 34–36.

42. Laderman, *The Sacred Remains*, 168.

43. Vanderlyn R. Pine, *Caretaker of the Dead: The American Funeral Director* (New York: Irvington, 1975), 16.

44. Iserson, *Death to Dust*, 216.

45. Farrell, *Inventing the American Way of Death*, 158; a status that is yet to be realized.

46. Laderman, *The Sacred Remains*, 29–30. See also Georganne Rundblad, "Exhuming Women's Premarket Duties in the Care of the Dead," *Gender and Society* 9, no. 2 (April 1995): 173–92.

47. Rundlad, "Exhuming Women's Premarket Duties in the Care of the Dead," 173–74.

48. Leroy Bowman, "The Effects of City Civilization," in *Passing: The Vision of Death in America*, edited by Charles O. Jackson (Westport, CT: Greenwood, 1977), 155.

49. Shirley Yee, *An Immigrant Neighborhood: Interethnic and Interracial Encounters in New York before 1930* (Philadelphia: Temple University Press, 2012), 87.

50. Yee, *An Immigrant Neighborhood*, 77–103, and F. C. Karla Holloway, *Passed On: African American Mourning Stories* (Durham: Duke, 2002), 6–17.

51. See Michel Foucault, *Discipline and Punish: Birth of the Prison* (New York: Random House, 1975).

52. John L. Konefes and Michael K. McGee, "Old Cemeteries, Arsenic, and Health Safety," in *Dangerous Places: Health, Safety and Archaeology*, edited by David A. Poirier and Kenneth L. Feder (Westport, CT: Bergin and Garvey, 2001). See also Jeremiah Chiappelli and Ted Chiappelli, "Drinking Grandma: The Problem of Embalming," *Journal of Environmental Health* 71, no. 5 (2008): 24–28. See also Alison L. Spongberg and Paul M. Becks, "Inorganic Soil Contamination from Cemetery Leachate," *Water, Air and Soil Pollution* 117 (2000): 313–27.

53. Chiappelli and Chiappelli, "Drinking Grandma," 25.

54. In 2011, the National Toxicology Program, an interagency program of the Department of Health and Human Services, named formaldehyde as a known human carcinogen in its *12th Report on Carcinogens* (3). It's also listed as a probable carcinogen by the Environmental Protection Agency. Studies show that embalming fluid, in fact, dissipates quite rapidly and that the greatest threat is to the embalmer.

55. Green Burial Council Statistic, 2014, that is the equivalent, the GBC says, to fill six Olympic-sized swimming pools.

56. Iserson, *Death to Dust*, 387–92.

57. Iserson, *Death to Dust*, 400.

58. Farrell, *Inventing the American Way of Death*, 171.

59. The word *casket* comes from the word *case*, and in the fifteenth century it referred to "a small ornamental box for holding jewels" (Oxford English Dictionary),

which may also reflect the shifting ideas of the value of the body at that time. Habenstein and Lamers suggest as much in *The History of American Funeral Directing* (Omnigraphics, 1990), as does James Farrell, who says that with the development of the casket the body comes to "supersede the soul in funeral service"; Farrell, *Inventing the American Way of Death*, 172.

60. Farrell, *Inventing the American Way of Death*, 148.

61. Farrell, *Inventing the American Way of Death*, 172.

62. Carlson, *Caring for the Dead*, 147.

63. Mitford, *The American Way of Death*, 85.

64. Stories of so-called exploding corpses are not the stuff of fiction. Under certain conditions, gases can build up in the abdomen, causing so much pressure that the organs and skin may break loose.

65. http://ensureaseal.com/and http://kryprotek.com/assembly/, accessed June 3, 2014.

66. Iserson, *Death to Dust*, 662.

67. Farrell, *Inventing the American Way of Death*, 99.

68. Anne Marie Somma, "Muslims Reconcile Burial Rights, State Rules," *The Courant*, February 18, 2008, http://articles.courant.com/2008-02-18/news/0802180012_1_united-muslim-masjid-islamic-law-mosque, accessed September 2, 2014; also see David Zinner, "Breathing New Life into Jewish Funeral Practice," *Kavod v'Nichum*, http://www.jewish-funerals.org/Breathing.

69. http://www.wilbert.com/funeral-professionals/tools-resources/videos/, accessed September 4, 2014.

70. GBC 2014 statistics, compiled with Mary Woodsen. That's the equivalent, the GBC says, to seventy-seven thousand trees and enough concrete to create a two-lane highway stretching from San Francisco to Kansas City.

71. Spongberg and Becks, "Inorganic Soil Contamination from Cemetery Leachate," 313–27.

72. Wilbert invented the first asphalt-lined vault in 1930, later developed one made of copper, and lastly one made of plastic in 1967.

73. The cremation was the body of a man named Baron Joseph Henry Charles De Palm. For more on this cremation, see Prothero's *Purified by Fire*.

74. Farrell, *Inventing the American Way of Death*, 164.

75. Prothero, *Purified by Fire*, 56.

76. Prothero, *Purified by Fire*, 39–40.

77. Farrell, *Inventing the American Way of Death*, 167.

78. Prothero, *Purified by Fire*, 107. Still, there were some who abhorred this take on burning and sought to sell cremation through other arguments, including a return to nature.

79. Prothero, *Purified by Fire*, 153–57.

80. Prothero, *Purified by Fire*, 168. The same year Mitford's book came out, the Vatican relaxed the ban on cremation, allowing Catholics the possibility of choosing cremation and still having a church funeral. See Prothero, *Purified by Fire*, 165.

81. Prothero, *Purified by Fire*, 178. He suggests that John Lennon's cremation played a key role in this shift.

82. Mitford, *The American Way of Death*, 16.

83. Ambrose Bierce, *The Devil's Dictionary* (London: Sovereign Classic, 2014), 46.

84. Prothero, *Purified by Fire*, 183.

85. NFDA Trends and Statistics, nfda.org/about-funeral-service-trends-and-statistics.html.

86. Iserson, *Death to Dust*, 303.

87. GBC 2014 statistic, compiled by Mary Woodsen with the Green Burial Council in "Trips to the Moon: Cremation and Energy Use in the U.S."

88. Iserson, *Death to Dust*, 309–10.

89. Mari Montse and Jose L. Domingo, "Toxic Emissions from Crematories: A Review," *Environmental International* 36, no. 1 (2010): 131–37.

90. Outside of the United States, recognition of the polluting effects of incineration (contained or uncontained, wood or petroleum fired) has led to the first experimental solar crematory near Goraj Ashram, in Gujarat, India.

91. "Dead May Face Emissions Controls," *Power Engineering*, September 2006.

92. Susan R. Maloney, Carol A. Phillips, and Allan Mills, "Mercury in the Hair of Crematoria Workers," *The Lancet* 352 no. 9140 (November 14, 1998). In parts of India, open-air pyres have come under considerable scrutiny for their pollution, and the government has been seeking out alternative "greener" solutions. Teo Kermeliotis, "India's Burning Issue with Emissions from Hindu Funeral Pyres," CNN World News, September 17, 2011, http://www.cnn.com/2011/09/12/world/asia/india-funeral-pyres-emissions/, accessed January 20, 2015.

93. Harry Bradford, "Cremation on the Rise Due to Struggling Economy," *Huffington Post*, December 14, 2011, http://www.huffingtonpost.com/2011/12/13/cremation-struggling economy_n_1146955.html?1323873627&ncid=webmail11, accessed June 3, 2014.

94. "Attorney Says Mercury Poisoning May Explain Tri-State Crematory Case," Chattanoogan.com, February 7, 2007.

95. Doug Grow, "Regulating Cremations' Mercury Emissions Proves as Hard as Pulling Teeth," *Minnesota Post*, February 18, 2013. See also "Final Report of the Senate Crematoria Study Committee," State Research Office, Atlanta, Georgia, 2012.

96. Kimberly M. Baga, "Taking a Bite out of the Harmful Effects of Mercury in Dental Fillings: Advocating for National Legislation for Mercury Amalgams," *Journal of Law and Health* 20 (2006): 169.

97. Minnesota, Maine, Vermont, and Colorado have all proposed legislation. Paige Christiansen and Mickensi Larson, "Mercury Removal Prior to Cremation: A Collaboration of Dentistry and Mortuary Science to Prevent Environmental Contamination," *DEC* 23, no. 10 (2009), 14–15.

98. MedicineNet.com, Mercury Poisoning Facts, http://www.medicinenet.com/mercury_poisoning/article.htm#mercury_poisoning_facts, accessed June 5, 2014.

99. Mad hatters is a term given to Huguenot hat makers who used mercury in their manufacturing.

100. It remains a peculiar truth that the story of Marsh's alleged mercury poisoning was never fully taken up outside the announcement of it. Even if it wasn't the whole truth, pursuing that environmental story in determining what transpired at the Tri-State Crematory might have opened up a better understanding of why it happened

and could have helped with long-sought-out answers. The feature film about the incident, *Sahkanaga*, foretells a different and, perhaps, repaired future. In Cherokee, *Sahkanaga* (pronounced sock-uh-nogga) means "Great Blue Hills of the Gods." In Summerour's summoning of the land and the spirits within it, he seems to know the gods were watching. Such deleterious acts may happen in spite of human blindness, but the land remains a witness to the dead all the same.

101. Prothero, *Purified by Fire*, 178.

102. Carlson, *Caring for the Dead*, 150. In nineteen states embalming is not required "under any circumstances." In other states, embalming can be required in certain circumstances. For example, if the body is being transported across state lines or if the body has a known infectious disease. See Slocum and Carlson, 2011, 57.

CHAPTER 4

1. Interview with Jodie Buller, June 13, 2014.

2. Interview with Lee Webster, September 14, 2014.

3. In the past two or three years, Woodsen estimates she's given about three dozen such talks, taking varied approaches to her groups. Mary Woodsen, email message to author, September 30, 2014.

4. Interview with Freddie Johnson, May 23, 2014.

5. https://amyacunningham.wordpress.com/contact/.

6. Michel Foucault, *Power/Knowledge: Selected Interviews and Other Writings, 1972–1977*, edited by Colin Gordon. New York: Pantheon Books, 1980, 81–85.

7. Gregory Dicum, "Green-Burial Movement Gets More Ambitious," *Grist*, July 28, 2006, http://grist.org/article/dicum2/, accessed November 4, 2014.

8. This culminated in the landmark book *Our Bodies, Ourselves*, published by the Boston Women's Health Collective, now in its ninth edition.

9. Jerri Lyons and Janell Va Melvin, *Final Passages: A Family-Directed Funeral Lying-in-Honor in a Home*, 1999.

10. In 2014 the NHFA touted more than five hundred members. http://www.homefuneralalliance.org/.

11. Interview with Lee Webster, September 14, 2014.

12. Email exchange with Amy Cunningham, January 20, 2015.

13. Interview with Bob Fertig, January 14, 2015.

14. Feminist theorists have also talked about subjugated knowledges, especially those wrought through racism, sexism, classism, and neocolonialism. See Patricia Hill Collins, *Black Feminist Thought: Knowledge, Consciousness, and the Politics of Empowerment*, 2nd ed. (New York: Taylor and Francis, 1999).

15. Over seventy zombie-themed feature films were released in 2013 in the United States. AMC's wildly popular *The Walking Dead* (2010) is now in its fifth season.

16. http://theconversationproject.org/, accessed September 1, 2014.

17. Interview with Ann Ellice Parker, June 16, 2014.

18. Shirley J. Yee, *An Immigrant Neighborhood: Interethnic and Interracial Encounters in New York before 1930* (Philadelphia: Temple University Press), 85–103.

19. Angelika Krüger-Kahloula, "On the Wrong Side of the Fence: Racial Segregation in American Cemeteries," in *History and Memory in African American Culture*, by Genevieve Fabre (New York: Oxford University Press, 1994), 141–42.

20. Karla F. C. Holloway, *Passed On: African American Mourning Stories* (Durham: Duke University Press, 2002), 202.

21. Holloway, *Passed On*, 203.

22. Holloway, *Passed On*, 201. See also Krüger-Kahloula, "On the Wrong Side of the Fence." See also Jacob Long, "Death and Burials: The Final Frontier for Segregation," *First Coast News*, April 30, 2014.

23. Krüger-Kahloula, "On the Wrong Side of the Fence," 134.

24. Krüger-Kahloula, "On the Wrong Side of the Fence," 140.

25. Holloway, *Passed On*, 151.

26. Interview with Adriana Corral, July 22, 2014.

27. http://deathcafe.com, accessed April 20, 2015.

28. Ann Hutton, "Death Café Convenes in Kingston," *Almanac Weekly*, August 23, 2013.

29. Interview with Lee Webster, September 15, 2014.

30. *The Basic Rules of Islamic Funerals*, compiled by Mohamed Baianonie, imam of the Islamic Center of Raleigh, North Carolina.

31. Code of Jewish Law, Yorah Deah, 348:3, 362:1.

32. Genesis 2:7; Genesis 3:19. Also see Maurice Lamm, *The Jewish Way in Death and Mourning*, (Jonathan and David Publishers, 2000), 54-55.

33. Email exchange with Rabbi Stuart Kelman, February 27, 2012 and January 11, 2015.

34. Amanda Pazornik, "'Today Is about Forever': 1st Green Jewish Cemetery Opens," JWeekly.com, April 1, 2010, http://www.jweekly.com/article/full/57642/today-is-about-forever-1st-green-jewish-cemetery-opens1/, accessed November 14, 2014.

35. Leon Cohen, "Greenwood Cemetery to Offer 'Green Burials,'" May 1, 2014, http://www.jewishchronicle.org/article.php?article_id=15132, accessed December 1, 2014.

36. Benjamin Stewart, "Committed to the Earth: Ecotheological Dimensions of Christian Burial Practices," *Liturgy* 27, no. 2 (February 2012): 70.

37. Brian Nearing, "To Lie Down in Green Pastures," Timesunion.com, June 22, 2012, http://www.timesunion.com/business/article/To-lie-down-in-green-pastures-3653992.php, accessed December 1, 2014.

38. Interview with Rick Touchette, January 29, 2015.

39. Interview with Father Charles Morris, June 20, 2014.

40. Harris, *Grave Matters*, 156.

41. David Abram, *The Spell of the Sensuous: Perception and Language in a More-Than-Human World* (New York: Vintage, 1997). Philosophers have long taught the value in truths gleaned through the kind of direct experience Abram believes in; see Environmental Phenomenology.

42. See F. Marina Schauffler, *Turning to Earth: Stories of Ecological Conversion* (Charlottesville: University of Virginia Press, 2003). Schauffler demonstrates that such ecological conversion experiences vary.

43. Val Plumwood, "Being Prey." *Utne Reader*, July/August 2000.

44. Aldo Leopold, *A Sand County Almanac* (New York: Oxford, 1949), 130.

45. Val Plumwood, "Tasteless: Towards a Food Based Approach to Death," in *The Eye of the Crocodile*, edited by Lorraine Shannon (Canberra: ANU E Press, 2012), 94.

46. Thomas Berry, "The World of Wonder," in *Spiritual Ecology: The Cry of the Earth*, edited by Llewellyn Vaughan-Lee (Golden Sufi Center, 2013), 19. Berry says this with respect to nature more generally.

47. Interview with Brian Flowers with Jodie Buller, November 27, 2013, "Speak Up, Speak Out," Skagit Valley College Radio http://24.113.141.253/mp3/suso-2013-11-27-Natural Burial With Brian Flowers. mp3, accessed August 4, 2014.

48. Interview with Freddie Johnson, May 23, 2014.

49. Mary Woodsen, email message to author, September 30, 2014. Also, informal conversation at Green Burial Council Summit, Santa Fe, October 2011.

CHAPTER 5

1. Interview with Lee Webster, September 15, 2014.

2. Interview with Freddie Johnson, May 23, 2014.

3. Interview with Jodie Buller, June 13, 2014.

4. NFDA, http://nfda.org/media-center/trends-in-funeral-service.html#personalization, accessed December 9, 2014.

5. Alyssa Newcomb, "Dead People Get Life-Like Poses at Their Funeral," ABCNews.com, June 13, 2014, http://abcnews.go.com/US/dead-people-life-poses-funerals/story?id=23456853, accessed September 14, 2014; Emma Green, "Burying Your Dead without Religion." *The Atlantic*, August 19, 2014; see Holy Smoke, LLC, http://www.myholysmoke.com/, accessed September 14, 2014; see Life Gem http://www.lifegem.com/, accessed September 14, 2014.

6. Clifford Geertz, *The Interpretation of Cultures* (New York: Basic Books, 1973), 112.

7. Val Plumwood, *Feminism and the Mastery of Nature* (London: Routledge, 1983), 101–2.

8. Ellen McCarthy, "'Green Burials' Are on the Rise as Baby Boomers Plan for Their Future, and Funerals," *Washington Post*, October 6, 2014.

9. NHFREA, NHfuneral.org brochure, http://www.nhfuneral.org/NHFREA_Green_Burial_brochure.pdf, accessed October 2, 2014.

10. Roberta Angerman, http://www.foxfieldpreserve.org/home/natural-burials/, accessed October 7, 2014.

11. Aldo Leopold, "The Round River: A Parable of Conservation," *A Sand County Almanac and Other Writings on Ecology and Conservation* (Library of America, 2014).

12. Gig Schlich, "Burying Tradition," *The Planet Magazine*, Winter 2005.

13. http://www.naturalburialcompany.com/, retrieved October 7, 2014.

14. Pearsall, Peter. "Green Burials" *The Planet Magazine*, Winter 2008.

15. Douglas Davies and Hannah Rumble, *Natural Burial: Traditional-Secular Spiritualities and Funeral Innovation* (London: Continuum, 2012), 98. Also see

Lewis Hyde's wonderful book *The Gift: Creativity and the Artist in the Modern World* (New York: Vintage, 2007).

16. Davies and Rumble, *Natural Burial*, 101–2.

17. Jane Caputi, "Feeding Green Fire," *Journal for the Study of Religion, Nature and Culture* 5, no. 4 (2011): 410–36.

18. Davies and Rumble, *Natural Burial*.

19. In Hannah Rumble, John Troyer, Tony Walter, and Kate Woodthorpe, "Disposal or Dispersal? Environmentalism and Final Treatment of the British Dead," *Mortality* 19, no. 3 (2014), the authors suggest that a "new ecological mentality is now framing the management of the dead. Along with green burial, new death care practices (like cremation and alkaline hydrolysis and promession) throughout Britian are "dispersing" rather than "disposing" of the dead—giving the dead back to "environments that sustain the living."

20. NHFA and FCA, "Restoring Families' Right to Choose: The Call for Funeral Legislation Change in America," May 2012.

21. Thomas G. Long and Thomas Lynch, *The Good Funeral: Death, Grief, and the Community of Care* (Louisville: Westminster John Knox Press, 2013), 210–11.

22. This was true with all the green burial ground owners and operators I've spoken with over the years. Green burial grounds also often express this through their literature. (See Duck Run website, for instance, where they say that "families are encouraged to be involved in services as much as they are comfortable with.")

23. Interview with Ed Bixby, October 5, 2014.

24. Interview with Jodie Buller, June 13, 2014.

25. Interview with Lee Webster, September 15, 2014.

26. Interview with Lee Webster, September 15, 2014.

27. Interview with Bob Fertig, January 14, 2015.

28. Benjamin M. Stewart, "Committed to the Earth: Ecotheological Dimensions of Christian Burial Practices," *Liturgy* 27, no. 2, (2012): 67.

29. Writer and funeral director Thomas Lynch has made much of this. See *The Undertaking: Life Studies from the Dismal Trade* (New York: W. W. Norton, 1997). Also, Long and Lynch, *The Good Funeral.*

30. Jessican Mitford. *The American Way of Death.* New York: Simon and Schuster, 1963.

31. See *The Good Funeral Store*, http://funerals.naturalburialcompany.com/, accessed November 10, 2014.

32. http://www.ecopod.co.uk/, accessed November 10, 2014.

33. This green burial ground was to be part of the not-for-profit conservation-based community development initiative put forth by Commonweal Conservancy's planned Stewardship Community. Director Ted Harrison insists the community is still in the works, which includes plans for a green burial ground, although it's been over ten years in the making.

34. Interview with Brian Flowers, October 7, 2014.

35. Interview with Brian Flowers, October 6, 2014.

36. Interview with Billy Campbell, September 26, 2014.

37. Email exchange with Bob Jenkins, October 3, 2014. The company has recently been endorsed by the Auckland Council (local New Zealand government) as a viable

organic solution for families wanting to scatter or bury human cremated remains. Email exchange with Bob Jenkins, February 2, 2015.

38. Interview with Billy Campbell, September 26, 2014.

39. Interview with Kenneth Kyger, June 10, 2014.

40. Email exchange with Brian Flowers, November 25, 2014.

41. Jae Rhim Lee's Mushroom Death Suit, functions on a similar premise. Lee calls it The Infinity Burial Suit. Now only a prototype, the dead are dressed in the garment, which is embroidered with mycelium spores. In addition, the body is also adorned with a mushroom slurry of sorts, a kind of makeup that is applied to the body. All this, Lee suggests, aids in decomposition, although there's no evidence the dead body needs additional help breaking down. http://infinityburialproject.com/burial-suit, accessed December 20, 2014.

42. Michael Pollan, "The Problem with Monocultures," Georgia Organics Conference, http://www.mnn.com/your-home/organic-farming-gardening/videos/michael-pollan-the-problem-with-monocultures, accessed November 22, 2014. Also see *The Omnivore's Dilemma: A History of Four Meals,* Penguin, 2006.

43. Wes Jackson, "Can We Restore the Prairie—And Still Support Ourselves?" *Yes! Magazine*, November 22, 2011.

44. Jane Caputi, "Mother Earth Meets the Anthropocene: An Intersectional Feminist Analysis," In *World Turning!: New Perspectives on Race, Class, Gender, and Global Climate Change and Sustainability*, edited by Phoebe C. Godfrey and Denise Torres. Forthcoming Routledge 2015.

45. Steelmantown, Ramsey Creek, White Eagle, and Greensprings, for instance, do not remound.

46. John Campanelli, "Ohio's Only 'Green' Cemetery Lets You Rest in Peace, in Nature," *The Plain Dealer*, March 20, 2011, http://www.cleveland.com/pdq/index.ssf/2011/03/ohios_only_green_cemetery_lets.html, accessed November 14, 2014.

47. Interview with Brian Flowers, October 6, 2014.

48. John Campanelli, "Ohio's Only 'Green' Cemetery Lets You Rest in Peace, in Nature," *The Plain Dealer*, March 20, 2011, http://www.cleveland.com/pdq/index.ssf/2011/03/ohios_only_green_cemetery_lets.html, accessed November 14, 2014.

49. Interview with Joel Rabinowitz, October 13, 2011.

50. Interview with Ed Bixby, October 5, 2014.

51. Val Plumwood, "The Cemetery Wars: Cemeteries, Biodiversity and the Sacred," *Local-Global: Indentity, Security, Community* 3 (2007): 67.

52. Jane Salmon, "Story of the Burial of Val Plumwood," https://www.google.com/?gws_rd=ssl#q=val+plumwood+burial, accessed January 15, 2015.

CHAPTER 6

1. Leopold, *A Sand County Almanac*, 216.

2. Leslie Marmon Silko, "Landscape, History and the Pueblo Imagination," *Antaeus* 57 (Autumn 1986).

3. Val Plumwood, "The Concept of Cultural Landscape: Nature, Culture and Agency in the Land," *Ethics & The Environment* 11, no. 2 (2006): 123–24.

4. Silko, "Landscape, History and the Pueblo Imagination," 2002.

5. Dan Shilling, "Aldo Leopold Listens to the Southwest," *Journal of the Southwest* 51, no. 3 (Autumn 2009).

6. Aldo Leopold, "Wilderness as a Form of Land Use," In *The Great Wilderness Debate*, edited by J. Baird Callicott and Michael P. Nelson (Athens: University of Georgia Press, 1998)..

7. Carolyn Merchant, *Ecological Revolutions: Nature, Gender & Science in New England*, 2nd ed. (Chapel Hill: University of North Carolina Press, 2010), 277–79.

8. Memorial Ecosystems, http://www.memorialecosystems.com/conservation-burial/tabid/110/default.aspx, accessed December 15, 2014.

9. Interview with Kimberley Campbell, May 18, 2014.

10. In "Proud and Humbled," Joe Sehee talks about coining the term *conservation burial*. Joe Sehee, "Proud and Humbled," *Natural Transitions* 3, no. 2 (2014): 18–21.

11. Sehee, "Proud and Humbled."

12. Right now Ramsey Creek stewards a total of seventy-eight acres.

13. Campbell's Memorial Ecosystems has consulted on a number of Conservation burial projects over the year, including Honey Creek Woodlands in Conyers, Georgia; Prairie Creek Conservation Cemetary in Gainesville, Florida; and Foxfield Preserve in Wilmot, Ohio.

14. Email exchange with Billy Campbell, January 16 and 19, 2015.

15. These make up the key criteria for Conservation burial. But there are other criteria. For a full breakdown of the standards for Conservation burial and for the other two certification levels, Natural and Hybrid, see Green Burial Council, "Burial Grounds Standards/Eco-Rating System," http://greenburialcouncil.org/wp-content/uploads/2014/11/CemeteryIntroInfo-Hybrid_Nat_Cons-2.pdf, accessed December 15, 2014.

16. The NHFA tracks the emergence of green cemeteries in the United States, those certified by the GBC and those not; http://www.homefuneralalliance.org/Resources/Documents/Green%20Cemeteries%20List%20.pdf, accessed December 28, 2014.

17. Upstate Forever, http://upstateforever.org/about-us/, accessed December 15, 2014. Ramsey Creek was the first burial grounds to be certified by the GBC at the conservation burial ground level. Joe Sehee talks about this too in "Proud and Humbled."

18. Interview with Billy Campbell, September 26, 2014; interview with Jodie Buller, June 13, 2014; interview with Sara Brink, June 10, 2014; interview with Freddie Johnson, May 23, 2014.

19. Stephen F. Christy Jr., "The Final Stop for Land Trusts," *The Land Trust Alliance*, Spring 2007. Also see Alexandra Harker's "Landscapes of the Dead: An Argument for Conservation Burial," in *Berkeley Planning Journal* 25, no. 1 (2012).

20. Phone interview with Stephen F. Christy, Jr., June 17, 2014.

21. Interview with Sara Brink, June 10, 2014.

22. Mandie Trimble, "Northeast Ohio Land Preserve Offers Alternative to Modern Burials," *WOSU Public Media*, http://wosu.org/2012/news/2012/07/17/northeast-ohio-land-preserve-offers-alternative-to-modern-burials/, accessed December 15, 2014.

23. Interview with Sara Brink, June 10, 2014.

24. Pam Graham, "The Tallgrass Prairie: An Endangered Landscape," *ProQuest Discovery Guides*, November 2011.

25. Bob Downing, "Ohio Pioneer Cemeteries Shelter Remnants of Tallgrass Prairie That Once Covered the Darby Plains," *Akron Beacon Journal*, October 24, 2014, http://www.ohio.com/lifestyle/ohio-travel/ohio-pioneer-cemeteries-shelter-remnants-of-tallgrass-prairie-that-once-covered-the-darby-plains-1.534910, accessed December 15, 2014.

26. Alachua Conservation Trust, http://alachuaconservationtrust.org/index.php?/alachua_v2/current_projects, accessed December 15, 2014.

27. Aldo Leopold, "Wilderness as a Form of Land Use," 77.

28. Interview with Stephen F. Christy, Jr., June 27, 2014.

29. Interview with Billy Campbell, September 26, 2014.

30. Interview with Jodie Buller, June 13, 2014.

31. Windward Education and Research Center, http://www.windward.org/internship/stprog.htm, accessed December 15, 2014.

32. Interview with Andrew Schreiber, June 17, 2014.

33. Interview with Stephen J. Christy, Jr., June 27, 2014.

34. Interview with Sara Brink, June 10, 2014.

35. Interview with Ed Bixby, October 5, 2014, and, also, Green Funeral Service Desk Reference, chapter 8, edited by Thomas A. Parmalee.

36. Interview with Ed Bixby, October 5, 2014.

37. Interview with Katey Bean, January 4, 2015.

38. Interview with Joel Rabinowtz, October 13, 2011

39. Interview with Ed Bixby, October 5, 2014.

40. Email correspondence with Ellen Macdonald, December 28, 2014.

41. Interview with Kenneth Kyger, June 11, 2014.

42. This green burial ground was established in 2011 and is featured in the film *A Will for the Woods*.

43. Email correspondence with Dyanne Matzkevich, January 7, 2015.

44. Interview with Dr. Bernard McEvoy, December 30, 2014.

45. Email correspondence with Billy Campbell, January 5, 2015.

46. http://www.greenburialma.org/, accessed January 16, 2015.

47. Interview with Judith Lorei, September 22, 2014.

48. http://greenburialcouncil.org/wp-content/uploads/2014/08/CemeteryIntroInfo-Hybrid_Nat_Cons-1.pdf, accessed January 15, 2015.

49. Phone correspondence with Kate Kalanick, January 5, 2015.

50. Email correspondence with Billy Campbell, January 5, 2015.

51. Interview with Kim Sorvig, January 10, 2015.

52. Interview with Joe Sehee January 6, 2015.

53. E-mail exchange with Billy Campbell, January 5, 2015.

54. The most revised standards will require that all burial containers be biodegradable for all three certification levels. This is a slight change in language from before. The hybrid level does not currently require them. Hybrids are in compliance if they "accommodate" them.

55. Interview with Kate Kalanick, January 5, 2015.

56. Email correspondence with Samuel Bar, June 11, 2014, and January 4, 2015.

57. Jodie Buller confirmed that one burial included a body flown in from Boston to White Eagle. Ed Bixby told me about a body flown in to Steelmantown, New Jersey, from somewhere in California.

58. D'Vera Cohn and Rich Morin, "Who Moves? Who Stays Put? Where's Home?" Pew Research—Social & Demographic Trends, December 29, 2008, http://www.pewsocialtrends.org/2008/12/17/who-moves-who-stays-put-wheres-home/, accessed January 3, 2015.

59. Interview with Katey Bean, January 4, 2015.

60. In academic circles this is most often referred to as "cultural landscapes." Still, Plumwood warns against the term. While "landscape" can have the effect of splintering nature and strengthening the human/nature split, "cultural landscapes" (which is meant to sew the human back into the realm of nature) can sometimes have the effect of denying agency in nature. For her, not unlike Silko, it's simply better to talk about the land (See Val Plumwood, "The Concept of a Cultural Landscape: Nature, Culture and Agency in the Land," *Ethics & the Environment* 11, no 2 [2006]).

61. Marty Durlin, "The Shot Heard Round the West," *High Country News*, February 1, 2010.

62. Greenville TEDx Talk with Dr. Billy Campbell, https://www.youtube.com/watch?v=OyA0VLzOPPA, accessed January 16, 2015. Campbell is admittedly influenced by the work of the restoration ecologist, William Jordan III, whose *Sunflower Forest* (2003) presents restoration ecology as an antidote to a conservation built on preservation—the kind that regards human presence as interference and trouble. As Jordan sees it, restoration ecology requires tending to the land through active methods (e.g., burning, removing invasive vegetation, sowing seeds), and in so doing puts us in direct relationship with a nature from which we've been severed. See William Jordan III, *The Sunflower Forest: Ecological Restoration and the New Communion with Nature* (Los Angeles: University of California Press, 2003). He mentions the work of Billy Campbell's memorial ecosystems in the book, 199.

63. Billy Campbell, email exchange, January 15, 2015.

64. Of course, this would require that Hybrids pay attention to landscape-level conservation, something that's not now required by the GBC. This is something Billy Campbell recommends. In fact, he provided a list of possible revisions to the GBC standards revision committee in 2014, including ways hybrids could begin to do this. Email exchange with Billy Campbell, January 15, 2015.

65. Mount Auburn website, http://mountauburn.org/2013/natural-burial/, accessed January 4, 2015.

66. Val Plumwood, *Feminism and the Mastery of Nature* (London: Routledge, 1993), 196. Plumwood is not saying this about green burial, only with respect to more generally giving back to the earth.

67. Interview with Andrew Schreiber, June 17, 2014.

68. Douglas Davies and Hannah Rumble, *Natural Burial: Traditional-Secular Spiritualities and Funeral Innovation* (London: Continuum, 2012), 97–108.

69. Davies and Rumble, *Natural Burial*, 101.

70. Nancy Bazilchuk, "Last Wishes: Green Cemeteries Fund Conservation," *Conservation Magazine* 8, no. 1 (January–March 2007).

CHAPTER 7

1. Leopold, *A Sand County Almanac*, viii.

2. In 2010, Cassity's father and brother would plead guilty to charges of insurance fraud, taking money from preneed sales that were to be held in trust. Tyler was not involved in the crime. In "Proud and Humbled (*Natural Transitions* 3, no. 2 [2014])," Joe Sehee said the fear that Tyler's father might become involved in Fernwood ultimately gave him great trepidation about the project.

3. Tad Friend, "The Shroud of Marin," *The New Yorker*, August 29, 2005.

4. Sehee, "Proud & Humbled." Also, interview with Joe Sehee, January 6, 2015.

5. Email exchange with Billy Campbell, January 15, 2015.

6. Email exchange with Billy Campbell, January 20, 2015.

7. Interview with Joe Sehee, January 6, 2015. Email exchange with Billy Campbell, January 19, 2015.

8. Sehee, "Proud & Humbled."

9. Interview with Joe Sehee, January 7, 2015.

10. Jordan wrote *The Sunflower Forest: Ecological Restoration and the New Communion With Nature* (Los Angeles: University of California Press, 2003).

11. Interview with Katey Bean, January 14, 2015.

12. Interview with Bob Fertig, January 14, 2015.

13. Interview with Katey Bean, January 4, 2015.

14. http://greenburialcouncil.org/, accessed December 15, 2015.

15. Certification for small farms runs between $600 and $1200, annually. http://www.ccof.org/, accessed January 11, 2015.

16. Interestingly enough, more and more municipalities are actually adopting LEED standards for their own codes, making them a regulatory body. Kim Sorvig, who actually served on the committee for the first major revision of LEED, said the standards have never been intended for such a use. Such green consumer authoritarianism is hotly debated at the local level.

17. Interview with Father Charles Morris, June 20, 2014.

18. Interview with Kim Sorvig, January 10, 2015.

19. The most recent GBC standards revisions were made in 2015.

20. Interview with Kim Sorvig, January 10, 2015.

21. http://greenburialcouncil.org/wp-content/uploads/2014/07/4PartBurialGuide.pdf.

22. At last count, in January 2015, there were fifty-three. Email exchange Kate Kalanick, January 12, 2015.

23. For example, the fee for second tier certification (Natural burial ground) runds $495 for the first year and $295 for each year thereafter.

24. Interview with Joe Sehee, July 7, 2015.

25. Kimberley Campbell, Green Burial Council Summit, Santa Fe, New Mexico, November 11, 2011.

26. Interview with Joe Sehee, July 7, 2015.

27. National Funeral Directors Association, http://nfda.org/about-funeral-service-/trends-and-statistics.html; Gary Laderman, *Rest in Peace: A Cultural History of Death and the Funeral Home in Twentieth Century America* (New York: Oxford

University Press, 2003), 15, 18–19; National Funeral Directors Association, http://nfda.org/about-nfda-.html.

28. Joshua Solcum and Lisa Carlson, *Final Rights: Reclaiming the American Way of Death* (Hinesburg: Upper Access, 2011), 98–112.

29. Vin Gurrieri, "FTC Approves Divestitures in $1.4B Funeral Co. Merger," *Law 360*, August 14, 2014, http://www.law360.com/articles/567083/ftc-approves-divestitures-in-1-4b-funeral-co-merger, accessed January 16, 2015.

30. https://www.funerals.org/about-the-fca, accessed January 16, 2015.

31. Slocum and Carlson, *Final Rights*, 143.

32. http://nfda.org/media-center/trends-in-funeral-service.html, accessed January 15, 2015.

33. http://nfda.org/green-funeral-practices-certificate.html, accessed January 10, 2015.

34. http://www.funerals.org/newsandblogsmenu/blogdailydirge/369-nfdaopenlettergreenburial, accessed January 12, 2015. The Green Certification program began to be offered around 2010.

35. http://www.classicplasticscorp.com/cooling-blankets.html and http://www.enigma-champion.com/encyclopedia/encyclo658.pdf, accessed January 15, 2015.

36. Andrew Martin, "Despite Risk, Embalmers Still Embrace Preservative," *New York Times*, July 20, 2011, http://www.nytimes.com/2011/07/21/business/despite-cancer-risk-embalmers-stay-with-formaldehyde.html?pagewanted=all&_r=0, accessed January 16, 2015.

37. Email exchange with Amy Cunningham, January 16, 2015.

38. Interview with Rick Touchette, January 29, 2015.

39. Interview with Kimberley Campbell, May 18, 2014.

40. Interview with Joe Sehee, January 6, 2015.

41. http://www.homefuneralalliance.org/Resources/Documents/Restoring%20Families'%20Rights%20to%20Choose%20Final.pdf.

42. Interview with Lee Webster, September 14, 2014.

43. Interview with Judith Lorei, September 22, 2014.

44. Interview with Ellen Macdonald, December 28, 2014.

45. Interview with Kenneth Kyger, June 11, 2014.

46. http://www.honeycreekwoodlands.com/about.aspx, accessed January 16, 2015. The Campbells were hired as consultants for this project.

47. Interview with Kimberley Campbell, May 18, 2014, and Mark Harris, *Grave Matters: A Journey through the Modern Funeral Industry to a Natural Way of Burial* (New York: Scribner, 2007), 159.

48. Interview with Ed Bixby, October 5, 2014.

49. Interview with Freddie Johnson, May 23, 2014.

50. http://www.mountgrace.org/green-cemetery-initiative-seeks-local-land, accessed January 16, 2015.

51. Interview with Billy Campbell, September 26, 2014.

52. Conversation with Three Valley Conservation Trust executive director, Liz Woedl, January 6, 2015.

53. Mei Mei Evans, "'Nature' and Environmental Justice," in *The Environmental Justice Reader: Politics, Poetics and Pedagogy*, edited by Joni Adamson, Mei Mei Evans, and Rachel Stein (Tucson: University of Arizona Press, 2002), 181–93.

54. Adamson, Evans, and Stein, *The Environmental Justice Reader*, 4.

55. 1850 census: 84.6 percent of the U.S. population was rural, while 15.4 percent was urban. https://www.census.gov/population/censusdata/table-4.pdf, accessed January 20, 2015. Moreover, apart from the rural South, poverty rates for urban and rural areas are, today, fairly neck and neck. USDA Economic Research Service, http://www.ers.usda.gov/topics/rural-economy-population/rural-poverty-well-being/geography-of-poverty.aspx.

56. Karen Washington (Bronx, New York) and Will Allen (Milwaukee, Wisconsin) are great examples of urban farmers working to tie women, the poor, and people of color back to food production in urban areas. See Dan Shaw, "A Believer in Vacant Lots—Urban Farming's Grand Dame: Karen Washington," *The New York Times*, September 19, 2014, http://www.nytimes.com/2014/09/21/realestate/urban-farmings-grande-dame-karen-washington.html and Growing Power, Inc., http://www.growingpower.org/.

57. Community Profile: City of Schenectady Comprehensive Plan 2020, http://www.cityofschenectady.com/Schenectady2020/Community_Profile.pdf, accessed January 22, 2015. Vale is one hundred acres set within, what is now, the inner city of Schenectady, New York. But in the 1850s, Vale was built like every other rural cemetery of its time, on the outskirts of town. Even though rural cemeteries were built as civic institutions that eschewed the divisions of religion, race, and creed, the history of legal and self-segregation in the United States originally rendered Vale a largely white place of burial. In 1880, however, graves from the "colored cemetery" across town were moved to Vale after they'd been uncovered in the pilfering of sand for building construction. A couple of those graves were of two men involved in the Underground Railroad, one a runaway slave from Maryland, Moses Viney, and the other, Richard P. G. Wright, who helped smuggle many slaves to freedom. In fact, the National Park Service recognizes Vale Cemetery as part of the Underground Railroad Network to Freedom. And yet, in time, the city would build up around the cemetery, positioning it no longer as a bucolic oasis outside the city center. Populations in the neighborhoods surrounding the cemetery would change too, with many Guyenese living in the vicinity today. Interview with Dr. Bernard McEvoy, president of Vale Cemetery, December 30, 2014.

58. I borrow this term from Terrell Dixon. "Environmental Justice: A Roundtable Discussion with Simon Ortiz, Teresa Leal, Devon Peña, and Terrell Dixon," *The Environmental Justice Reader: Politics, Poetics and Pedagogy*, edited by Joni Adamson, Mei Mei Evans, and Rachel Stein (Tucson: University of Arizona Press, 2002), 19.

59. Interview with Kenneth Kyger, June 11, 2014.

60. Dan Blottenberger, "Final Resting Place isn't always so final in Germany," *Stars and Stripes,* June 29, 2010.

61. Email exchange with Bob Jenkins, February 2, 2015.

62. http://www.letyourlovegrow.com/, email exchange with Bob Jenkins, October 3, 2014.

63. See Hannah Rumble, John Troyer, Tony Walter, and Kate Woodthorpe, "Disposal or Dispersal? Environmentalism and Final Treatment of the British Dead," *Mortality* 9, no. 3 (2014): 243–60. In Europe, by 2020, all crematoria must reduce their mercury emissions to 100 percent. "In order to achieve these targets, crematoria emissions are cooled so the mercury can liquefy and be collected, which means that much of the emissions heat goes into the cooling system rather than up the chimney. The equipment that reduces emissions can, thus, also recycle heat, which can be used to heat either the crematorium building or other buildings nearby."

64. Only one place in the United States does open-air burning—less than a dozen a year, by permit—Crestone Cemetery in Colorado.

65. http://www.resomation.com/index_files/Page347.htm, accessed January 22, 2015.

66. Anthropologists Douglas Davies and Hannah Rumble wonder whether these two methods can contribute to an imagining of a future self after death in the way that green burial offers—"as an animate site that allows for a sense of participation of its present and future life form." *Natural Burial: Traditional-Secular Spiritualities and Funeral Innovation* (London: Continuum, 2012), 145.

67. Email exchange with Katrina Spade, January 27, 2015.

68. Interview with Katrina Spade, October 2, 2015.

69. John Collins Rudolf, "Into the Great Green Beyond," *New York Times*, June 30, 2010, http://green.blogs.nytimes.com/2010/06/30/into-the-big-green-beyond/?hp, accessed December 15, 2014.

70. Doug Manning, "Personalization Is More Than a Product," *The Director*, June 2002.

71. Derrick Jensen, "Forget Shorter Showers," *Orion Magazine*, June 2009.

CHAPTER 8

1. Interview with Kimberley Campbell, May 18, 2015.

2. Mary Daly makes the argument for a struggle for knowledge with the rise of gynecology in *Gyn/Ecology: The Metaethics of Radical Feminism* (Boston: Beacon Press, 1978). Also see Barbara Ehrenreich and Deirdre English, *Witches, Midwives and Nurses: A History of Women Healers* (New York: The Feminist Press, 1975).

3. *Moyers & Company*, television show, May 10, 2013.

4. Ibid.

5. *A Will for the Woods* (2013), feature documentary, Amy Browne, Jeremy Kaplan, Tony Hale, and Brian Wilson.

6. Online Etymology Dictionary, http://www.etymonline.com/index.php?term=social, accessed January 29, 2015.

7. Neil Evernden talks about "relationship as context" in *The Natural Alien: Humankind and Environment* (Toronto: University of Toronto Press, 1985), 133–44.

8. Supposedly from *The Origin of Species*. Darwin Correspondence Project.

9. Interview with Joel Rabinowitz, October 13, 2014.

10. "A. Carl Leopold Answers *Grist*'s Questions," June 12, 2007, http://grist.org/article/leopold/, accessed January 22, 2015.

11. Email exchange with Ellen Macdonald, December 28, 2014.

12. Interview with Kimberley Campbell, May 18, 2014.

13. Interview with Ann-Ellice Parker, June 16, 2014.

14. Interview with Adriana Corral, July 22, 2014.

15. Final Passages, http://finalpassagesbeta.com/?q=home.

16. http://www.homefuneralalliance.org/, accessed January 29, 2015. http://www.finalpassages.org/, accessed January 29, 2015.

17. https://www.funerals.org/. Also see these two books written by current FCA executive director and former FCA executive directors, Joshua Slocum and Lisa Carlson. Slocom, *Final Rights: Reclaiming the American Way of Death* (Hinesburg: Upper Access, 2011); Carlson, *Caring for the Dead: Your Final Act of Love* (Hinesburg: Upper Access, 1987).

18. Interview with Lee Webster, September 14, 2014.

19. Lisa Carlson, *Funeral Ethics Organization Newsletter,* "Black Eye for Green Burial Council," Spring/Summer 2008. Though Carlson has been critical of the GBC, her attacks in this piece are based on factually inaccurate information. Carlson was a prominent figure in death care reform in the United States, having acted as executive director of the Funeral Consumers Alliance for many years before writing this piece. She later founded FEC. Writer and funeral director Thomas Lynch, who is also criticized by Carlson in the newsletter, responded to her remarks in this letter: http://www.funeralethics.org/lynch.pdf. Lynch's letter incited an internal storm; the entire board of the FEC resigned. In a September 2008 edition of *Funeral Service Insider,* former FEC board member Ron Hast made the following statement about Carlson's attack on the GBC and Lynch: "What it ended up being was [Carlson's] bully pulpit with the credentials of the people that she pulled onto the board. For me, this came down to the fact that it was the straw that broke the camel's back. Lisa was completely out of order in this whole issue and went way beyond the level of ethics in her reporting."

20. Email exchange with Joe Sehee, January 29, 2015.

21. Ibid.

22. Joe Sehee resigned as executive director in 2012, although he remained a program manager for the GBC until January of 2014. He still works in an ex-officio capacity.

23. Interview with Kimberley Campbell, May 18, 2014. Campbell said this was the case with Ramsey Creek.

24. The Green Burial Council held two meetings to discuss its organizational structure and future, one just before founder Joe Sehee stepped down as executive director, in Santa Fe in November 2011 and another two-and-a-half years later in Ann Arbor, Michigan, in June 2014. I was in attendance at both organizational meetings and education was a top priority at both.

25. Interview with Freddie Johnson, May 23, 2014.

26. Interview with Lee Webster, September 14, 2014; interview with Kimberley Campbell, May 18, 2014.

27. Email exchange with John Eric Rolfstad, January 16, 2015.

28. Email exchange with Joe Sehee, January 31, 2015.

29. Ibid.

30. Interview with Ted Hollingsworth, October 17, 2014.

31. See Thomas Bender's "The 'Rural' Cemetary Movement: Urban Travail and the Appeal of Nature," *The New England Quarterly*, Vol. 47, no. 2 (June, 1974), 196–211.

32. Christopher G. Boone, Geoffrey L. Buckley, J. Morgan Grove, and Chona Sister, "Parks and People: An Environmental Justice Inquiry into Baltimore, Maryland," *Annals of the Association of American Geographers* 99, no. 4 (2009): 767–87.

33. American Society of Landscape Architects, "Interview with Majora Carter, Sustainable South Bronx, and Majora Carter Group," http://www.asla.org/contentdetail.aspx?id=20586, accessed January 29, 2015.

34. Cynthia Beal, "The Cemetery as a Habitat," *American Cemetery* (March 2012): 36–37.

35. Interview with Joellen Lampman, May 20, 2014.

36. Interview with Joe Sehee, January 30, 2015.

37. White Haven was the first cemetery to join Audubon International in 1998. Andrea Vittum, CCE, "The Cooperative Sanctuary Program: Enhancing Your Cemetery's Image and its Bottom Line," *International Cemetery & Funeral Management,* December 1998.

38. Interview with Tara Pepperman, Director of the ACSP Program, February 10, 2015.

39. Interview with Joellen Lampman, May 20, 2104.

40. Email exchange with Billy Campbell, January 19, 2015. See also Horatio Clare, "Coronation Meadows: A Flight for the Flower of England," The Telegraph, June 7, 2013, http://www.telegraph.co.uk/news/earth/countryside/10106160/Coronation-Meadows-A-fight-for-the-flower-of-England.html, accessed January 26, 2015.

41. Interview with Fr. Charles Morris, June 20, 2014.

42. In the Hudson Valley, for instance, the Roman Catholic Church owns more lands on the banks of the Hudson River than any other religious institution.

43. Benjamin Stewart, PhD, is associate professor of worship at Lutheran School of Theology at Chicago.

44. Interview with Benjamin Stewart, May 28, 2014.

45. Susan L. Flader and J. Baird Callicott, *The River of the Mother of God and Other Essays by Aldo Leopold* (Madison: The University of Wisconsin Press, 1991), 281.

46. Alice Walker, "Everything Is a Human Being," in *Living By the Word: Selected Writings, 1973–1987* (San Diego: Harcourt Brace & Company, 1981), 148.

EPILOGUE

1. I borrow this phrase from Jane Caputi. See Jane Caputi, "Feeding Green Fire," *Journal for the Study of Religion, Nature, and Culture* 5, no. 4 (2011): 410–36.

2. Thomas Cole, "Essay on American Scenery," *American Monthly Magazine* 1 (January 1836).

Bibliography

"A. Carl Leopold, Nature Activist, Answers *Grist*'s Questions," June 12, 2007. http://grist.org/article/leopold/. Accessed January 22, 2015.

Abram, David. *The Spell of the Sensuous: Perception and Language in a More-Than-Human World*. New York: Vintage Books, 1996.

Adamson, Joni, Mei Mei Evans, and Rachel Stein, eds. *The Environmental Justice Reader: Politics, Poetics & Pedagogy*. Tucson: University of Arizona Press, 2002.

American Society of Landscape Architects. "Interview with Majora Carter, Sustainable South Bronx, and Majora Carter Group." http://www.asla.org/contentdetail.aspx?id=20586. Accessed January 29, 2015.

Ariès, Philippe. *Western Attitudes toward Death: From the Middle Ages to the Present*. Baltimore: Johns Hopkins University Press, 1974.

Associated Press, "Three Philadelphia-Area Funeral Directors Nabbed in Scheme Selling Body Parts." Foxnews.com, October 4, 2007. http://www.foxnews.com/story/2007/10/04/three-philadelphia-area-funeral-directors-nabbed-in-scheme-selling-body-parts/. Accessed August 13, 2014.

Baga, Kimberly, M. "Taking a Bite out of the Harmful Effects of Mercury in Dental Fillings: Advocating for National Legislation for Mercury Amalgams." *Journal of Law and Health* 20 (2006): 169.

Barrett, Paul M. "Huge Funeral Chain Settles Graveyard Desecration Suit, Buries Financial Details." *Bloomberg Business Week*, February 28, 2014. http://www.businessweek.com/articles/2014-02-28/huge-funeral-chain-settles-graveyard-desecration-suit-buries-financial-details. Accessed November 22, 2014.

Battacharya, Shaoni. "Elephants Pay Homage to Dead Relatives." *New Scientist*, October 26, 2005. http://www.newscientist.com/article/dn8209-elephants-may-pay-homage-to-dead-relatives.html#.VLvfCGTF8mc.

Bazilchuk, Nancy. "Last Wishes: Green Burial Fund Conservation." *Conservation in Practice* 8, no. 1 (January–March 2007).

Beal, Cynthia. "The Cemetery as a Habitat." *American Cemetery*, March 2012.

Bender, Thomas. "The 'Rural' Cemetery Movement: Urban Travail and the Appeal of Nature," *The New England Quarterly*, Vol. 47, No. 2, (June, 1947), 196–211.

Berry, Thomas. *The Great Work: Our Way into the Future.* New York: Bell Tower, 1999.

———. "The World of Wonder." In *Spiritual Ecology: The Cry of the Earth.* Edited by Llewellyn Vaughan-Lee. Point Reyes: The Golden Sufi Center, 2013.

Blottenberger, Dan. "Final Resting Place isn't always so final in Germany," *Stars and Stripes,* June 29, 2010.

Boone, Christopher G., Geoffrey L. Buckley, J. Morgan Grove, and Chona Sister. "Parks and People: An Environmental Justice Inquiry into Baltimore, Maryland." *Annals of the Association of American Geographers* 99, no. 4 (2009).

Bosman, Julie, and Joseph Goldstein. "Timeline for a Body: 4 Hours in the Middle of a Ferguson Street." *New York Times*, August 23, 2014. http://www.nytimes.com/2014/08/24/us/michael-brown-a-bodys-timeline-4-hours-on-a-ferguson-street.html.

Boston Women's Health Book Collective. *Our Bodies, Ourselves.* New York: Touchstone, 2011.

Bowman, Leroy. "The Effects of City Civilization." In *Passing: The Vision of Death in America.* Edited by Charles O. Jackson. Westport: Greenwood, 1977.

Bradford, Harry. "Cremation on the Rise Due to Struggling Economy." *Huffington Post*, December 14, 2011. http://www.huffingtonpost.com/2011/12/13/cremation-struggling economy_n_1146955.html?1323873627&ncid=webmail11. Accessed June 3, 2014.

Buber, Martin. *I and Thou.* New York: Scribner and Sons, 1958.

Bynum, Caroline Walker. *Fragmentation and Redemption: Essays on Gender and the Human Body in Medieval Religion.* New York: Zone Books, 1991.

———. *Resurrection of the Body in Western Christianity.* New York: Columbia University Press, 1995.

Campanelli, John. "Ohio's Only 'Green' Cemetery Lets You Rest in Peace, in Nature." *Plain Dealer*, March 20, 2011. http://www.cleveland.com/pdq/index.ssf/2011/03/ohios_only_green_cemetery_lets.html. Accessed November 14, 2014.

Caputi, Jane. "Green Consciousness: Earth-Based Myth and Meaning in Shrek," *Ethics & the Environment* 12, no. 2 (2007): 23-44.

———. "Feeding Green Fire." *Journal for the Study of Religion, Nature, and Culture* 5, no. 4 (2011): 410–36.

———. "Introduction." *Journal of American Culture* 35, no. 1 (2012): 1–3.

———. "Mother Earth Meets the Anthropocene:An Intersectional Feminist Analysis" In *World Turning!: New Perspectives on Race, Class, Gender, and Global Climate Change and Sustainability*, edited by Phoebe C. Godfrey and Denise Torres. Forthcoming Routledge 2015.

Carlson, Lisa. *Caring for the Dead: Your Final Act of Love.* Hinesburg: Upper Access, 1987.

Carson, Rachel. *Silent Spring.* New York: Houghton Mifflin, 2002.

Carter, David O., and Mark Tibbett. "Does Repeated Burial of Skeletal Muscle Tissue (*Ovis aries*) in Soil Affect Subsequent Decomposition?" *Applied Soil Ecology* 40 (2008): 529–35.

Chiappelli, J., and T. Chiappelli. "Drinking Grandma: The Problem of Embalming." *Journal of Environmental Health* 71, no. 5 (December 2008): 24–28.

Christy, Jr., Stephen F. "The Final Stop for Land Trusts." *The Land Trust Alliance*, Spring 2007.

Clare, Horatio. "Coronation Meadows: A Flight for the Flower of England." *The Telegraph*, June 7, 2013. http://www.telegraph.co.uk/news/earth/countryside/10106160/Coronation-Meadows-A-fight-for-the-flower-of-England.html. Accessed January 26, 2015.

Cohen, Leon. "Greenwood Cemetery to Offer 'Green Burials.'" *Jewish Chronicle*, May 1, 2014. http://www.jewishchronicle.org/article.php?article_id=15132. Accessed December 1, 2014.

Cohn, D'Vera, and Rich Morin. "Who Moves? Who Stays Put? Where's Home?" Pew Research, Social & Demographic Trends, December 29, 2008. http://www.pewsocialtrends.org/2008/12/17/who-moves-who-stays-put-wheres-home/. Accessed January 3, 2015.

Collins, Patricia Hill. *Black Feminist Thought: Knowledge, Consciousness, and the Politics of Empowerment*, 2nd edition. New York: Taylor and Francis, 1999.

Creed, Barbara. "Horror and the Monstrous-Feminine: An Imaginary Abjection." *Screen* 27, no. 1 (1986): 44–71.

Daly, Mary. *Gyn/Ecology: The Metaethics of Radical Feminism*. Boston: Beacon Press, 1978.

Davies, Douglas, and Hannah Rumble. *Natural Burial: Traditional-Secular Spiritualities and Funeral Innovation*. London: Continuum, 2012.

"Dead May Face Emissions Controls." *Power Engineering*, September 2006.

Douglas, Mary. *Purity and Danger: An Analysis of Concepts of Pollution and Taboo*. New York: Routledge, 1966.

Downing, Bob. "Ohio Pioneer Cemeteries Shelter Remnants of Tallgrass Prairie That Once Covered the Darby Plains." *Akron Beacon Journal*, October 24, 2014. http://www.ohio.com/lifestyle/ohio-travel/ohio-pioneer-cemeteries-shelter-remnants-of-tallgrass-prairie-that-once-covered-the-darby-plains-1.534910. Accessed December 15, 2014.

Duffy, John. *The Sanitarians: A History of American Public Health*. Chicago: University of Illinois Press, 1992.

Dunlap, Riley E., and Angela G. Mertig, eds. *American Environmentalism: The U.S. Environmental Movement, 1970–1990*. Washington, DC: Taylor & Francis, 1992.

Durkheim, Émile. *The Elementary Forms of Religious Life*. London: G. Allen & Unwin, 1915.

Durlin, Marty. "The Shot Heard Round the West." *High Country News*, February 1, 2010.

Eggert, Jacob C. "Life Cycle Impact Analysis of the Average Death in the United States: Inputs, Residuals, and Opinions of Primary Disposition Methods." Master's Thesis, University of Wisconsin-Green Bay, Environmental Science and Policy.

Ehrenreich, Barbara, and Deirdre English. *Witches, Midwives and Nurses: A History of Women Healers*. New York: The Feminist Press, 1975.

Evernden, Neil. *The Natural Alien: Humankind and the Environment*, 2nd edition. Toronto: University of Toronto Press, 1993.

———. *The Social Creation of Nature*. Baltimore: The John Hopkins University Press, 1992.

Farmar, Alfred. "The Modern Cemetery: The Perpetual Care Lawn Plan." *Overland Monthly* 29 (April 1897): 440–47.

Farrell, James J. *Inventing the American Way of Death, 1830–1920*. Philadelphia: Temple University Press, 1980.

Faust, Drew Gilpin. *This Republic of Suffering: Death and the American Civil War*. New York: Vintage, 2008.

Firestone, David, with Robert D. McFadden. "Scores of Bodies Strewn at Site of Crematory." *New York Times*, February 17, 2002. http://www.nytimes.com/2002/02/17/national/17CREM.html. Accessed November 22, 2011.

Flader, Susan L., and J. Baird Callicott. *The River of the Mother of God: And Other Essays by Aldo Leopold*. Madison: The University of Wisconsin Press, 1991.

Foucault, Michel. *Discipline and Punish: Birth of the Prison*. New York: Random House, 1975.

Foucault, Michel. *Power/Knowledge: Select Interviews and Other Writings, 1972–1977*, edited by Colin Gordon, New York, Pantheon Books, 1980.

Friend, Tad. "The Shroud of Marin." *The New Yorker*, August 29, 2005.

Gibbs, Janice. "Green Burials See Jump in Popularity." *Killeen Daily Herald*. http://kdhnews.com/news/green-funerals-see-jump-in-popularity/article_601ac430-3b92-11e4-a3f6-001a4bcf6878.html?mode=jqm. Accessed December 15, 2014.

Gilbert, Sandra. *Death's Door: Modern Dying and the Ways We Grieve*. New York: W. W. Norton, 2007.

Graham, Pam. "The Tallgrass Prairie: An Endangered Landscape." *ProQuest Discovery Guides*, November 2011.

Green, Emma. "Burying Your Dead without Religion." *The Atlantic*, August 19, 2014.

Greenberg, Brad A. "Jewish Cemetery Accused of Desecrating 500 Graves." Jewishjournal.com, September 12, 2009. http://www.jewishjournal.com/thegodblog/item/jewish_cemetery_accused_of_desecrating_500_graves_20090912/. Accessed November 22, 2014.

Gurrieri, Vin. "FTC Approves Divestitures in $1.4B Funeral Co. Merger." *Law 360*, August 14, 2014. http://www.law360.com/articles/567083/ftc-approves-divestitures-in-1-4b-funeral-co-merger. Accessed January 16, 2015.

Habenstein, R. W., and W. M. Lamers. *Funeral Customs the World Over*. Milwaukee: Bulfin, 1960.

———. *The History of American Funeral Directing*. Omnigraphics, 1990.

Haglund, William D., and Marcella H. Sorg, eds. *Forensic Taphonomy: The Postmortem Fate of Human Remains*. Boca Raton: CRC Press, 1997.

Harker, Alexandra. "Landscapes of the Dead: An Argument for Conservation Burial." *Berkeley Planning Journal* 25, no. 1 (2012).

Harris, Mark. *Grave Matters: A Journey through the Modern Funeral Industry to a Natural Way of Burial*. New York: Scribner, 2007.

Hogland, Sarah. "Hidden Agendas: The Secret to Early Nineteenth-Century British Reform." In *Victorian Secrecy: Economies of Knowledge and Concealment*. Edited by Albert D. Pionke and Denise Tischler Millstein. Surrey: Ashgate, 2010.

Holloway, Karla F. C. *Passed On: African American Mourning Stories*. Durham: Duke, 2002.

Hutton, Ann. "Death Café Convenes in Kingston." *Almanac Weekly*, August 23, 2013.

Irish, Donald P., Kathleen F. Lundquist, and Vivian Jenkins Nelsen, eds. *Ethnic Variations in Dying, Death and Grief: Diversity in Universality*. Philadelphia: Taylor & Francis, 1990.

Iserson, Kenneth, V., MD. *Death to Dust: What Happens to Dead Bodies?* New York: Galen Press, 2001.

Jackson, David. "Obama: We Treated bin Laden Better Than He Treated 9/11 Victims." *USA Today*, May 5, 2011.

Jackson, Wes. "Can We Restore the Prairie—And Still Support Ourselves?" *Yes Magazine*, November 22, 2011.

———. *Nature as Measure: The Selected Essays of Wes Jackson*. Berkeley: Counterpoint, 2011.

Jensen, Derrick. *Consulting the Genius of the Place: An Ecological Approach to a New Agriculture*. Berkeley: Counterpoint, 2010.

———. "Forget Shorter Showers." *Orion Magazine*, June 2009.

Jordan, William III. *The Sunflower Forest: Ecological Restoration and the New Communion with Nature*. Los Angeles: University of California Press, 2003.

Kelly, Suzanne. "Dead Bodies That Matter: Toward a New Ecology of Human Death." *Journal of American Culture* 35, no. 1 (2012): 37–51.

Kermeliotis, Teo. "India's Burning Issue with Emissions from Hindu Funeral Pyres." CNN World News, September 17, 2011. http://www.cnn.com/2011/09/12/world/asia/india-funeral-pyres-emissions/. Accessed January 20, 2015.

Knight, Sam. "Bodysnatchers Steal Alistair Cooke's Bones." *Times Online*, December 22, 2005. Accessed October 25, 2011.

Konefes, John L., and Michael K. McGee. "Old Cemeteries, Arsenic, and Health Safety." In *Dangerous Places: Health, Safety and Archaeology*. Edited by David A. Poirier and Kenneth L. Feder. Westport: Bergin and Garvey, 2001.

Kristeva, Julia. *Powers of Horror: An Essay on Abjection*. New York: Columbia University Press, 1982.

Krüger-Kahloula, Angelika. "On the Wrong Side of the Fence: Racial Segregation in American Cemeteries." In *History and Memory in African American Culture*. New York: Oxford University Press, 1994.

Laderman, Gary. *Rest in Peace: A Cultural History of Death and the Funeral Home in the Twentieth-Century America*. Oxford: Oxford, 2003.

———. *The Sacred Remains: American Attitudes toward Death, 1799–1883*. New Haven: Yale, 1996.

Lamm, Maurice. *The Jewish Way in Death and Mourning*, Jonathan and David Publishers, 2000, Laqueur, Thomas, W. "The Deep Time of the Dead." *Social Research: An International Quarterly* 78, no. 3 (2011).

———. "Spaces of the Dead." *Ideas: The National Humanities Center* 8, no. 2 (2001).

———. "Why Do We Care for the Dead?" Presented at Radcliffe Institute for Advanced Study, Harvard University, April 29, 2014.

Leopold, Aldo. "The Round River: A Parable of Conservation." *Writing–Unpublished Manuscripts–*AL's Desk File, Philosophic and Literary, 1940–1948.

———. *A Sand County Almanac*. New York: Oxford, 1949.

———. "Wilderness as a Form of Land Use." In *The Great New Wilderness Debate*, J. Baird Callicott and Michael P. Nelson. Athens: Univesrsity of Georgia Press, 1998.

Linden, Blanche M. G. *Silent City on a Hill: Picturesque Landscapes of Memory and Boston's Mount Auburn Cemetery*. Amherst: University of Massachusetts Press, 2007.

Long, Jacob. "Death and Burials: The Final Frontier for Segregation." *First Coast News*, April 30, 2014.

Long, Thomas G., and Thomas Lynch. *The Good Funeral: Death, Grief, and the Community of Care*. Louisville: Weestminster John Knox Press, 2013.

Lynch, Thomas. *The Undertaking: Life Studies from the Dismal Trade*. New York: W. W. Norton, 1997.

Lyons, Jerri, and Janell Va Melvin. *Final Passages: A Family-Directed Funeral Lying-in-Honor in a Home*, 1999.

MacDonald, Helen. *Human Remains: Dissection and Its Histories*. New Haven: Yale University Press, 2005.

Maloney, Susan R., Carol A. Phillips, and Allan Mills. "Mercury in the Hair of Crematoria Workers." *The Lancet* 352 (November 14, 1998).

Manning, Doug. "Personalization Is More Than a Product." *The Director*, June 2002.

Marsh, Tanya D. "Ebola, Embalming and the Dead: The Spread of Infectious Diseases," *Wake Forest Law Review*, Volume 2, 2014, 113-123

Marcuse, Herbert. *One-Dimensional Man*, 2nd edition. Boston: Beacon Press, 1991.

Martin, Andrew. "Despite Risk, Embalmers Still Embrace Preservative." *New York Times*, July 20, 2011. http://www.nytimes.com/2011/07/21/business/despite-cancer-risk-embalmers-stay-with-formaldehyde.html?pagewanted=all&_r=0. Accessed January 16, 2015.

McCarthy, Ellen. "'Green Burials' Are on the Rise as Baby Boomers Plan for Their Future, and Funerals." *Washington Post*, October 6, 2014.

McKibben, Bill. "Movements without Leaders: What to Make of Change on an Overheating Planet." Tomdispath.com, August 18, 2013. http://www.tomdispatch.com/blog/175737/. Accessed December 6, 2014.

Merchant, Carolyn. *The Death of Nature: Women, Ecology and the Scientific Revolution*. San Francisco: Harper, 1980.

———. *Ecological Revolutions: Nature, Gender & Science in New England*. Chapel Hill: University of North Carolina Press, 1989.

Metcalf, Peter, and Richard Huntington. *Celebrations of Death: The Anthropology of Mortuary Ritual*, 2nd edition. Cambridge: Cambridge University Press, 1991.

Mitford, Jessica. *The American Way of Death*. New York: Simon and Schuster, 1963.

Montse, Mari, and Jose L. Domingo. "Toxic Emissions from Crematories: A Review." *Environmental International* 36, no. 1 (2010): 131–37.

Morgan, Oliver, and Claude de Ville de Goyet. "Dispelling Disaster Myths about Dead Bodies and Disease: The Role of Scientific Evidence and the Media." Special Report, *Pan American Journal of Public Health* 18, no. 1 (2005).

Nearing, Brian. "To Lie Down in Green Pastures." Timesunion.com, June 22, 2012. http://www.timesunion.com/business/article/To-lie-down-in-green-pastures-3653992.php. Accessed December 1, 2014.

Newcomb, Alyssa. "Dead People Get Life-Like Poses at Their Funeral." *ABC News*, June 13, 2014. http://abcnews.go.com/US/dead-people-life-poses-funerals/story?id=23456853. Accessed September 14, 2014.

Patterson, Randall. "The Organ Grinder." *New York Magazine*, October 16, 2006. http://nymag.com/news/features/22326/. Accessed August 10, 2014.

Pazornik, Amanda, "'Today Is about Forever': 1st Green Jewish Cemetery Opens." JWeekly.com, April 1, 2010. http://www.jweekly.com/article/full/57642/today-is-about-forever-1st-green-jewish-cemetery-opens1/. Accessed November 14, 2014.

Pearsall, Peter. "Green Burials," *The Planet Magazine*, Winter 2008.

Pearson, Mike Parker. *The Archeology of Death and Burial.* College Station: Texas A&M University, 2000.

Petropoulos, Thrasy. "Seat at the Autopsy Sideshow." *BBC News*, November 21, 2002. http://news.bbc.co.uk/2/hi/health/2497889.stm. Accessed August 10, 2014.

Pine, Vanderlyn R. *Caretaker of the Dead: The American Funeral Director.* New York: Irvington, 1975.

Plumwood, Val. "Being Prey." *Utne Reader*, July/August 2000.

——. "The Cemetery Wars: Cemeteries, Biodiversity and the Sacred." *Local-Global: Identity, Security, Community* 3 (2007): 54–71.

——. "The Concept of a Cultural Landscape: Nature, Culture and Agency in the Land." *Ethics & the Environment* 11, no. 2 (2006): 115–50.

——. *Environmental Culture: The Ecological Crisis of Reason.* London: Routledge, 2002.

——. *Feminism and the Mastery of Nature.* New York: Routledge, 1993.

——. "Tasteless: Towards a Food Based Approach to Death." In *The Eye of the Crocodile.* Edited by Lorraine Shannon. Canberra: ANU E Press, 2012.

Pollan, Michael. *The Omnivora's Dilemma: A Natural History of Four Meals*, Penguin, 2006.

Prothero, Stephen. *Purified by Fire: A History of Cremation in America.* Berkeley: University of California Press, 2001.

Proust, Marcel. *In Search of Lost Time, Volume 6, Time Regained.* New York: Random House, 1993.

Raymunt, Monica. "Down on the Body Farm: Inside the Dirty World of Forensic Science." *The Atlantic*, December 2, 2010. http://www.theatlantic.com/technology/archive/2010/12/down-on-the-body-farm-inside-the-dirty-world-of-forensic-science/67241/. Accessed November 20, 2011.

Richardson, Ruth. *Death, Dissection and the Destitute.* Chicago: University of Chicago Press, 2000.

Roach, Mary. *Stiff: The Curious Lives of Human Cadavers.* New York: W. W. Norton and Company, 2003.

Rosenblatt, Adam. "Sacred Graves and Human Rights." *Human Rights at the Crossroads.* Edited by Mark Goodale. Oxford: Oxford University Press, 2012.

Rousseau, Jean-Jacques. *Emile or On Education.* Introduction, translation and notes by Allan Bloom. New York: Basic Books, 1979.

Rudolf, John Collins. "Into the Great Green Beyond." *New York Times*, June 30, 2010. http://green.blogs.nytimes.com/2010/06/30/into-the-big-green-beyond/?hp. Accessed December 15, 2014.

Rumble, Hannah, John Troyer, Tony Walter, and Kate Woodthorpe. "Disposal or Dispersal? Environmentalism and Final Treatment of the British Dead." *Mortality* 9, no. 3 (2014).

Rundblad, Georganne. "Exhuming Women's Premarket Duties in the Care of the Dead." *Gender and Society* 9, no. 2 (1995).

Schauffler, Marina F. *Turning to the Earth: Stories of Ecological Conversion*. Charlottesville: University of Virginia Press, 2003.

Shaw, Dan. "A Believer in Vacant Lots – Urban Farming's Grand Dame: Karen Washington," *The New York Times*, September 19, 2014.

Schertow, John Ahni. "Police Arrest Hawaiian Activists Protesting the Desecration of Sacred Site." *IC Magazine*, May 5, 2011. https://intercontinentalcry.org/police-arrest-hawaiian-activists-protesting-the-desecration-of-sacred-site/m. Accessed July 12, 2014.

Schlich, Gig. "Burying Tradition." *The Planet Magazine*, Winter 2005.

Sehee, Joe. "Proud & Humbled." *Natural Transitions* 3, no. 2 (2014).

Selzer, Richard. *The Exact Location of the Soul: New and Selected Essays*. New York: Picador, 2001.

Shilling, Dan. "Aldo Leopold Listens to the Southwest." *Journal of the Southwest* 51, no. 3 (Autumn 2009).

Shiva, Vandana. *Biopiracy: The Plunder of Nature and Knowledge*. Boston: South End Press, 1999.

———. *Staying Alive: Women, Ecology and Development*. London: Zed Books, 1989.

Silko, Leslie Marmon. "Landscape, History and the Pueblo Imagination." *Antaeus* 57 (Autumn 1986).

Slocum, Joshua, and Lisa Carlson. *Final Rights: Reclaiming the American Way of Death*. Hinesburg: Upper Access, 2011.

Slotnik, Daniel E. "Michael Mastromarino, Dentist Guilty in Organ Scheme, Dies at 49." *New York Times*, July 8, 2013. http://www.nytimes.com/2013/07/09/nyregion/michael-mastromarino-dentist-guilty-in-organ-scheme-dies-at-49.html?_r=0. Accessed August 13, 2014.

Smith, Joy Lukachick. "10th Anniversary of Bodies Discovered at Tri-State Crematory in Noble, Georgia." *TimesFreePress*, Sunday, February 12, 2012. http://www.timesfreepress.com/news/2012/feb/12/horror-in-noble/. Accessed July 25, 2014.

Somma, Anne Marie. "Muslims Reconcile Burial Rights, State Rules." *The Courant*, February 18, 2008. http://articles.courant.com/2008-02-18/news/0802180012_1_united-muslim-masjid-islamic-law-mosque. Accessed September 2, 2014.

Spongberg, Alison L., and Paul M. Becks. "Inorganic Soil Contamination from Cemetery Leachate." *Water, Air and Soil Pollution* 117 (2000): 313–27.

Stewart, Benjamin M. "Committed to the Earth: Ecotheological Dimensions of Christian Burial Practices." *Liturgy* 27, no. 2 (2012): 62–72.

———. "The Place of Earth in Lutheran Funeral Rites: Mapping the Current Terrain." *Dialog: A Journal of Theology* 53, no. 2 (2014): 121–29.

Trimble, Mandie. "Northeast Ohio Land Preserve Offers Alternative to Modern Burials." *WOSU Public Media.* http://wosu.org/2012/news/2012/07/17/northeast-ohio-land-preserve-offers-alternative-to-modern-burials/. Accessed December 15, 2014.

Tuana, Nancy. *The Less Noble Sex: Scientific, Religious and Philosophical Conceptions of Woman's Nature.* Bloomington: Indiana University Press, 1993.

Ulaby, Neda. "Origins of Exhibited Cadavers Questioned." NPR News, August 11, 2006. http://www.npr.org/templates/story/story.php?storyId=5637687. Accessed July 9, 2014.

Vass, Arpad A. "Dust to Dust." *Scientific American* 303, no. 3 (2010): 56–59.

Vernant, Jean-Pierre. *Mortals and Immortals: Collected Essays.* Princeton: Princeton University Press, 1991.

Walker, Alice. *Living by the Word: Selected Writings, 1973–1987.* San Diego: Harcourt Brace & Company, 1981.

Wilkerson, Isabel. "Michael Brown's Shooting and Jim Crow Lynchings Have Too Much in Common. It's Time for America to Own Up." *The Guardian*, August 25, 2015. http://www.theguardian.com/commentisfree/2014/aug/25/mike-brown-shooting-jim-crow-lynchings-in-common. Accessed September 10, 2014.

Wollstonecraft, Mary. *A Vindication of the Rights of Woman.* Cambridge: Cambridge University Press, 1995.

Yee, Shirley J. *An Immigrant Neighborhood: Interethnic and Interracial Encounters in New York before 1930.* Philadelphia: Temple University Press, 2012.

Zinner, David. "Breathing New Life into Jewish Funeral Practice." *Kavod v'Nichum*, http://www.jewish-funerals.org/Breathing. Accessed January 30, 2014.

Index

Abram, David, 17, 65, 105, 152n6,
164n41
advanced care planning, 60–61, 133
African American: bodies, 24, 41,
62; community and death care
conversations, 61–62; death care
discrimination, 61–62; funeral
directors, 44, 133
*History and Memory in African
American Culture*, 164n19, 181
*Passed On: African American Mourning
Stories*, 160n50, 164n20, 181
Alachua Conservation Trust, 88, 91, 92,
120, 169n26
arsenic: based embalming fluid, 42, 44,
160n52, 181
alkaline hydrolysis, 28, 124, 125,
156n37, 166n19
American Academy McAllister Institute
of Funeral Service, 59
American Forests, 136
The American Way of Death, 4, 27,
42, 49–50, 114, 156n36, 159n34,
161n63, 161n67, 161n74, 161n77,
161n82, 166n30, 182
anatomists, 25–26
ancient Greece, 16, 24, 27
Antigone, 24, 27

Association for Death Education &
Counseling Conference, 59
Audubon International, 139–41, 176n37

backgrounding, 18, 19, 36, 45, 48, 75,
82
Bacon, Francis, 17
Beal, Cynthia, 72, 74, 93, 139, 176
Bean, Katey, vii, 96, 104, 111, 169n37,
170n59, 171n11
Belleplain State Forest, 95, 138
Bentham, Jeremy, 26
Berry, Wendell, 85
Bigelow, Jacob, 106
biotic community, 20, 71, 83, 85,
104–6, 142
Bixby, Ed, vii, 73–74, 78, 94–97, 119,
138, 166n23, 167n50, 169nn35,
169n39, 172n48
black market in body parts, 22
biomass, 76, 78, 81
Bin Laden, Osama, 24
birthing practices, 60, 129
body farms, 29, 157
bodies: African American, 24, 41, 62;
women's 2, 16
Bodyworlds and Bodyworlds 2, 26,
156n31

187

About the Author

Suzanne Kelly, PhD, is an independent scholar whose work spans the topics of the environment, feminism, sex, and death. She writes and farms in New York's Hudson Valley.